The Death and Life of the Music Industry in the Digital Age

The Death and Life of the Music Industry in the Digital Age

JIM ROGERS

BLOOMSBURY

LONDON · NEW DELHI · NEW YORK · SYDNEY

Bloomsbury Academic
An imprint of Bloomsbury Publishing Plc

175 Fifth Avenue	50 Bedford Square
New York	London
NY 10010	WC1B 3DP
USA	UK

www.bloomsbury.com

First published 2013

Library of Congress Cataloging-in-Publication Data
Rogers, Jim, 1969-
The death and life of the music industry in the digital age / by Jim Rogers.
pages cm
Includes bibliographical references and index.
ISBN 978-1-78093-160-9 (hardcover : alk. paper) –
ISBN 978-1-62356-001-0 (pbk. : alk. paper)   1. Sound recording industry–
Social aspects.   2. Music and technology.   I. Title.
ML3790.R63 2013
384–dc23
2012041382

ISBN: HB: 978-1-7809-3160-9
PB: 978-1-6235-6001-0

Typeset by Newgen Imaging Systems Pvt Ltd, Chennai, India
Printed and bound in the United States of America

ML
3790
.R63
2013

Contents

List of tables

Acknowledgements

I would like to extend my sincere gratitude to colleagues and friends from the Dublin City University community (past and present), all of whom have served to generate a stimulating and engaging academic environment as well as providing a much appreciated source of friendship and support over recent years. In particular, Ciaran Dunne, Frank Byrne, Pat Brereton, Barbara O'Connor, Mark O'Brien, Farrel Corcoran, Sheamus Sweeney, Henry Silke, Declan Tuite, Bill Dorris, Neil O'Boyle, Trish Morgan and Darryl D'Souza. To Des McGuinness, particular thanks must go for all of his encouragement and generosity. Special thanks also go to Sergio Sparviero at Universtät Salzburg (Austria) and Anthony Cawley at Hope University, Liverpool (United Kingdom). I would like to express my sincere gratitude to Prof. Paschal Preston at Dublin City University, whose guidance and mentorship has been (and continues to be) immense, and extends way beyond the call of duty. A debt of gratitude must also be paid to Cormac McCanney for so frequently volunteering to act as a sounding board and for being such a reliable source of practical advice. To Katie Gallof, Emily Drewe and all the team at Bloomsbury, many thanks for your support and patience. I also wish to acknowledge the financial support provided by the Irish Research Council for Humanities and Social Sciences (IRCHSS) and the Irish Social Science Platform (ISSP) at different times during the course of my doctoral and postdoctoral research studies (which provide the empirical data for this book). However, the biggest 'thank you' off all is reserved for Carol Redican . . . for her love and encouragement.

1

Digital deliria and transformative hype

In some ways we are the canary down the mine,
the first battle ground, but behind us goes anyone
who creates anything that can be turned into data . . .

PETER GABRIEL

Since the 1960s Simon Napier-Bell has worked as a songwriter, record producer and author. However, he is best known as the manager of a number of successful international recording acts including Eric Clapton and the Yardbirds, Marc Bolan and T-Rex, Boney-M, Japan and Wham. In a 2008 newspaper article entitled 'The Life and Crimes of the Music Biz', he somewhat gleefully describes the music industry as 'careering towards meltdown' (*The Observer*, Music Monthly, 20 January 2008: 41). Focusing on six key music industry executives from the present and recent past, Napier-Bell dramatically outlines how just four major music companies[1] have usurped almost all rivals and grown to increasingly dominate a business that is 'distinctly

---

[1] The companies that Napier-Bell refers to are the Universal Music Group (UMG), the Warner Music Group (WMG), Sony Music Entertainment and EMI – the four corporate players whose combined share of the global recorded music market has, over the past decade, fluctuated between 70 per cent and 80 per cent and, by 2008 (when Napier-Bell was writing) had grown to account for 92 per cent of the Irish market. By late 2011, the market had concentrated further when EMI was acquired by Universal.

medieval in character: the last form of indentured servitude' (ibid.). In Napier-Bell's sensational account, a core group of notorious moguls control and operate these companies and use bullying and thuggery to extract products and performance from their employees and artists. He accuses these companies of being 'intentionally fraudulent' and practising 'systematic thievery' from their artists (ibid.: 45). However, he now sees each passing week heaping more gloom on these majors who are seeing their record sales plummet, and are consequently losing their grip on the industry as the internet renders the machinery of the music corporation obsolete. The music companies, Napier-Bell concludes, were never the 'guardians' of the music industry, rather they were its greedy 'bouncers' who have now become irrelevant. The internet has produced, for artists and managers:

> the moment to take things into their own hands. Artists no longer need to be held [by a label] for ten years, and they no longer need to sign away ownership of their recorded copyrights. These days, an artist working closely with his manager can ensure that everything is done in the artist's best interest. (Napier-Bell, 2008: 41)

Napier-Bell's account is decidedly sensational and we might consider that it reflects the biases he evolved over decades of negotiating and battling with the big industry players. Sensationalism aside, his perspective on the situation of the music industry in an evolving digital environment is illustrative of two commonly held and frequently relayed assumptions on the matter:

1   The first is that major music companies – the 'bad guys' of the music industry – are facing potential ruin in light of recent and ongoing technological developments primarily centred around the internet.

2   The second is that such technological developments, which enable the distribution and promotion of music online, have revolutionized the industry's core structure by enabling interface between artists and consumers like never before. These developments are thus perceived as diminishing the power of major music companies in acting as intermediaries in artist-consumer relationships.

There is a commonly held assumption that new information and communication technologies (ICTs) are liberative for artists and that structural change in artist-intermediary-consumer relationships have been a net gain for the artist. Thus, the internet is widely perceived as having severely disrupted the roles and interests of established industry actors, thus producing a 'new music order'. In short, radical change driven by technology is widely viewed as the order of the day for the music industry in the digital era. Arguments that either celebrate or bemoan the advent of the internet as a medium for the distribution and promotion of music have dominated much commentary on the industry since the mid-1990s. Many column inches have been devoted to commenting on the ethics (or lack of) associated with unauthorized music file-sharing online, and the plights of musicians and music companies as such activities have evolved and spread. The ongoing persistence and topicality of such debates is perhaps best illustrated by the recent levels of coverage given to, and controversy generated by such subjects as the 'Emily' case[2] or the proposed monitoring of network users activities by internet service in the United States in a move aimed at combating online 'piracy'.[3] Such debates around the seemingly existential threats new digital technological innovations (and their uses and misuses) hold for the music industry have been common since the mid-to-late 1990s when unauthorized sharing of music became common on US university campus networks.

Popular music forms the basis of a major international industry that, as Patrik Wikström notes, possesses a nature that is 'as chaotic and unpredictable as any other complex dynamic system' (2009: 170). The final decades of the twentieth century saw the music industry (itself a core constituent element of the broader media and cultural industries) significantly increase its importance in economic and

---

[2] Summer 2012 saw Emily White, an NPR intern, post a notice on the NPR blog stating that she possessed a music library of 11,000 songs, but had only ever purchased 15 CDs. The posting generated widespread media coverage and a multitude of responses from both proponents and opponents of free music 'sharing'.

[3] In spring 2012, ISPs such as Comcast, Time Warner and Verizon were widely reported to be entering a joint initiative with the Record Industry Association of America (RIAA) and Motion Picture Association of America (MPAA) whereby the ISP would track, warn, and ultimately restrict or deny services to copyright 'infringers' in the United States. [Similar developments in other territories are outlined in Chapter 3 of this book.]

employment terms. Since the mid-to-late 1990s, innovations in the realm of digital media technologies have evolved to threaten the medium-to-long-term viability of the record industry – the music industry's most important economic sector over many decades. The unauthorized use of copyrighted material is undermining the record industry's ability to make money and has produced a 'crisis' for a sector that had grown exponentially on the back of the CD-boom. Equally, the record industry has been contending with the challenge of moving from physical to digital formats. Moreover, if this is the 'moment' to strike for independence and for musicians to rid themselves of corporate intermediaries and gatekeepers (as Napier-Bell celebrates), then the established music industry 'actors' are indeed navigating turbulent waters.

The music industry, as we shall see, is much more than the record industry. As a whole, it has proved itself to be resilient and innovative in responding to the challenges of digitalization. This book is primarily concerned with examining and understanding how the music industry has negotiated the digital coalface. In the chapters that follow we will consider some of the key problems and challenges facing the music industry since the turn of the millennium, and some of the core response strategies of the industry over that period. We will consider what has changed and what has stayed the same. Ultimately we will seek to draw some conclusions regarding the form and extent of disruption that the 'digital revolution' (which is feted and feared in equal measure) has visited upon this cultural industry sector.

Musical dystopia

Since the late 1990s, a few core themes have grown to dominate much commentary and discussion on the music industry. First there is the marked decline in the value of record sales that has raised questions around the long-term viability of the music industry, with online 'piracy' seen as the primary factor in this contraction. Also, for the established music labels, the transition to a digital environment has brought with it several problems regarding how they can monetize their content. Besides the issue of piracy, the shift to digital has not been without its setbacks as record companies have sought new revenue streams and new means of distribution in a less than surefooted manner. Against this backdrop, the concept of an industry in crisis has taken hold. 'Crisis' is a concept that has become embedded in discourse around the music industry since the late 1990s. For example:

> We run the risk of witnessing a genuine destruction of culture . . . The internet must not become a high tech wild west, a lawless zone where outlaws can pillage works with abandon, or worse, trade in them in total impunity. And on whose backs? On artists' backs. (Nicolas Sarkozy, president of France, 23 November 2007)

Sarkozy's much publicized comments were delivered in the wake of an agreement struck between French internet service providers (ISPs), the French government and movie and music companies aimed at curbing unauthorized file-sharing on the internet. Subsequently, Paul McGuinness (the manager of U2) did little to modify Sarkozy's picture of an impending digital Armageddon:

> I believe President Sarkozy truly caught the spirit of the age with that statement . . . It is a good rule of thumb that when it is the manager and not the artist getting the headlines, something is out of kilter. Well there is certainly something out of kilter with the music business today . . . The record industry is in crisis. (Paul McGuinness, speech delivered at *Music Matters* conference, Hong Kong, 4 June 2008)

In the same speech, McGuinness appealed to governments around the world to force ISPs to be proactive in combating online copyright infringement.

Much commentary and analysis of the music industry in the mainstream press has also centred around such crisis rhetoric in recent years. Arguing that the internet has resulted in the evolution of an 'everything is free culture', Willie Kavanagh, (MD of EMI Ireland and chairman of the Irish Recorded Music Association [IRMA]) writes that it is 'impossible for any business to compete with free' (*The Irish Times*, 8 August 2010: 14). Media and journalistic accounts detailing the decline of the music industry have remained commonplace in news stories, features and opinion columns. For example, 'Piracy continues to cripple the music industry' (*The Guardian*, Thursday, 21 January 2010); 'The music industry . . . knee deep in a downloading crisis' (*The Sunday Business Post*, 6 April 2008); 'Downloads keep going up . . . Music giants lose fortune in 1.2bn song thefts' (*The Times*, 17 December 2010); 'Industry crisis as album sales drop' (*The Irish Independent*, 14 January 2008); and 'Music industry in a flat spin' (*The Sunday Times*, 27 January 2008). Internationally, such commentary is replicated: 'Music labels feel the music pirating pain' (*Sydney Morning Herald*, 21 November 2011); The 'scourge of the illegal copying and downloading of music from the internet' represents 'a competition monster for music retailers and distributors' (*Africa News*, 12 October 2011); 'No cure for piracy since the day the music started dying' (*The Australian*, 12 September 2011); The 'illegal downloading of music and videos . . . [is] a problem that robs billion from music and movie businesses' (*New York Times*, Sunday, 17 July 2011: 11); 'Want a snapshot of an industry in crisis? Take a look at the music business right now' (*Globe and Mail*, 31 January 2008).

Overall, these notions of change have become common-sense assumptions in much discourse surrounding the recent evolution of the music industry. But such reporting is nothing new. In 2003 the *Financial Times* reported how the downturn in record sales revenues experienced by the Universal Music Group 'underlined the severity of the crisis facing the world's biggest record companies . . . a crisis created by the combination of stagnant sales, internet theft and rampant piracy' (*The Financial Times*, 17 June 2003). Even technology periodicals enthusiastically joined the choir. For example, *Wired* magazine declared 2003 as 'the year the music dies' (Mann, 2003).

Furthermore, in 2002 Britney Spears, Eminem and Luciano Pavorotti headed a coalition of 90 recording artists and songwriters that placed full-page advertisements in *The New York Times* and *Los Angeles Times* condemning the practice of internet downloading on the grounds that it threatened their careers. In the ad, the Dixie Chicks are quoted as saying: 'It may seem innocent enough, but every time you illegally download music, a songwriter doesn't get paid' (*The Associated Press & Wire*, 26 September 2002). Subsequently, established international artists such as Metallica and The Corrs have appeared on main evening news bulletins denouncing the use of peer-to-peer file-sharing services and claiming the future of the industry that enables them to pursue their artistic endeavours is under threat, as are their livelihoods and the conditions that facilitate musical creativity and the production of music recordings. Summer 2009 saw English pop singer Lily Allen, supported by counterparts James Blunt and Gary Barlow launch a blog campaigning against internet music 'piracy' (idontwanttochangetheworld.blogspot.com). Soundings from industry seminars and trade fairs have consistently echoed similar sentiments.

Perhaps the overall scenario of doom and gloom that has grown tó characterize the music industry is most vividly stated by *Irish Times* journalist Conor Pope who asks:

> Has music had its day? . . . Of the all the upheavals wrought by the internet revolution over the last fifteen years, the shake up in the world of music has been amongst the most profound. The consequence of free music downloads could end up destroying not just the shops that used to sell music, but an entire industry. (*The Irish Times*, Monday, 27 April 2009: 15)

Pope's language is stark and strident. The terms he employs ('upheavals wrought', 'revolution', 'profound', 'destroying . . . an entire industry') imply the most radical disruption to the existing order.

In short, the very existence of a recorded music industry in the short-to medium-term future is commonly perceived as hanging in the balance with artists, record companies and retailers all facing the prospect of economic destruction. Media commentary and analyses critiquing these accounts of crisis and the extent of the claims made by the music industry regarding its collapse have been extremely rare, although not unheard of. For example, 'The big question: Is the crisis facing the music industry as bad as the big record labels claim?' (*The Independent*, 14 February 2007).

Beyond the perceived effects of online copyright infringement on music industry revenue streams, other media accounts point to internet platforms as effectively rendering obsolete the artist and repertoire (A&R) and marketing and promotion functions traditionally associated with major music companies. Sites such as Bandcamp, ReverbNation, MySpace and Soundcloud have all evolved as platforms for the promotion of artists and recordings. Aside from cyberspaces such as these and other 'mass-user' sites like Facebook and YouTube, a wave of other 'niche' music social networking sites are increasingly regarded as rendering redundant the machinery of the major media corporation in mediating the relationship between artist and music end-user. As *Irish Times* columnist Brian Boyd tells us, music's 'digital revolution isn't discriminatory' with music journalists the latest casualties of technological innovation (*The Irish Times*, Friday, 4 February 2011: 32). In this account, Boyd outlines how he perceives the role of the professional music critic being diminished and replaced by online social networks. Technology, he argues, has made music journalism 'redundant'. For Boyd, music journalists are left 'clinging to the wreckage . . . playing catch-up with a technological revolution' in an environment where music enthusiasts increasingly rely on each other for recommendations and reviews (ibid.).

Musical utopia

The promise and potential of the internet to destroy pre-existing industrial structures and transfer power into the hands of the individual has been soundly celebrated. The transformative hype surrounding digital technologies is perhaps best exemplified by Nicholas Negroponte, one of the founders of the MIT Media Lab and a celebrated *guru* of the information age. For Negroponte, social and economic structures would be revolutionized by digital technological innovations. Writing in high-tech publication *Wired.com* in February 1995, he argued that transfer to digital would lead copyright to 'disintegrate', with everything that was capable of being digitized being potentially 'up for grabs'. If Negroponte's claims were to be realized, then such developments would hold serious ramifications for the music industry as we know it. In such an environment, traditional power structures could potentially collapse. But with the demise of the major labels would come the promise of liberation for artists. Kevin Kelly, the associate editor of *Wired* magazine, argued that:

> The recording industry as we know it is history . . . [with] digital
> file-sharing technologies . . . undermining the established

economics of music'. (*New York Times Magazine*, 17 March 2002: 19–21).

While digital technologies would serve to dismantle the power of the major record companies, Kelly equally points to those same technologies empowering individual recording artists to act independently like never before. In the evolving digital world, those 'musicians with the highest status are those who have a 24-hour net channel devoted to streaming their music' (ibid.).

Equally, while Boyd (2011) laments the role of online social networks in heralding the demise of music journalism, other accounts point more positively to such developments. For example, David Haynes, the founder of Soundcloud (a music-based social networking site) states that:

> In the past, there were just a few gatekeepers . . . and you had a powerful network of labels, A&R, radio and TV executives and magazines who decided what you should be listening to. Now it's so much easier to find out . . . what other people . . . on the other side of the world are recommending. (David Haynes cited in *The Guardian*, 5 September 2010)

In the same article, journalist Alexandra Topping points to such online platforms transferring power into the hands of music fans regarding the discovery of new music.

The purpose and structure of this book

The sum of the above accounts is that the music industry is experiencing radical upheaval in the wake of the digital 'revolution'. In the more extreme cases, these accounts spell out changes that are leading to the potential destruction of an entire industry. These notions of negative or insidious change have become common-sense assumptions in much discourse surrounding the recent evolution of the music industry. Equally, as we have seen, other accounts herald the arrival of a more level-playing field in the music industry where both creators and consumers of music are enabled to access each other without, as Burnett puts it, requiring 'the machinery of a multinational corporation mediating this relationship' (2011: 441). It is against this background that the research from which this book has derived initially evolved.

I'll now briefly outline the purpose of this book. Its central concern is to examine change in the twenty-first-century music industry. The key questions it asks are:

- *What* has changed in the twenty-first-century popular music industry?

- *Why* has it changed?

- *How* has it changed?

These questions in turn direct us to ask a number of others: Is the internet, as some of the aforementioned accounts have reported, inducing a 'crisis' that is signalling the collapse of the music industry? Or is it the case that it is producing a period of pressure that is resulting in an intensified restructuring and reordering within the industry? What, if any, implications do the widely reported decline in recorded music sales have for other music industry sub-sectors? Over a decade after the internet first emerged as a medium for the distribution and promotion of music, has the structure and organization of the overall music industry been significantly altered? What are the characteristics of the contemporary music industry? To draw on Kelly's words, does the contemporary music industry illustrate the 'new rules for the new economy' that were predicted to arise from the ability to digitize content and the rapid and widespread diffusion of internet technologies? Does this signal, as Negroponte predicted, the disintegration of copyright law? Or to what extent has the music industry 'playing field' been 'democratized'? – By this, I refer to the increased opportunities offered to smaller businesses and recording artists for self-promotion and distribution. And how have the established music companies responded to the threats, challenges and opportunities associated with 'being digital'? Furthermore, what continuities have been carried into the digital era? Do the changes that have occurred mark a radical transformation of this cultural industry sector, or do they merely mark new ways of doing the same things? These are the questions that prompted the research that has ultimately led to this book.

Napier-Bell (2008) details an industry that has been and is controlled, almost exclusively, by a small group of very powerful players. Since the late 1970s concentration has increased significantly and, for the first two of these decades so too did profits. Global compact disc sales reached their peak in 1999 when their retail value was placed at US$38.7 billion (IFPI, 2000). However, since then (and in stark contrast to the previous decade) the early years of the new millennium showed that sector to be in significant decline. When we also consider the extensive staff cuts that have occurred in major record labels and, the demise of many 'bricks and mortar' music retailers, the record industry as a whole appears to paint a gloomy picture.

Developments in the sphere of digital technologies are commonly cited as carrying severe consequences for the major record labels, and their established roles and interests. At the production end, the finance and resources required to generate recordings have diminished considerably over the years. The necessary technology is cheaper and more accessible than ever before. Equally, when it comes to the distribution and consumption of music, the arena has changed radically since the mid-to-late 1990s. Developments such as the MP3 file and the widespread adoption and popularity of online peer-to-peer networks mean that music can be copied and shared with increasing ease.

As noted above, much media commentary has placed the music industry on a steep downward slope, with illicit file-sharing presented as the primary culprit charged with bringing about its downfall. Similar sentiments are also to be found in some academic writing (see, e.g. Liebowitz, 2002).

Like many other commentators, Napier-Bell heralds this digitally induced disruption and turbulence as an absolute good as it democratizes the entire music industry by giving greater power to both creative artists and music consumers and freeing them from the shackles of multinational entertainment/media corporations. In essence, the music industry is in the throes of significant change and is still in the process of negotiating an extremely turbulent and critical junction. The first decade or so of the new millennium has been a time of 'digital incunabula' for the record industry as it has endeavoured to come to terms with the change in how consumers access music and how their established tactics and strategies for maintaining market dominance have been challenged. As it is the first of the media and cultural industries to experience many of the challenges arising from the transition to digital, the outcome of the music industry in this arena is being keenly observed by many other actors across the media and cultural industry sectors (Hesmondhalgh, 2010). To recall the words of Peter Gabriel, the music industry is the 'canary down the mine, the first battleground'. For Willie Kavanagh, chairman of the IRMA, the music industry is precisely that, a 'canary down the mine for the digital economy' (*Irish Times*, Friday, 8 August 2010: 14).

For Boyle (2008), an assumption held by society is that in order for the market to 'work', goods must be 'rivalrous' – to use Boyle's analogy of a petunia farmer: 'If I have the petunia, you can't have it'; and also 'excludable' – 'The farmer only gives you petunias when you pay for them' (Boyle, 2008: 2–3). The received wisdom is that the transfer to digital brings with it non-rival and non-excludable products, thus making digitized content extremely difficult to monetize. Hence, music is increasingly conceived of as 'free' content. As such, the record industry has been 'working extensively to control the flood of copyrighted music on the internet' (Burnett and Wikström, 2006: 579).

Facebook, YouTube, internet blogs and other social media are now perceived as key intermediaries necessary for the generation of profile at consumer/user level. Traditional intermediaries such as radio and the music press are perceived to carry a decreasing level of significance. Furthermore, in this era of crisis for the record industry, we are increasingly told of the growth of the live music market, and the necessity for artists to be able to generate income through this, and other sources such as synchronization fees as the market for recordings declines, possibly terminally.

In short, we are being invited to accept that prevailing relationships of power within the record industry are currently undergoing radical transformation. However, Boyle invites us to 'pause . . . and inquire how closely reality hews to the economic story of non-rival and non-excludable public goods' (2008: 3). This book accepts Boyle's challenge and interrogates the 'received wisdom' regarding the impact of digitalization on the music market. It will proceed to question the extent of the change that has occurred in the music industry in the internet era, and ultimately contend that we are witnessing not only change, but also significant continuity in the structure and character of the music industry. Here, despite the 'flood' of free music available online, it is useful to evoke the 'bottled water' analogy: water falls freely from the sky, yet people pay a premium to have it nicely packaged. This book will remain mindful of this analogy and Boyle's request for 'inquiry'.

The core research drawn upon to examine the evolution of the music industry in the digital era has primarily involved an extensive series of in-depth interviews with 30 key popular music industry informants mainly conducted across the period 2007–10. They were initially conducted during the course of an Irish-based doctoral research project. The majority of the interviewees are thus operating in Ireland, with a number of others UK-based. The interviewees comprise personnel and key informants across a broad spectrum of music industry activities, core and ancillary. Many of the comments and quotes continue to hold true, yet in such a dynamic and fast moving industry, some of the comments detailed in the chapters that follow may already seem a little dated. Three or four or five years add up to a long time in the music industry. But while this is so, they still provide a most valuable set of tools for the exercise at hand. It is important to remember that their value here lies in the light they shed on many of the common-sense assumptions we hold in relation to the digital technology/music industry relationship, and by extension, to the assumptions we make as a society to the role of technology in general. The data deriving from those interviews combines to complicate many of the straightforward assumptions that we routinely make in relation to the roles and outcomes of new and recent digital technological innovations in the context of the music industry. Perhaps more significantly, they paint a picture of innovations occurring outside the realm of technology that ultimately serve to emphasize strong strands of continuity contrasting with the more conventional images of radical change and upheaval implied by the host of media and journalistic accounts referred to above. In short, while many things change, many things don't.

All of the interviews drawn upon in this book were conducted over a decade after the internet first became a medium for the mass circulation of music. They provide interesting and useful insights into the experiences, activities and perspectives of a variety of key informants spanning a broad range of music industry sectors and related spheres. Their accounts illustrate the core issues, challenges and opportunities as they have evolved for the industry on that 'first battle ground' as music has turned into data. These accounts ultimately combine to offer a much more complex and nuanced perspective on the music industry in the digital age than many of the techno-centric accounts of radical disruption that point largely, or only to crisis and decline.

The 30 interviewees were as follows: Stuart Bailie (music journalist); Ben Barrett (artist manager); Jim Carroll (music journalist); P. J. Curtis (record producer); John D'Ardis (record/CD manufacturer and studio owner); Dick Doyle (national record industry trade organization representative); George Ergatoudis (music radio executive); Bruce Findlay (artist manager); Ross Graham (director, Northern Ireland Music Industry Commission [NIMIC]); Dermot Hanrahan (media entrepreneur); Jackie Hayden (music journalist); Gerry Harford (artist manager); Shay Hennessy (independent label owner); Peter Jenner (artist manager); Úna Johnston (music industry trade fair organizer); Willie Kavanagh (major label executive); John Kennedy (ex-international record industry trade organization representative); Johnny Lappin (independent music publisher); Steve Lindsey (independent music publisher); Jim Lockhart (musician / music radio producer); Fachtna O'Ceallaigh (artist manager); Dave O'Grady (independent label owner); Michael O'Riordan (independent music publisher); Petr Pandula (independent label owner); John Sheehan (retired major label executive); Julian Vignoles (TV commissioning editor); Alison Wenham (international independent record industry trade organization representative); Bill Whelan (composer and record producer); John Williamson (artist manager); and Ian Wilson (music radio producer). The activities listed after each name represents each interviewee's principal occupation at the time of the interview. A short biography for each interviewee is contained in the appendix at the back of this book.

However, it should be noted that a number of these interviewees have worked in more than one area of the music industry (or related sphere of activity) during their career. The overall 'occupational' breakdown of the 30 interviewees is as follows: eight are (or were) employed by a major record company in either senior management or personnel roles; six work (or have worked) for an independent record company; three are (or were) employed in senior management or personnel roles by a major music publishing company; five own, work (or have worked) for an independent music publishing company; six are (or were) artist managers; four work (or worked) in live music promotion; three work (or worked) as record producers; three serve (or served) on the board of management of music royalty collection societies; three are (or were) music retailers; three are (or were) professional musicians/composers/creative artists; four are (or were) senior representatives of industry trade bodies; four are (or were) music journalists; eight work (or worked) in the management and production of music radio; three have produced specialized music programming for television; one is a record/CD/DVD manufacturer; one is a former music industry lawyer; two have worked in training and education for the music industry; one is a music industry trade fair co-ordinator/event manager.

So, as the sums above indicate, a significant number of those interviewed have worked across two or more spheres of activity throughout their careers. The assembly of such an array of informants serves to offer a unique, and extremely rich information resource, based on the accumulated (and often tacit) knowledge of highly experienced actors across a broad range of music industry activities. While each individual interviewee offered a unique angle on the music industry in digital times, the artist managers interviewed provided particularly interesting and insightful accounts. As managers representing the interests of recording artists, they engage with all of the other actors throughout the music industry chain and surrounding spheres of activity and, as such, offer an additional insight into and perspective upon the role of other actors.

Historical context

At this point, it is perhaps useful to offer some historical context to the evolution of the music industry. If everything is supposed to be changing, then what is it changing from? What was the world of music like before the internet entered the equation?

As we will see in this book, the popular music industry is much more than just the record industry. Rather, it has been aptly described as a 'scaffold of intense alliances between diverse and often conflicting interests and motivations' (FORTE Task Force, 1996: 21). As an industry, popular music encompasses a variety of dimensions comprising a range of actors including songwriters, composers, performers, artist management services, record labels, distributors, retailers, music publishing companies, live music agents and promoters and a host of other related realms of business. At the industry's core lie three primary spheres of activity: the record industry, the music publishing industry and the live music industry.

Out of all the sub-sectors in this industrial network, the most important in terms of economic significance has been the record industry. As the twentieth century progressed, the record industry multiplied its value. In the mid-1940s the value of record sales in the United States was US$109 million; by 1980 this figure had risen to US$3.7 billion (Gronow, 1983). The other major international markets for records (United Kingdom, Germany, France and Japan) also expanded significantly across this period. By 1990 the retail value of the US recorded music market was US$7.5 billion with estimated global revenues in excess of US$24 billion (IFPI, cited in Negus, 2011: 59–60). The compact disc (CD) proved to be a real boom technology for the record industry and provided the platform for a decade-long period of super-profits driving global revenues to a record high of US$38.7 billion in 1999 (IFPI, 2000).

It is also important to emphasize that the story of the record industry throughout the twentieth century was not entirely a picture of year-on-year growth. As Hesmondhalgh (2007) points out, cycles of boom and decline have characterized the sector. Worldwide recession saw record sales experience a downturn in the early 1930s and again at the turn of the 1980s. Overall, however, the record industry has experienced a very significant swelling of its value up until 1999.

Throughout its history, the music industry has experienced a high degree of concentrated ownership (Chapple and Garofalo, 1977; Negus, 2011; Peterson and Berger, 1990). By the early 1990s, shortly before the internet first evolved as a medium for the widespread dissemination of music, five major transnational music labels controlled over 70 per cent of the global market for recorded music (Negus, 2011). Soon after, these five became the four major labels we noted in reference to the above Napier-Bell article. More recently, the sector has experienced further consolidation and reduced to just three – Universal, Sony and Warner. Such 'oligopolistic concentration' of the record industry was traditionally 'maintained by control of the total production flow from raw materials to wholesale sales' (Peterson and Berger, 1990: 143). Within this, governance over the sphere of music distribution – the key control stage or 'moment' in the overall value chain in the music industry (as in other media industries) – has, as a matter of course been exercised by a very small number of very powerful interests.

This concentration of power has at times led to accusations of the major record labels acting against the interests of their own consumers. For example, the past 15 years has seen a number of CD price-fixing investigations in Europe and the United States. Also, Longhurst (1995) points to a House of Commons Committee monopoly enquiry into the overpricing of CDs in Britain in the 1990s which concluded that copyright restrictions artificially inflated CD prices by restricting the import of cheaper recordings. The Committee recommended that the UK Department of Trade and Industry re-examine legislation around copyright issues with particular reference to its anticompetitive effects in the recorded music industry.

In addition to consumers losing out, the independent recording sector also failed to make gain from the premium profit market in CD sales. As Burnett explains, by largely removing vinyl from the marketplace in the latter part of the 1980s, the major music companies 'effectively eliminated' the independent sector (1996: 59). This was because much of the new CD market derived from reissuing vinyl recordings in this evolving digital format. Some of the larger independent labels with established back catalogue were acquired by the major labels during this period for the potential opportunities arising from such rereleases. Burnett points to the Motown label as an example here. Island and Virgin provide others. However, the lack of any back catalogue placed newer and emerging independent companies at a disadvantage as they had little to use as leverage in negotiation with the majors.

The great promise of the internet was that all of this would change, and it is against this backdrop that the outcome of the internet in the music industry to date needs to be measured.

Also, we must be mindful of how core activities and revenue streams have been evolving in recent decades. The record industry was initially based around manufacturing, but as Simon Frith declared a quarter of a century ago: 'For the music industry, the age of manufacture is now over' (Frith, 1987: 57). Frith was referring to the growing importance of the 'secondary' use of recordings through broadcasting and synchronization in terms of the revenue generation for rights owners. Such a declaration regarding the demise of manufacturing was premature given how the CD would continue to drive profits for the record industry for another dozen years. However, attention to the expansion of revenue streams through secondary uses for music is important when it comes to developing a more holistic understanding of how the music industry has evolved in recent decades. Thus, we can see the term 'music industry' referring to 'a complex network of rights owners and network users, a continual flow of rights income which seems inexhaustible, and sometimes, indeed, quite random' (Frith, 2004: 176).

As we shall see in the chapters ahead, close attention to this seemingly bountiful 'flow of rights income' serves to paint a more complex and multidimensional picture of the outcome of the music industry in the digital era than the one-dimensional narrative of online piracy crippling its efforts to sustain itself.

Theoretical context

As Mark Latonero notes: 'Music and technology have been entwined in a close relationship for millennia' (2003: 2). Given the centrality of digital technologies, particularly the internet, to arguments surrounding the apparent crisis in the music industries and to debates surrounding change in music production, distribution and consumption practices, it is useful to incorporate some key perspectives on relationships between technology and actors in the social world into the analytical framework underpinning this book. There is much debate among theorists regarding the role of technology in society. While some theoretical approaches label technology as an independent, seemingly autonomous force that drives change in society (i.e. technological determinist approaches), others argue that it is impossible to separate technology from the social environment within which it emerges, and that the reification of the technological is flawed (social shaping of technology approaches).[4] This book implicitly draws upon the tensions between these two broad theoretical perspectives to produce an informed analysis of recent developments in the music industry.

Sentiments of the radical transformative power of technologies are well established in the chambers of academia. The work of such authors as Marshall McLuhan (1962, 1964), Alvin Toffler (1970, 1980), Daniel Bell (1973), Nicholas Negroponte (1996) and Kevin Kelly (1999) comprises some of the most robust and substantial literature labelled as 'technological determinism'. This term, which is widely attributed to the US economist Thorstein Veblen, is effectively an umbrella term referring to a range of theoretical perspectives which, put crudely, operate to a greater or lesser degree on the fundamental assumption that society is forced to change in order to adopt technological innovations, innovations that 'progress' along a linear trajectory, heightening efficiency. Such thinking is pervasive in debates around the evolution of the music industry in the digital era.

Perhaps the predominance of technological determinist thinking in society is evidenced by the way in which society codifies historical periods according to their most salient, characteristic technologies, each referring to the presumed dominant technical form of a specific era (Winston, 1998). We live in 'the age of the internet', or 'the digital era'. The branding of Ireland as a 'knowledge economy' (and more recently 'smart economy') illustrates this trend for apotheosis through technological innovation, and it mirrors a similar campaign in Thatcher's Britain in the 1980s (Preston, 2001). Even the title of this book reflects society's labelling of the early twenty-first century as a technological epoch!

Conversely, social shaping theories essentially challenge technological determinist assumptions regarding the nature and trajectory of technological change and its impacts upon the social world. Following the lead of Raymond Williams (1974), authors such as Bijker, Pinch and Hughes (1987), MacKenzie and Wajcman (1985), Marvin (1988), and Winston (1995, 1998) all essentially shifted the focus

---

4 See, for example, Lister et al. (2008) and Preston (2001) for a detailed synthesis of the core arguments across this spectrum.

from a techno-centric perspective on social relations to an approach that afforded primacy to social forces, and the effects of society on technology. As with technological determinism, the aforementioned authors represent a range of different approaches towards analysing the role of technologies from a social shaping perspective. Ultimately however, in one way or another, these authors all emphasize the role of sociocultural conditions in shaping the development of technologies. Lister et al. summarize social shaping approaches as:

> Implicitly arguing that technology on its own is incapable of producing change, the view being that whatever is going on around us in terms of rapid technological change, there are rational and manipulative interests at work driving the technology in particular directions and it is to these that we should primarily direct our attention. (Lister et al., 2008: 74)

Social shaping theorists, thus, argue against the primacy of technologies in society. Rather, they forward an approach based upon society shaping the outcome of technologies to its own needs, or perhaps more appropriately, technological innovations and evolutions as the products of struggles and conflicts and struggles between different interest groups in society, many of which are removed from any predominantly technological logic or trajectory.

Raymond Williams (1974) emphasizes the role played by 'real decision-making groups' in society, such as political and economic elites in shaping the outcome of technologies in our social world. Winston (1998) serves to illuminate these processes by providing a 'model for the nature of change in media technologies'. Here Winston outlines a range of historical continuities that underlie apparently radical technological innovation. He illustrates how new technologies are suppressed by 'general social constraints' that 'coalesce to limit the potential of the device to radically disrupt pre-existing social formations' (ibid.: 11). This is what Winston refers to as 'the law of the suppression of radical potential'. This aspect of Winston's model is particularly pertinent to the overall approach of this book.

As we have already established, the internet is commonly regarded as possessing the potential to produce radical disruption to the role and interests of major music labels, and in particular to the relationships those labels have traditionally enjoyed with music fans. However, as Winston's (1998) analysis of the evolution of media technologies (spanning from the telegraph to the internet) indicates, the actual outcomes of technological innovations in the media and communications spheres often differ from those envisaged and proposed by their designers and suppliers. Rather, as Preston (2001) argues, the widespread adoption and appropriation of radical technological innovations is accompanied by a diverse set of 'matching' innovations which must be considered as relatively autonomous from any 'inherent' technical considerations, characteristics or trajectories. These include organizational, industrial, social and institutional (including policy) innovations. Hence, the precise outcome of any radical technological innovation (in terms of its socio-economic effects) is the product of conflicts and struggles between different interest groups in domains that can be far removed from any predominantly 'technological' logic or trajectory. The full working out and embedding of such complex sets of innovations involves, according to Preston (ibid.), a process of social learning which may require a relatively extended phase of social struggles and trial and error experimentation.

Such perspectives indicate that we must move beyond technology-centred analysis to address the empirical interplay of key socio-economic interests and powers that are framing the practical application and/or appropriation of the internet in the context of the music industry. This book is thus concerned with how such interplay shapes the form and extent of the internet's disruptive potential in the music industry. To borrow and bend Winston's (1998) phrasing, this book will probe the key 'suppressants' of the internet's 'radical potential' to disrupt the music industry.

Outline of chapters to follow

The responses of interviewees to questions about change in the music industry fall into three broad categories:

1   They offer perspectives on the problems or challenges generated for the music industry either directly or indirectly by digitalization.

2   Their combined accounts serve to place these problems or challenges in context by highlighting opportunities that have evolved for established music industry actors both within and beyond the digital realm during the first decade or so of this century.

3   They offer perspectives on how to get music to mass markets in the digital era, thus shedding light on those utopian visions advanced by Negroponte, Kelly and the like regarding the promise and potential of digital technologies to make the media 'playing field' more democratic and accessible.

Each of these issues is dealt with in turn in the chapters that follow. A brief outline of the remaining chapters of this book is outlined below.

Chapter 2 outlines interviewee perceptions of the challenges being faced by the contemporary popular music industry. Here, interviewees are initially asked to consider key 'headline-level' changes they perceive to have occurred in the music industry since the turn of the millennium. Perhaps unsurprisingly, almost all signal the internet as the most significant development, and most link this directly to an overall downturn in record sales revenues. These arguments centre on the perceived loss of scarcity resulting from the inability to apply effective copyright control mechanisms in cyberspace. However, beyond this they advance additional factors that they claim provide evidence of severe record industry decline, as well as forwarding perspectives on a range of phenomena that they perceive as causing these problems. While some of these factors extend beyond technological logic, most are related to various aspects of digitalization. This leads us to consider recent employment trends across the major music companies; the decline of 'bricks and mortar' retailing; criticisms levelled at the major music companies over long-term inefficiencies and a failure to realize or grasp opportunities afforded by the internet at an earlier stage; consequences arising from the shift from physical to digital formats; and the effects of supermarket retailing.

Chapters 3 and 4 see interviewees advancing what might best be categorized as strategies or responses of the established music industry to the 'problems' raised in Chapter 2, as well as highlighting opportunities that have arisen through new digital platforms and, the expansion of some more traditional revenue streams for the music industry. Chapter 3 primarily focuses on issues surrounding the digital sphere, and recent licensed platforms for the digital distribution and promotion of music. This chapter will first consider legal developments (in the domain of copyright law) that were unfolding during the course of the interviews, as well as the development of new business models and licensing systems that enable music copyright owners to exploit evolving opportunities in the digital realm. Overall we will see how the emergence and proliferation of digital music stores, ad-supported streaming partnership and various other licensed online and mobile platforms for music is serving to grow of the overall digital music market, and increase the number of revenue streams open to music companies relating to recording, publishing and other related products and services. The chapter also considers digital games as a site of music revenue and promotion and, the potential that exists in emerging markets such as the BRIC countries.

Chapter 4 then sees interviewees first consider how opportunities for revenue generation from secondary sources have evolved, and how this shapes the overall picture of the music industry. Here, emphasis is placed on the overall growth of the music publishing sector from the mid-1990s onwards and in particular, the synchronization opportunities for music in film, TV and advertising. Beyond this, the chapter sees interviewees reflect upon the recent evolution of the live music industry in the context of its increasing convergence with other core music industry sub-sectors. It proceeds to consider aspects of the relationship between the content and technology sectors and highlight how some of the key players on the music content stage are linked to, and have interests in the technology sphere. Finally, this chapter moves to consider the evolution of broader, all-encompassing '360 degree' deals for music artists.

Chapter 5 primarily concerns itself with the promise and potential of the internet to enable music artists to take control of their own destiny and bypass the more traditional structures associated with the established music industry in getting their music to market. As such, it asks interviewees to consider if and how the 'do-it-yourself' approach to a music industry career has been enhanced in the digital era, and to what extent, if any, the music industry playing field has been levelled by the internet. The chapter examines the composition of the recorded music market and proceeds to consider the roles of and relationships between major and independent companies. It sees interviewees reflect upon earlier techno-centric predictions which point to more independent actors achieving increased and easier access to the marketplace and offer their perspectives on and experience of the current relationship between major and independent actors. Beyond this, drawing largely on the contributions of some of the artist managers who participated in interviews, the chapter examines contemporary processes for getting new music to market and considers, among other things, the role of blogs, online audio- and video-streaming services, social networking sites and other online music discussion and review platforms in assisting an emerging artist to independently generate a public profile.

Leading on from Chapter 5, Chapter 6 moves to consider the role of tastemakers in the internet age, and which 'intermediaries' are most effective in growing a consumer base. While highlighting some potential benefits associated with social networking sites, interviewees almost invariably switched the conversation to the medium of radio as crucial tastemaker. Television and music press were also highlighted, but only to signal their limited and diminishing effectiveness in the contemporary environment. Beyond this, interviewees are asked to reflect upon and advance their concepts of the contemporary music consumer and the consumer bands that constitute the music consumer market.

Finally, Chapter 7 summarizes some of the key changes and continuities that have occurred in the music industry well over a decade after the internet established itself as a medium for the promotion and distribution of music. While acknowledging the role of digital technological innovations in evolving change in the music industry, this chapter also contends that key restructuring and reconfiguration of the broader music industry that has taken place, thus serving to suppress the radically transformative potential of file-sharing technologies and other digital innovations in the context of the music industry. As such, it points to many of the more traditional music industry structures remaining in place despite the promise of digital innovations to dismantle such frameworks. Furthermore, it points to a re-conceptualization of the recording artist in the internet era that serves to bolster and sustain such oligopolistic structures.

2

Death by digital?

The starting point of this book was the assumption that the music industry has undergone radical change in recent years, driven by a digital 'revolution'. The key challenge for this book is therefore to probe and examine how the music industry has evolved in the context of a changing technological environment. The raw materials drawn upon for constructing this reality are the insights and perspectives of 30 industry professionals and key informants from across the spectrum of music industry sub-sectors and related spheres.

These interviewees were invited to reflect upon and articulate their particular perceptions of change across a wide range of aspects of the music industry. In many instances, the responses of interviewees to questions about change may best be categorized under two headings: first, they offered perspectives on problems generated for the music industry either directly or indirectly by digitalization; beyond that, they highlighted strategies formulated by the industry to provide 'solutions' to these problems, or to compensate in other ways for any losses incurred through falling record sales. While subsequent chapters will be dedicated to mapping the responses and solutions they perceive as evolving, this chapter focuses specifically on interviewee's perceptions of the challenges being faced by the contemporary music industry, that is, problems.

At the outset, each participant was asked to identify the most fundamental 'headline-level' changes that occurred in the music industry since the late 1990s. Perhaps unsurprisingly, all interviewees signalled the arrival of the internet as a medium for the circulation of music as the most significant development, and most initially linked this to a downturn in the economic fortunes of the record industry. However, beyond this they advanced additional factors that they claim provide evidence of severe record industry decline, as well as forwarding perspectives on a range of phenomena that they perceive as causing these problems. While some of these factors extend beyond technological logic, most are related to various aspects of digitalization. This leads us to consider recent employment trends across the major music companies; the decline of 'bricks and mortar' retailing; criticisms levelled at the major music companies over long-term inefficiencies and a failure to realize or grasp opportunities afforded by the internet at an earlier stage; consequences arising from the shift from physical to digital formats; and the effects of supermarket retailing.

Primary perception of change: File-sharing = downturn in sales

When asked to consider if change has occurred in the music industry over the past decade, the starting point for almost all interviewees is two factors: the rise of the internet; and the simultaneous fall of record sales. These responses follow closely many of the media and journalistic accounts referred to in chapter one. In some cases, the 'effects' of the internet are presented as being more extreme or fatalistic than in others, but ultimately, *most* interviewees concur that very significant change has occurred and it's mostly for the worse. For example:

> People aren't paying for music anymore. That's the problem. I think the majors have collapsed and it is over for them. (Dave O'Grady, artist manager, personal interview)

> With moving online . . . the bottom has fallen out of the music industry's sales. (Michael O'Riordan, music publisher, personal interview)

> Digitalisation has totally rattled the industry. The internet is certainly hurting the industry . . . The big record companies have taken a

real pounding in the last few years. (Peter Jenner, artist manager, personal interview)

There is now a perception that music is actually free, that recorded music is something that you don't actually need to pay for . . . Under the current structure this is a form of thievery, but people say 'lighten up, everybody's doing it'. Because of consensus there is a new morality. People expect then that they don't have to pay for music. (Bill Whelan, composer, personal interview)

We put the downturn almost exclusively down to peer-to-peer networks and illegal uploading of music. (Dick Doyle, IRMA, personal interview)

In 2009, the International Federation of Phonographic Industries (IFPI) estimated that 95 per cent of all music traffic on the internet related to illicit file-sharing and distribution (IFPI, 2009a: 3). They subsequently predicted a cumulative loss of €240 billion to European creative industries across the 2008–2015 period with the simultaneous loss of 1.2 million jobs in these sectors (IFPI, 2011a: 5).

Media entrepreneur (and former manager of Virgin music retail in Ireland) Dermot Hanrahan describes the record industry of the 1980s and 1990s as being dominated a small number of 'aggressive, domineering businesses' that 'oozed arrogance' (personal interview). Hanrahan described each of the major record labels as 'a monopoly in their own right' as they held exclusive access to the stars on their label and thus dictated the terms upon which retailers or third parties accessed the recording and publishing copyrights they owned. However, Hanrahan sees such an era of dominance as having been 'destroyed' by the advent of the internet file-sharing technologies: 'Peer-to-peer means the game is up for the big record labels. It's over. Finito' (personal interview).

For former Pink Floyd manager, Peter Jenner, the 'crisis' he perceives facing the record industry derives from that industry's inability to generate opportunities for monetizing creativity in an internet environment:

The internet means the whole funding of music is now in question. How do we fund it? Where does the money come from? Where can we make money? How can we make money? What do we have to do to make money? This is not just about money to the artist but about the investment that is often required to bring an act to the point where they have enough recognition and support to be able to make a living from creating, recording and performing music. (Peter Jenner, personal interview)

Record industry trade body representatives from the IFPI, IRMA, AIM and Phonographic Performance Ireland (PPI) advanced a number of specific cases of mass infringements of copyrights to support their argument that file-sharing is severely damaging their market. These accounts also suggest a large quantity of users 'stealing' vast quantities of recorded music. The implication is often that having access to free music on the internet means that many users will only consume pirated music, and many cases they will pirate all files at their disposal. For example:

> Peer-to-peer sharing, it's a bit like this: a kid records something at home, and it's like he's stealing a chocolate from Willy Wonka's factory, but the problem with peer-to-peer is that it opens up the whole factory and they steal the lot. You know, there is this kid we are suing now who has uploaded 37,000 copyrights . . . People go: 'the poor kid, you shouldn't be doing that to him', but the problem is he's hurting us . . . 37,000 copyrights stolen . . . 37,000 copyrights . . . 37,000 copyrights. (Willie Kavanagh, EMI Ireland, personal interview)

Dick Doyle cites an additional case where IRMA is pursuing an individual who has 30,000 song files on their personal computer (PC): 'When you think of it, 30,000 songs being shared worldwide – the loss to our industry is colossal' (personal interview). It remains extremely unlikely that every illicitly shared music file would otherwise correspond to a 'legitimate' sale on the part of the record industry, but, as Doyle continues (speaking in 2007):

> How much is file-sharing hurting [the record industry]? It's definitely hurting badly. In Ireland you can see that we are down from about 145 million to 110 million so that's about a 35 million drop since 2001 . . . that's 25%. So it is definitely hurting it badly. (Dick Doyle, personal interview)

According to Alison Wenham, chair of the AIM:

> The major industry has always controlled the means of distribution up until the digital era, and that control has been lost. Not just the major companies, *all* copyright owners have lost that control with the internet. (Alison Wenham, personal interview)

Wenham proceeds how state that 'everything' can be accessed for free on the internet. Speaking in our 2007 interview, then IFPI chairman and CEO John Kennedy advanced that there were no historical comparisons to the challenges faced by the record industry since the advent of peer-to-peer networks. What makes the plight of the record industry unique in his eyes is the perpetration of:

> wholesale theft which is tolerated by society, governments and the media. It is sometimes even seen as virtuous that people are indulging in taking music for free . . . A small microcosm of one of the problems we have with society nowadays is whilst the music industry has suffered from illegal copying, copying has become part of kids instinct now to the extent that it's such a problem in education that teachers and university lecturers are having huge problems with plagiarism which is damaging our education system and the young people within it in a very material way. (John Kennedy, personal interview)

Dick Doyle stated that his organization was involved in an ongoing process of issuing lawsuits against individual network users, and that all individuals they were pursuing had infringed a minimum of five hundred copyrights:

> Obviously the pricing of the CD was very good before because people saw it as a high value product and they were prepared to pay for it, where as now people think music should be for free. A lot of young people have been brought up on the fallacy that music is for nothing because they can get it on the internet and they can share it with friends. So there is a whole cultural change going on now compared to what was happening twenty years ago . . . We have spawned a whole generation of people who have never

bought music . . . and they have never appreciated that there is an economic value in music . . . Maybe with the next generation we can try to get back to where there is a value in music . . . where we can say that there is an artist who needs to be fed. (Dick Doyle, personal interview)

Doyle's argument regarding the 'artist who needs to be fed' is echoed among many of my interviewees. Both major and independent record and publishing company representatives alike ultimately reduce debates surrounding copyright infringement to an attack on the creative artists who produce the industry's raw material. Thus, some interviewees saw this problem not only leading to the decline of record companies and broader music companies, but also the demise of musical creativity resulting from mass copyright infringement. They regard the evolution of a culture that regards music as a 'free' service as removing incentives for artists to engage in creativity and produce music and recordings. A number of key informants from the spheres of recording and music publishing point to an impending crisis around creativity arising from a dirge of artistic endeavour amidst a culture that fails to place economic value on musical texts. For example:

This is *the* problem. The culture has seeped in where by people are beginning to think that music is *free*. If you take that to its logical conclusion, well when the music runs out there'll be *no more music* . . . That is the flux that we are in at the moment . . . If people think that music is free, songwriters are going to stop making music because there will be no point. They are not going to make any money from their efforts so they'll go and do something else . . . *There'll be no more music.* (Johnny Lappin, music publisher, personal interview)

Because it is there for nothing on the internet, people think music is free. Music should *not* be free, but it is . . . If copyright law can no longer protect you against somebody running off copies, then you will no longer have any creativity. This is what people don't realise. (Michael O'Riordan, music publisher, personal interview)

Former IFPI chairman and CEO John Kennedy agrees that removing incentives to produce creative works, courtesy of a 'broad devaluing of music' resulting from mass copyright infringements serves to make performing and creative careers in music less attractive propositions. Pointing to the mid-teens to mid-twenties age bracket as the 'key offenders' in terms of illegal file-sharing, Kennedy outlines how this section of consumer society has traditionally been the group providing the ignition for new artists, new investment and new revenues. The large-scale withdrawal of this group from the recorded music industry revenue chain holds implications for the long-term 'health' of the industry as it 'hurts those who provide its raw material' (personal interview). However Kennedy rejects ideas of a potential dearth of creativity killing the music industry. As he explains, for the organizations he represents, 'the plus' is that more music than ever is being consumed, 'the minus' is that less music is being paid for. Kennedy's optimism for the survival of his industry derives from what he considers to be a shift in attitude towards the internet by broader society. He sees such change as primarily driven by society's concerns over such issues of pornography, and the need for commercial operators to measure their bandwidth in a more effective way. As such, the internet is becoming an increasingly regulated environment:

> Some years ago the idea of any policing of the internet would have been considered sacrilege, but the idea now that the internet wouldn't be policed for any number of reasons is just naïve. (John Kennedy, personal interview)

Kennedy sees such a shift in attitude as 'potentially breeding hope' for a record industry as it implies governments are now displaying an increasing willingness to act on online activities that 'cannot be good for society'. Kennedy argues that the extent of actions taken by legislative and judicial systems against file-sharers, technology suppliers and networks within various nation states around the world is 'too little, but I will not say too late'. He contends that governments are beginning to understand the problems faced by the member companies that the IFPI represents, and are beginning to play a role that will assist the record industry in transforming consumption habits towards a point where more people start purchasing music again.

All of the above comments must be considered in the context of IFPI statistics which report how the global recorded music market has largely been in decline throughout the first decade of the new millennium (Table 2.1). They indicate an initial drop of 17.3 per cent from a record high of US$38.7 billion sales in 1999 to US$32 billion in 2003 (IFPI, 2004). While there was a modest recovery of 4.7 per cent throughout 2004 and sales held (almost) steady throughout 2005, the subsequent period to the end of 2006 saw a further drop of 5.4 per cent to an overall global retail value of US$31.8 billion (IFPI, 2007c). By the end of 2010 this figure had dropped to US$24.3 (IFPI, 2011c). This pattern is also reflected in an Irish context where record sales revenues dropped from a high of €145.6 million in 2001 to €72.2 million by the end of 2010 (ibid.).

TABLE 2.1 Global retail value of recorded music sales 1999–2010 (combined physical and digital formats in $US billions)

	1999	2000	2002	2004	2006	2008	2010
Total	38.7	36.9	32.2	33.6	31.8	26.5	24.4

Source: Author, compiled from various IFPI Recording Industry in Numbers reports 2000–11.

However, while many media and industry accounts imply that there is a general consensus that peer-to-peer file-sharing technologies have led to a significant decline in record sales revenues, the responses of some interviewees in this research study complicates this picture. The source of record sales revenue data is the IFPI, the trade body the represents the interests of, primarily, the major record labels. On an annual basis, the IFPI collects and publishes sales statistics from its various member bodies across the world. As some interviewees highlight, in most cases, these figures are uncritically relayed to the public via the media. Instances questioning their accuracy are extremely rare. As artist manager Williamson advances:

the whole 1999 meltdown period . . . who knows whether that's true or not because we're relying on the figures that come from guess where? The major record companies themselves. (John Williamson)

As Hesmondhalgh (2007b) emphasizes, we must recognize how such a picture of declining revenues offers support to the lobbying power of the record industry in their quest to encourage the legislative and judicial arms of different regions to extend the reach of copyright law. The IFPI and its local partners around the world have consistently and robustly canvassed for the expansion of intellectual property control mechanisms across the years since the internet emerged as a medium for distributing music. During the course of my interviews with current or former record industry trade body representatives, these informants emphasized their roles as lobbyists, both at international and local level.

The picture of declining record sales revenues and its conflation with a wider music industries downturn also strengthens the arguments of major players in the music industries when it comes to receiving the blessing of institutions of governance for mergers, joint ventures and alliances such as the Sony-BMG merger in 2004. In 2006, the European Court of First Instance annulled the European Commission's original clearance decision from 2004 on foot of an appeal from IMPALA, an independent record industry umbrella group. However, the merged parties successfully appealed this decision. In obtaining the original go-ahead for the merger they cited, among other factors, the necessity for consolidation 'to help our artists realise their creative goals while at the same time . . . address the important issues that will enable this artform to evolve and prosper' in the face of a shrinking market (Sony Music Entertainment press release, 5 August 2004). Ironically, 2004 was the first year since 1999 that the IFPI posted an (albeit mild) upturn in global record sales. Sony subsequently subsumed BMG in 2009 and now operates as Sony Music Entertainment. 2012 similarly saw the European Commission raise antitrust concerns regarding the takeover of EMI by the Universal Music Group.

Interviewee John Williamson focuses less on the statistics produced by the IFPI and more on the media's reporting of same. He advances that the IFPI sales data might be 'exactly right . . . close to right . . . or nowhere near right'. The point for Williamson is that these statistics are rarely if ever analysed in the media and are most often uncritically relayed as fact:

> Nobody actually questions the figures. Journalists don't or cannot either. So you are in a situation where anyone who has got the resources to put together something that is reasonably impressive and has a whole lot of figures in it is going to get somewhere with the politicians. (John Williamson, personal interview)

Furthermore, all of the above statistics relating to recorded music sales revenues must be considered in the context of reported revenues for the combined music industries as a whole. A 2008 economic report issued by the Performing Rights Society in the United Kingdom indicates that despite a decade-long decline in the value of recorded music sales, overall revenues have been on the increase in that territory. The royalty collection society estimate a year-on-year rise of 4.7 per cent with total combined revenues from recording, publishing and live streams rising from ST£3.2 billion in 2007 to ST£3.6 billion in 2008 (PRS for Music, 2009a). Marketing and media research analysts eMarketer estimated that the global combined revenues from these core streams rose from US$60.7 billion in 2006 to US$62.6 by the end of 2008 billion (Verna, 2009). Placed in an even wider context incorporating musical instrument sales, portable digital players, music reproduction hardware and advertising revenues generated by music radio, Price Waterhouse Cooper estimated the 2007 value of 'music driven' industries at US$130 billion (PWC, 2007). A later study (Winseck, 2011) estimated that while the record industry is in decline, the combined value of a broader range of music industry sub-sectors, encompassing recording, live performances, publishing and others has actually risen from US$51 billion in 1998 to more than US$71 billion in 2010. This represents an overall growth of 40 per cent across those sectors over that 12-year period. Thus, it is important to note that music has an economic relevance that extends far beyond the scope of record sales, and such data indicates a global music industry that is actually growing rather than one in decline.

Conflicting research on the 'effects' of file-sharing

A further point regarding the relationship between the internet and the decline in record sales stems from a range of research reports and surveys that have been produced at various points during the past number of years on the outcome to date of internet file-sharing technologies regarding user behaviour and practice. These accounts, outlined in reports by trade bodies, consumer lobby groups, industry consultants, policymakers and the academic world serve to complicate 'conventional wisdom' on the 'effects' of internet file-sharing on the recorded music market. While some reports and studies point to online 'piracy' inflicting significant harm on the music industry, others are more ambivalent in their findings regarding the effects of file-sharing activities. Moreover, others argue that unauthorized file-sharing serves to drive consumer spending on other music services (e.g. concert tickets). Outlined below is a brief overview of some of these studies.

Examining a range of potential causal factors for the decline in recorded music sales revenues, Liebowitz (2006) ultimately concludes that file-sharing is the primary, if not exclusive reason behind the downturn. Liebowitz's (2008) analysis of album sales in 99 US cities over a five-year period from 1998 to 2003 ultimately concludes that file-sharing activities are directly responsible for a decline in recorded music sales that is larger than the actual decline that has occurred. In other words, but for peer-to-peer file-sharing, record sales would have continued to increase throughout this period. Liebowitz estimates that the annual rate of growth would have averaged approximately 4.46 per cent throughout this five-year period, keeping with the average achieved by the recording industry over the previous 25 years. For Liebowitz, these findings 'confirm the worst nightmares of the recording industry' (ibid.: 859).

While acknowledging that file-sharing held benefits for new and emerging artists by enhancing their profile and helping to establish a potential consumer base, Blackburn (2004, 2007) ultimately concluded that the free availability of online music files caused significant harm to the record industry by diminishing the sales of established acts. Zentner (2006), in his analysis of an earlier European consumer survey by Forrester Research, concludes that 'peer-to-peer usage reduces the probability of buying music by 30%' (ibid.: 63). In their analysis on US college students, Rob and Waldfogel (2006) estimate that illicit downloading results in a 10 per cent reduction in expenditure on albums. Peitz and Waelbroeck's (2004) analysis of music downloading across 16 countries over a four-year period concluded that file-sharing activities resulted in a 20 per cent downturn in CD sales. However, the same authors' later study on the role the internet plays in facilitating users to sample music concluded that consumers are now ultimately willing to pay more for music because file-sharing allows for a better match between individual tastes and music products (Peitz and Waelbroeck, 2006).

In their analysis of 'currently available research that sheds light on file-sharing', Oberholzer-Gee and Strumpf conclude that the 'empirical evidence on sales displacement is mixed' (2010: 25). Their survey indicates that while 'some studies find evidence of a substitution effect, other findings, in particular the papers using file-sharing data, suggest that piracy and music sales are largely unrelated' (ibid). Van Eijk, Poort and Rutten (2010) conclude that while there is little likelihood that a majority of downloaded music files will ever come from an authorized source, the effects of illicit file-sharing are in fact less threatening to the viability of the music industry than the major rights holders argue. Rather, they find that only a small percentage of music exchanged on peer-to-peer file-sharing networks 'comes at the expense of industry turnover. This renders the overall welfare effects of file sharing robustly positive' (ibid: 51). That particular study draws upon earlier Dutch-based (Huygen et al., 2009) research on the economic and cultural aspects of file-sharing which concludes:

> The degree of substitution is difficult to determine, and controversial . . . Measuring the possible harmful effect of a specific uploader's content is even more difficult, if not downright impossible. (ibid.: 103–4)

While Mortimer et al. (2010) point to file-sharing activities leading to a reduction in the level of recorded music sales, they also highlight a simultaneous increase in live performance revenues, particularly for smaller acts.

Contradiction and ambivalence have been characteristics of reports from earlier years. A 2007 market research survey by NPD Group indicated that legal download sales were the fastest growing digital music category in 2006, and, despite having increased by 47 per cent over the previous 2 years, activities on peer-to-peer file-sharing networks was slowing (NPD, 2008). The report further argued that it was likely that the annual number of legal downloaders would surpass peer-to-peer file-sharers by the end of 2007. Conversely, in its annual digital music survey for 2007, Entertainment Media Research suggested pirated downloads had reached an all-time high in 2007 and were continuing to rise (cited in *The Guardian*, Monday, 30 July 2007). However, the same report also found online social networking sites to be boosting interest in music that translates into recorded music sales. Social networks such as MySpace are listed as the most popular sites with 30 per cent of respondents in a survey of 1,700 users claiming to make regular or occasional physical and/or digital purchases based on music they had discovered on a social networking site.

While the annual IFPI *Digital Music Reports* and *World Recording Industry in Numbers* reports illustrate strong year-on-year growth in overall digital sales since 2003, these reports invariably point to proliferating file-sharing activities preventing digital market increases from offsetting physical sales losses, and thus plunging their industry into crisis. However, according to Jim Carroll, journalist and ex-MD of the Lakota Record label:

> We need to draw a line here: In terms of the death of the record industry, it is a *story*, a media story. That's all . . . a *story* that is being fed through the media. (Jim Carroll, personal interview)

Carroll argues that popular media accounts of crisis in the record industry are based on 'half-truths' in so far as evidence of any downturn in terms of recorded music sales revenues has long since existed. However, overall revenues from recording and music publishing remain high. As Carroll continues:

> They are still making money and people are still buying music. Every year I go into Grafton Street [Dublin] as near to Christmas as I can stand and I just marvel at the amount of people in there buying CDs and I wonder why it can't be like that all year round. And sure there will be times like Christmas or when there is a big release, like Coldplay or U2 when there will be big fast sales. (Jim Carroll, personal interview)

Regarding the legitimate digital market, a 2006 sales analysis report by Forrester Research on the iTunes Digital Music Stores indicated a 65 per cent drop in sales at the Apple store throughout 2006, with file-sharing labelled as the primary cause. Their findings on iTunes were based on analyses of credit card transactions over a 27-month period. While Apple labelled this report as 'simply incorrect', it did not publish any statistics. However, while growth rates have slowed down in recent years, IFPI statistics illustrate the overall digital music market to have increased by more than 1,000 per cent between 2004 and 2010 (IFPI, 2011a). Furthermore, Nielssen Soundscan data points to the digital album market in the United States still growing by 14 per cent in the year to June 2012 (McDaniel, 2012). iTunes remains by far the most dominant player in the digital music store market. Furthermore, with Apple and Google on the verge of launching cloud-based digital music subscription services, independent telecoms analyst Ovum (2011) predict that such services will experience annual growth in the region of 60 per cent up to 2015, bringing the overall value of the digital music market to approximately US$20 billion.

Other reports indicate a significant level of ambivalence regarding the outcome of peer-to-peer file-sharing for the record industry. Research commissioned on the domestic recorded music market in Canada – compiled by Andersen and Frenz (2008) for Canadian government department *Industry Canada* – found that music file-sharing has no detrimental effect on recorded music sales; in fact it is associated with generating physical sales. Upon garnering responses from 2,100 participants, Andersen and Frenz concluded in their government sponsored research report, that among Canadians who engage in peer-to-peer file-sharing, for every 12 songs-files shared, physical sales increase by 0.44 CDs. In effect this means that for every two albums shared on peer-to-peer networks (or the equivalent amount of songs in single-track downloads), one additional 'legal' sale is generated. Overall, Andersen and Frenz found that:

> Analysis of the Canadian population does not uncover either a positive or negative relationship between the number of files downloaded from peer-to-peer networks and CDs purchased. That is, we find no direct evidence to suggest the net effect of P2P file-sharing is either positive or negative for Canada as a whole. (Andersen and Frenz, 2008: 24)

Furthermore, a 2005 study conducted by research agency The Leading Question claimed that active file-sharers spend four-and-a-half times more money on legal music purchases than consumers who only download from licensed sites (cited in *Billboard*, 2011a).

While initially attacking peer-to-peer file-sharing as a major contributory factor to a crisis within the record industry, EMI MD Willie Kavanagh, speaking in 2007, proceeded to place such 'piracy' into a perspective that was, in the longer term, somewhat less threatening to his industry:

> I don't think that this is a bad kind of analogy: When television took off in the sixties the idea was that film companies were screwed. Why would anybody go to the cinema when you could watch moving pictures for free on your telly? But decades later the reality is that there are still new movies released in cinemas every single week. Cinema is a business model that works . . . It's about consuming, and how people want to consume. There will always be illegal ways to consume music, but there are illegal ways to consume most things and these really hurt legitimate producers. (Willie Kavanagh, personal interview)

Kavanagh was also eager to stress that when it comes to file-sharing, the level of tolerance society possesses for the 'illegality of it all' is currently at a point that is 'way beyond being palatable'. He views file-sharing technology as a 'damaging but not fatal' development for the record industry.

Jim Carroll is equally at pains to emphasize that file-sharing, while significantly hurting the record industry, must be placed in a broader context. Carroll related an account of his attendance at the 2007 South By South West (SXSW) international music industry conference in Texas:

> I sat in on one very interesting panel where this guy actually broke down, in terms of file-sharing, how an album gets spread around – where it begins and where it starts getting shared and downloaded. It was amazing to me that the likes of Limewire and eDonkey are only number five in the sequence – There are four levels before that, four levels before it gets to the commoner garden peer-to-peer file-sharing services that we have all heard about. And the amount of people doing this are a tiny, tiny number relatively speaking. (Jim Carroll, personal interview)

Research on the symbiosis of peer-to-peer and iTunes at the Harvard Business School argues that the major record labels should give greater consideration to peer-to-peer traffic when formulating online pricing schemes. A study compiled in conjunction with the Universtat Autonoma de Barcelona advances that prices low enough to encourage users away from peer-to-peer networks are not optimal in large markets (Casadesus-Masanell et al., 2007). Rather, the study argues that the licensed suppliers of music are better off setting higher prices and attracting those consumers that are willing to pay due to congestion on peer-to-peer networks. Furthermore, the study finds that legal attacks by the record industry against software suppliers and individual file-sharers carry a harmful effect for peer-to-peer networks. Casadesus-Masanell and Hervaes-Drane (2010) offer a similar argument regarding the pricing strategies of authorized outlets.

An earlier study published by the Berkman Centre at Harvard University and Gartner in December 2005 based on a survey of 475 early adopters suggests that the capacity to share music files with other consumers is an important consideration for users when choosing an online music service. The report also highlights file-sharing to play significant role in determining subsequent recorded music purchases.

It is also worth remembering at this point, that claims of new technological developments harming established content producers are nothing new. In his testimony to the US House of Representatives in 1982 as part of their hearing on 'Home Recording and Copyrighted Works', Jack Valenti, then president of the Motion Picture Association of America (MPAA) accuses VCR technology of carrying detrimental consequences for the movie industry:

> I say to you, the VCR is to the American film producer and the American public what the Boston strangler is to the woman home alone . . . It's like a great tidal wave just off the shore . . . One does not have to be trained in sophisticated marketing and creative judgement to understand the devastation on the after-theater marketplace caused by the hundreds of millions of tapings hat will adversely impact on the future of the creative community in this country [US]. It's simply a question of basic economics and plain common sense. (Valenti cited in Committee of Judiciary records, Monday, 12 April 1982)

Valenti subsequently labelled the MPAAs campaign against internet 'piracy' as his 'own personal war' (see, for example, Lessig, 2004: 26). The record industry's 'home taping is killing music' campaign in the 1970s and 1980s in response to the widespread diffusion of cassette duplication technologies as standard in home stereo systems echoed similar sentiments.

Other key evidence of record industry decline

Beyond declining recorded music sales statistics, interviewees advanced two key strands of evidence pointing to record industry decline:

1 The shedding of jobs at major music companies in recent years;

2 The collapse of 'bricks and mortar' retail outlets for recorded music

Job cuts at the major labels

Referring to the Irish context, radio producer Jim Lockhart tells of 'swathes of people cut out of the record labels here'. In his ongoing dealings with labels regarding the acquisition of licensing rights among other factors, Lockhart is more frequently referred to the London offices of the companies who increasingly administer their Irish operations. Lockhart's testimony is borne out in the closure of Sony's distribution depot in Dublin. Sony was the last major label to retain an Irish-based distribution facility. Its closure also coincided with the stripping back of its local marketing personnel.

Many other interviewees describe the major record companies evolving into a smaller, tighter more controlled set of businesses than they previously were, in an environment where their ongoing viability is threatened. For example, according to Dave O'Grady (speaking in 2008):

> If you look at how many people they lay off and have being laying off in the last couple of years . . . I heard a figure quoted recently at the South by South-West trade fair that in America three years ago there were 500 major label A&R men, now there is 70. It is as simple as that. (Dave O'Grady, personal interview)

Speaking in 2007, AIM chair Alison Wenham echoes a similar message:

> Within major labels, there have been massive cutbacks worldwide. They have lost about one-third of their workforce in the last four years and one-third of their artist rosters too so there is increasing contractions in labour and artists and repertoire activity. (Alison Wenham, personal interview)

Such comments come in the wake of a series of staff-cutting announcements by major labels and, for Ross Graham, former chairman of NIMIC, these cuts are:

> solid evidence that the majors are becoming less profitable. There have been savage staff cuts left, right and centre because the

margins are so slim. It's all about survival in a retracting market. (Ross Graham, personal interview)

Supporting evidence can be drawn from a range of major label 'downsizing' measures taken in recent years. In late 2011 RCA Records announced the 'retirement' of its Arista, Jive and J Records labels with their respective rosters now being administered directly by RCA itself. In 2008, Universal announced the downsizing of its Island-Def Jam and Geffen-Interscope-A&M label groups. However, by far the most notable staff-cutting exercise came in January 2008 when EMI's recorded music division sliced two thousand jobs internationally reducing its workforce to 2,500 following a three-month review by then owners Terra Firma. According to Guy Hands, the founder and CEO of Terra Firma, this was a direct response 'to the challenges posed by a digital environment' that required the company to reduce costs by £200m a year (cited in *The Guardian*, Tuesday, 15 January 2008). For John Williamson, the case of EMI is the most stark example of the major labels developing 'much more efficient mechanisms' of operation:

> Suddenly, jobs started getting cut back. There are far fewer staff now, that's an obvious change, and obviously that has a knock on effect as regards what a record company can actually do. Similarly the way that they were structured and how much they would actually pay people at a junior level has actually changed downwards over the past few years. If you are at entry level in these industries it's like 'you should be privileged to be working for us' so you'll get taken in on work experience and get virtually no money and you might actually get a job at some point in the future. (John Williamson, personal interview)

In 2007 Sony announced the cutting of an undisclosed number of job cuts as part of a broader restructuring operation with its internet music retailing division. Furthermore, in October 2007, the Sony website predicted up to 60 imminent or near-future job losses from US and international offices after announcing an US$8 million loss over the previous month alone which it blamed on the depleting CD market. This move followed the closure or downsizing of some of its regional/

national offices earlier in 2007, including its Canadian head office in Toronto.

All of the above comes on the context of the IFPI predicting 1.2 million job losses in creative industries in Europe by 2015 (IFPI, 2011a).

The collapse of 'bricks and mortar' retail outlets for recorded music

Another factor that is flagged by interviewees as a symbol of crisis is the phenomenal decline of physical retail chains and outlets for music. Primarily, the transfer from physical to digital and the related spread of peer-to-peer file-sharing is perceived as reducing the market for recorded music, with physical retailers a resultant prime casualty. As a result, the latter years of the last decade saw the closure of numerous of 'bricks and mortar' outlets.

According to artist manager Peter Jenner: 'what's really on the frontline of query is what's happening to retail and what that means' (personal interview). Jenner explains that a combination of falling 'legal' consumption and shifting purchasing patterns are combining to 'kill off' physical retail outlets. Jenner's comments come in the midst of ongoing closures of record 'megastores' and retail chains. Such comments are also echoed by Bill Whelan who states that 'record retailing has gone to the dogs because internet downloading and home copying and the distribution of music amongst the community via itself' (personal interview). For Ross Graham, CEO of NIMIC, music retail was:

> bound to collapse. Physical retail has become the most dangerous business to be in in this game. It has been in decline for years, sometimes reducing steadily, and sometimes you get very sharp large jumps downward. You can get a quarter in a year now where suddenly there will be a 12% drop in sales. (Ross Graham, personal interview)

Peter Jenner further explains that, primarily as a result of digital distribution, the turnover time for hit records is becoming shorter and shorter as record companies 'front-load the charts' in a strategy to combat falling sales. Jenner sees the proliferation of formats upon which a single recording is now released as an attempt to 'maximise the return on any one fan of a record'. Jenner's experience is that consumers of singles are likely to purchase multiple remixes of one song and he argues that the growing importance that record labels afford to this market sector indicates a level of desperation on the part of the labels, aiming products at an increasingly focused fan base.

For John Sheehan, former chairman of Sony Ireland:

> It all comes back to the technological developments that are ongoing. Digitalisation places question marks over the future of all aspects of the industry, but in particular retail is really suffering . . . the record shops. They got a second lease of life with the emergence of DVD and the back catalogue of films. It was that which really sustained their revenue growth. But that is slowing down now . . . The sad aspect for me is that I don't see the physical carrier in the music business growing at all. (John Sheehan, personal interview)

Beyond this, former independent retailer Bruce Findlay highlights the rise of online 'dispensers' of physical recordings such as Amazon and other mail order services in 'forcing bricks and mortar guys off the map' (personal interview). All of these comments come in the context of a series of physical retail closures over the recent years. December 2008 saw retail chain Zavvi (formerly Virgin Megastores) go into administration. It subsequently closed the majority of its stores throughout January and February 2009, with HMV purchasing 19 of the Zavvi outlets across the United Kingdom and Ireland. HMV itself had earlier announced that its annual profits had fallen by more than 50 per cent.

2009 saw the High Court in Dublin appoint an examiner to the Golden Disc music retail group, which at that point in time operated 20 stores across Ireland. A range of media accounts detailing the court proceedings stated that the retailer was insolvent and carrying liabilities of €9.5 million. These stories pointed to increased competition from a range of online sources as the source of Golden

Disc's problems. While subsequently closing several of its outlets, the chain continued to operate some 15 stores across Ireland. 2010 saw the company report a loss of €1.6 million.

Beyond the decline (and in some cases demise) of the bigger music retail chains, smaller independent operators also been forced to close their doors. For example, Dublin-based retailer Road Records ceased trading in spring 2009. Despite an attempted re-launch later that year (supported by a series of fund-raising shows performed by a range of local musicians), the store ultimately closed down in early 2010. A much larger independent retailer, the Scottish-owned Fopp chain, shut down all but eight of its stores across the United Kingdom in summer 2007. Those that survived were taken over by HMV. According to the BBC, the 'surging popularity of downloading music from the internet' was primarily responsible for the decline of Fopp (*BBC News* online, Friday, 29 June 2007) Just after Christmas 2012, HMV went into administration putting over 200 stores in the United Kingdom and Ireland at risk.

Having detailed declining sales revenues, job losses across the industry the demise of physical retail as evidence of crisis in the record industry, many interviewees proceeded to outline a number of different causal factors relating to these negative trends. Based primarily on these accounts, the remaining sections of this chapter outline and summarize these various factors in turn.

Other digital factors perceived as causing record industry decline

Beyond file-sharing on the internet, interviewees identified three additional factors relating to developments in network technologies and consumer electronics that they perceive to be damaging their industry: first, CD-duplication technologies combined and digital media libraries as standard utilities on personal computers; second, the increased capacities associated with portable digital storage devices; and third, changing consumption habits in the context of shifting formats and the 'unbundling' of recorded music.

CD-burning technologies

For John Kennedy, digitalization has spawned an even bigger problem than peer-to-peer file-sharing on the internet. He details how the CD has been available on the market since 1982 and remains the standard playback medium for commercial music recordings to the present day. While the earliest CD recorders cost in the region of ST£25,000 in the early 1980s, CD-burning technology has been mainstream in personal computers since the late 1990s. According to Kennedy, the copying of CDs has now become 'a major problem around the world' for the music industries because it crosses much greater demographics than the early adopters who embrace new and emerging internet file-sharing technologies. This sentiment is shared by record producer and manufacturer John D'Ardis who argues that CD burners have delivered 'a devastating blow' to the broader music industry:

> I would seriously think the whole music industry model is seriously in trouble. The main problem is that it is so easy to burn a good quality copy of what you like and transfer it to everybody that likes it without charge. Given that situation, it is very difficult for a company to try and make money. (John D'Ardis, personal interview)

D'Ardis proceeds to state that digital libraries can be used to 'infinitely' store material ripped from CDs from where the material can be transferred, shared and copied repeatedly. Furthermore, he argues that such digital libraries potentially remove the necessity for the user to upgrade their music collection to a newer format at a future stage. This factor was a key driver of the CD market, where users re-bought on CD what they had previously bought on vinyl or cassette. Echoing a similar perspective, former Sony Ireland chairman John Sheehan argues that it is a remarkable achievement for record companies to have maintained the level of revenue generation that they have in such an environment where the ripping of CDs was now a 'commonplace activity'.

According to former CBS Records and Polydor marketing and promotions manager Jackie Hayden, the concept of buying music is alien to a growing percentage of young music users. A combination of free access to internet databases and the proliferation of CD burners as standard devices within personal computers makes purchasing music 'so out of date as to be almost laughable' to a generation of 'rip and burn merchants'. Hayden details much anecdotal evidence in support this argument. For example:

> A guy recently told me that he was going out with his mate for a few drinks. He called to his mate and while he was waiting for him to come downstairs or whatever he was talking to his mate's son who was watching MTV. The video for the new My Chemical Romance single came on and this guy said 'That's a fucking great song, I must get that'. Within about 15 seconds the mate's son had downloaded it, burned it and gave it to him on a CD. (Jackie Hayden, personal interview)

As with peer-to-peer file-sharing, some interviewees regard CD-burning activities as not only depleting recorded music sales revenues, but also removing any incentive to produce creative works. For example:

> You can copy CDs so easily now, everything can be burned, Jesus, so what's the point in recording anymore? At the end of it you get nothing out of it. What's the point? . . . But that's the way that life is going to be because nobody wants to pay. And nobody wants to pay for it because they can copy it and get it for free. So they are stifling creativity, they are stifling it. (Michael O'Riordan, personal interview)

Interviewees also identify side-loading is a key activity that drives down revenues. CD recordings that may have been purchased legally in the first instance, and/or tracks that have been downloaded from the internet are entered into digital libraries such as Windows Media Player, Real Player or iTunes from which CD copies may be burned. Windows Media Player or Real Player come as standard on many PC/ laptop packages. The widespread existence of such digital libraries casts doubt over the need to replace music collections in the future in the way that new formats such as the CD have been used to replace vinyl or cassette in the past. As such, some interviewees argue that back catalogue will lose its value in the future.

Portable storage devices

In response to a general question about the evolution of the digital era, former MD of Virgin Ireland Dermot Hanrahan argued that we must place the advent of the internet and MP3 files in a longer-term historical context. Hanrahan described a series of technological developments that either served to transform, or sought but failed to transform music consumption up until the advent of the MP3 file. He outlined how vinyl, cassette and CD technologies grew the market for music companies and bolstered the dominance of the most powerful ones. While minidisc and digital compact cassette technologies were employed to do likewise, they failed to repeat the success of the CD.

Hanrahan proceeds to argue that with these technologies, the dominance of the major record companies was assured by their ownership of the content these formats carried. The copying and sharing of music prior to the internet and MP3 technologies was never significant enough to stunt the growth of the record industry and, was largely the preserve of organized crime. However, Hanrahan, John Kennedy and other interviewees argue that digitalization has transformed the arena of duplication and circulation to a point where 'the masses have become the pirates' (Dermot Hanrahan, personal interview).

As a number of interviewees explained, an additional key difficulty for the record business is the growing capacity of storage devices, and the increasing ease with which music can be transferred. In 2001 Apple used the slogan '1,000 Songs in Your Pocket' to promote the original iPod. During the course of our interview Dermot Hanrahan produced a 60 GB Apple iPod with sufficient storage capacity for approximately 20,000 songs. This, as Hanrahan pointed out, was roughly the equivalent of 2,000 CD albums which vastly exceeds the average record collection in the average home. Such rapidly increasing memory capacity on portable media players combined with the ready availability of free music files and ever-improving speed of networks serves to:

> spread free music at a rate that was never conceived of before . . . Ten years from now iPods will theoretically have enough space to store the recorded catalogue of all the major record labels and carry it around in your pocket. Can you imagine what a nightmare this is for the music industry? The game is up. (Dermot Hanrahan, personal interview)

Although less fatalistic than Hanrahan in his analysis, former Sony Ireland chairman John Sheehan sees the damaging potential of such storage devices for the record, arguing that 'there's no doubt about it, that kind of technology is already in the stocks' (John Sheehan, personal interview). Also, EMI Chief Executive Willie Kavanagh argues that file-sharing and duplication are severely hurting the record business, and acknowledges a very significant threat posed by evolving storage devices. However, he rejects such doomsday scenarios as outlined by Hanrahan. Kavanagh explained that EMI conduct market research on a biannual basis, each time updating, refining and building on a model encompassing 'the broadest possible base of music consumers'. Conceiving of this recorded music market consumer base as 'complex and multilayered' comprising of 'whole different levels or categories' of music users, Kavanagh argues that beyond a minority of early adopters who purchase or acquire large amounts of music, many consumers fail to possess sufficient interest or technological knowledge to update their files or music library on a weekly or even monthly basis. Kavanagh further makes the point that while new releases generate big sales in the short term, back catalogue is hugely important to his company and constitutes upwards of 50 per cent of sales in any given year. He explains that one of the biggest groups of buyers of back catalogue are people that buy either physical or digital recordings as a replacement product for recordings they already have in an earlier format:

> But are the buyers of back catalogue hugely technically savvy? And are they likely to improve to in their savvyness? Would they,

for example, ever have known to go to Kazaa? They could have got anything they wanted there for free, but they still came to us. (Willie Kavanagh, personal interview)

Shifting formats and associated consumption habits driving revenues down

While interviewees largely related peer-to-peer file-sharing technologies, CD-burning appliances and digital storage devices to the 'illegal' distribution and duplication of recorded music, further problems arise from the restructuring of the 'legitimate' recorded music retail market in the internet era. The core argument here is that the decline of the album as the key industry format is resulting in lower profit margins. This is as a result of a process known as 'unbundling' that has produced a marketplace where consumers now purchase single tracks at digital music stores such as iTunes for 99 cents per song, rather than buying entire 'bundled' albums or collections.

According to the British Phonographic Institute (BPI) (2009), sales of singles in the United Kingdom grew by 33 per cent in 2008 alongside a 3.2 per cent decline in album sales. As Table 2.2 indicates, single sales over the five-year period to the end of 2008 in the UK market increased by in excess of 350 per cent. So, while the market for singles is expanding rapidly, the market for albums is simultaneously contracting.

TABLE 2.2 UK unit sales 2004–11 (combined physical and digital formats in millions)

	2004	2005	2006	2007	2008	2009	2010	2011
Albums	163.4	159.0	157.7	138.1	133.6	128.9	119.9	113.2
Singles	32.3	47.9	67.0	86.6	115.1	152.7	161.8	177.9

Sources: British Phonographic Industry (BPI) 2009, 2011; *Music Week*, 2012.

One interviewee, Fachtna O'Ceallaigh outlines how music as a 'unit' has been unbundled from whole albums to single songs via MP3s and subsequently unbundled further in ringtones to clips of music no more than a few seconds long. This, for O'Ceallaigh, is changing the habits and patterns associated with the music consumer in a manner that is causing the market to shrink:

> The Western consumer that consumes music is demanding instant gratification. They will download maybe two songs from an album on iTunes, and some of them might eventually pay for the whole album . . . but many who might previously have bought the album will now remain satisfied with their two 99c songs. (Fachtna O'Ceallaigh, personal interview)

Music publisher Steve Lindsey goes much further, stating that the shift in formats to single-track downloading is the primary cause of crisis in the recording industry:

> I think unbundling certainly has had a massive effect on the business as a whole. I have a bit more of a generalized view on all this. The public have more options now before them upon which to spend their money. When I was young, I'd go out and buy albums. I'd plan what I wanted to buy, I'd be in the record shops leafing through stuff for ages and ages, and the cost of an album was relatively high so you'd have to save your money to get them. Then the internet hadn't been invented, there was no such thing as computer games, cinemas were fleapits – there were no multiplexes. But these days you have cinema and DVDs as commonplace. People, with their leisure time and leisure money spend it on things other than music. This is the main reason that the music business is in trouble. People don't place any importance on albums anymore. For music, they just cherry-pick the tunes the want from iTunes. They are not necessarily interested in the albums that people are making anymore. (Steve Lindsey, personal interview)

Here, Lindsey's contention echoes with a report commissioned by the Value Recognition Strategy. This working group was created in the United Kingdom in 2006 primarily through the endeavours of independent music companies and royalty collection societies, but with the backing of the industry as a whole. A 2007 report commissioned by this group to examine the declining value of revenue from sound recordings, and compiled by IT (information technology) and business consultancy firm Capgemini, lays a greater degree of the blame for falling sales revenues with format changes rather than piracy (Orlowski, 2007). According to the Capgemini report, sound recording revenues in the United Kingdom have dropped by ST£480 million between 2004 and 2007. However their research indicates that only ST£86.4 million of this can be attributed to piracy, that is 18 per cent of the total estimated loss. Rather, the primary cause of revenue loss they identify is the unbundling of CDs into an individual selection of digital songs. This process, according to Capgemini, has cost record industry ST£368 million over the same period, that is 77 per cent of the total estimated loss. As such, the report suggests that lawsuits against illegal file-sharers and the suppliers of file-sharing software should not be the primary concern of the major music labels. Rather they should apply themselves to finding a consumer-friendly digital bundle.

Former IFPI chairman and CEO John Kennedy also outlined a shift from an album to a non-album world in which he argued that single-track downloads were costly to produce and disseminate, and fail to offset physical losses:

> The digital business is not in its overall business as profitable as the physical, not least because the album model has fallen out in the digital world. It is not true that there are no distribution costs, or manufacturing costs just because it's all done on the net. These are replaced by different types of costs like digitisation. On a single-track model, in theory it is possible for that model to be more profitable, but you have marketing monies and promotion monies and recording cost investment which in the past would have driven an investment that would have given a return more often on an album than a single, and online it's a much more per track business. So the economic model is much worse from that point of view. And remember too there are credit card costs. (John Kennedy, personal interview)

However an earlier assertion made by then EMI chairman Eric Nicoli offers another perspective. In a keynote address delivered at the 2006 Midem Music Industry Trade Fair in Cannes, Nicoli argued that allowing consumers to download individual songs from an album – the so-called unbundling of music – rather than requiring them to buy all of the tracks in an album package, is crucial to the ongoing success of the digital market. Nicoli stated that 'the day is surely within our sights when digital growth outstrips physical decline and we can all compete for a share of a growing pie' (cited in Smith, 2006).

Elsewhere, Terry McBride, founder and CEO of the Nettwerk Music Group in Canada goes much further by arguing that profit margins from the 'digital space' are approximately 300 per cent greater than with physical formats. For McBride, 'you're going to hit a tipping point where physical continues to go down more than digital goes up and yet the company becomes more profitable' (cited in *Musictank* newsletter, September 2008). Based on this account, the sale of three to four single-track digital downloads can generate the equivalent profit of one CD album for record labels.

This is in turn countered by ex-independent record company owner Jim Carroll who views the logic of reduced costs surrounding manufacture, duplication and distribution as resulting in greater profit margins from single-track download as:

> a very sensible 'bean-counter economics' approach to things. *But* you must remember that the record labels are still spending the same amount getting the product to market in the first place. The recording budgets haven't shrunken, the amounts spent on marketing and distribution hasn't shrunken. The packaging might be gone, but they are still paying out big advances to bands. They are still paying for recording studios. They are still paying big producers big fees. In terms of the major labels, there hasn't been any cognisance taken of the fact that they are recording and dealing in reduced revenues form digital downloading. (Jim Carroll, personal interview)

However, John Williamson contests this point somewhat, arguing that reductions in costs regarding packaging and physical manufacturing 'ensures that the profit margins remain as high as possible from both dealer price and subsequently retail price' (personal interview).

As such there are arguments and counterarguments regarding to the benefits and drawbacks of the proliferation of single-track downloads for music companies.

Perceptions of record industry inefficiency?

A number of interviewees raised issues regarding the record industry's own role in failing to respond as quickly and effectively as it might have done to the challenges arising from the transition to digital.

One such criticism relates to the industry ignoring the emergence of the internet as a medium for the distribution of music, and for failing to recognize or grasp the opportunities it offered by the internet for monetizing digitized music files. Another is that it became complacent during the CD-boom years which yielded super-profits for the major labels and, that those same major labels were careless and wasteful in their investment in new talent.

Given that MP3s and digital distribution originated outside of the realm of the dominant players in the record industry (unlike key previous innovations regarding cassette and CD technologies), some interviewees argued that the record industry was slow to evolve a response to such developments. For example:

> The record industry has got itself into a lot of trouble by doing a lot of short-term thinking and short-term planning and by failing to look at long-term shifts. I can't say that that isn't a very difficult thing to do, but they are left trailing in the wake of every key digital change. They weren't on board with file-sharing early on trying to legitimise it in any sensible way . . . So regarding key areas, key drivers that have been fundamental on how the music industry goes, they've been late at looking at how they can monetise those. (George Ergatoudis, personal interview)

> They [record industry] have been incredibly sluggish about developing some kind of system for dealing with this [unauthorised

sharing and copying]. It's not like it just came out of nowhere. This has been a very distinct possibility for the past ten to fifteen years. The record companies have not been creative in terms of dealing with the advance of technology. (Bill Whelan, personal interview)

Other interviewees emphasized a wastefulness that they traditionally associated with the major labels, and an incompetence that grew from the complacency of having long maintained a stranglehold on the channels of recorded music distribution:

Having worked for two companies, I think the major companies have squandered obscene amounts of money carelessly on artists who took the money that record companies should never have given them in the first place. A good example here would be the band An Emotional Fish. Record people tend to give people money, people who have no experience of dealing with it . . . They just give money away, and then if they have a big hit, they forget. The issue becomes blurred as to where all of the other money went . . . It all became a bit fanciful really. In one sense they deserve everything they've got from letting the whole situation get out of control . . . Burying their heads in the sand from the internet is just another example of the same attitude. (Jackie Hayden, personal interview)

Such actions as described by Hayden also emphasize the extremely loose control they maintained over the process of music production. Hayden continues:

You could build up mountains of anecdotal evidence about how inefficient they used to be. Even recently [2008] there was that report about how the new owners of EMI were deciding that they had to cut back on the £20,000 a year budget for candles that they had! That sort of story can be replicated across all of the major record labels in terms of sheer wastefulness. The number of bands in the eighties and nineties that were using their taxi accounts to take them half way across the country. (Jackie Hayden, personal interview)

However, others argued that while record companies were guilty of such ignorance, this is now irrelevant as technology has rendered the outcome to be out of their hands:

> The record industry has been playing King Canute for a decade now. They are almost like a version of the 1920s Detroit Guild of Blacksmiths, trying to stop the rollout of the motorcar. They ignored the internet and have done everything in their power to try and block the advantages of the internet . . . They ignored it and believed that the world would remain theirs forever. But now they are running around in a flap wondering what to do next, so they sue the kids. (Dermot Hanrahan, personal interview)

Such an outlook, viewing technology in such stark deterministic terms, implies a futility to the actions of the record labels or their representative trade bodies, and a hopelessness regarding their future.

One particular development, concomitant to the early digital start-ups such as MP3.com in the 1990s, serves to support views that the major music companies misjudged the potential associated with developments in the digital domain. The inclusion of enhanced CD/CD ROM tracks as bonus tracks became standard on many CD album releases throughout the mid-to-late 1990s. Such add-ons often featured the video relating to one of the single releases from the album, or documentary footage or photographs pertaining to the making of the album. The widespread use and promotion of such a format for pitching their products at PC-using music consumers suggests that the major music companies treated the personal computer primarily as a stand-alone reproduction device without considering or engaging with the possibilities associated with networks.

Unsurprisingly, record industry trade body representatives defended the actions, or lack of action of their members. Former IFPI chairman and CEO John Kennedy argues that the response of the record business could not have been any faster or any different:

> As I travel around the world and speak to governments and media, when they continually throw the criticism at me that the record

industry didn't do enough to help itself, or didn't move quickly in response to the internet, I always ask them to tell me what we should have done differently. Nobody has ever given me a great answer to that. (John Kennedy, personal interview)

Kennedy, speaking in 2008, further argues that the response of the record industry to the advent of the internet is exemplified in how it migrated to a very successful online model initially via a-la-carte download digital music stores, and subsequently via other platforms. He then presented the mobile model as an example of the record industry 'flying the flag' for creative industries at the digital coalface:

In 2007 digital music went from two billion dollars to three billion dollars. Our digital industry has grown fifty per cent over the past year. Any industry would be very proud of that. (John Kennedy, personal interview)

However, Belle and Sebastian manager John Williamson is fast to highlight what he regarded as an obvious solution that could have been implemented almost a decade ago. He focuses on the rapid and widespread diffusion of the Napster software programme between 1999 and 2001:

What strikes me most is what a wasted opportunity Napster was for the record companies. The number of chances they had during the 1999–2001 period to monetise things like Napster and set up a model at the beginning that would yield them profits for years, but they didn't. I still think the really obvious one was, that when the Napster court cases were going on in 2001, at one point there was an offer of compensation, and there was the opportunity to take it as well. Napster had however many users globally, and at that point, if they had had the vision to see forward. (John Williamson, personal interview)

Napster had started unauthorized sharing of copyrighted music files in 1999. By 2001 had become one of the world's most popular peer-to-peer file-sharing services. According to Napster's own newsletter in 2000, it had 50 million users. Williamson continues:

I think a lot of people bought into Napster more so than the subsequent file-sharing services, because everything was there, it had absolutely everything. You could find the most obscure seven-inch single from the seventies there and you could find the latest Madonna album there and everything in between, because it was there, somebody would have digitised it and uploaded it. People love the idea of being able to find anything. You could never get access to that much stuff in any record shop. So there was, through this mechanism, an opportunity to access and rope in a vast percentage of Napster users if, at that point, the record companies had decided to just take the compensation, buy out Napster, keep everything – all of the content, and pick up a small subscription fee every month. I've seen the calculations before – If 10% of all of the people who used Napster subscribed, then the turnover of the global record industry would have been bigger than it was from physical at the time. That was the opportunity they had. (John Williamson, personal interview)

A number of interviewees detailed how the major companies were unable to agree on an appropriate business model for any such prospective digital venture. While subscription models and pay-per-download models were considered, none were pursued at the time. Dick Doyle offers a reason as to why no swift decisions were taken at the time, and why it was only in the years subsequent to the Napster case that digital business models emerged:

It is much, much more difficult to set up a legitimate business model than it is an illegal business model. An illegal business model is simple – you just put someone else's content up, and you make your money out of advertising. But to set up a legitimate business, you have to negotiate with all of the stakeholders in the industry. I'm not just talking about record companies here – record companies are just part of the industry. You also have publishers, the artists, and then you have to negotiate with the people who are going to deliver the service, so you buy SPs. Then once you've done all of that, you've got to set up a secure system for payment. So out of every ninety-nine cent track that you sell, there are about 5 or 6 stakeholders taking a cut. *That's* a legitimate business model. You *have* to talk to everyone. To set up an illegal one, it's simple, you just don't talk to anybody. *This* is why it took so long to respond. *This* is why it took so long to get everyone involved. (Dick Doyle, personal interview)

Williamson, however, contests such explanations arguing that there were solutions the major companies could have taken much earlier, but the most potentially 'dangerous' factor was their indecisiveness. He contends that 'any bold decision' taken by the major companies during the MP3.com and Napster period such as the 'full-scale launch' of either à la carte, subscription or other models of service 'would have worked' because at that point in time the major record companies 'were so powerful that they could almost make the market bend around them'.

Furthermore, until recently the majors have adamantly refused to do the kind of deals necessary to replicate what the original Napster, Kazaa or eDonkey had provided – that is, they consistently refused to issue blanket licenses that would enable ISPs to sell music via an 'all you can eat' music buffet to network users whereby users could download, burn and swap files in return for a subscription fee. This, according to John Williamson, was a key mistake. However, in the light of legal successes against the ISPs, by the end of the last decade the reticence of the major labels to engage in such licensing agreements was relenting somewhat. According to John Kennedy, 'the labels would be willing to engage' in discussion 'should ISPs want to explore such a move as part of a wider process of assisting the record labels in the fight against piracy' (personal interview). Kennedy's remarks reflect a significant change in the attitude of the major labels towards online business models, and the potential for revenue generation now seen from blanket subscription.

At the time of my initial interview with Kennedy in 2007, such moves were already underway in the United Kingdom with a venture called Playlouder MSP. Playlouder subsequently evolved as an internet access service that included the right to download songs, transfer them to portable devices and subsequently share them. Copyright owners are compensated from a royalty pool deriving from subscription fees based on the popularity of their recordings on the service. To monitor the network and enforce its borders, Playlouder MSP uses technology that can identify songs as they pass through the network, and if necessary, block them.

Recognizing that such agreements held some potential for music companies, a number of interviewees advanced that revenue streams would be limited as record companies would be competing over a fixed pool of money. However the fees that consumer would pay under subscription to such services account for only a portion of the monies that such ISP music services can generate for recording and music publishing copyright holders. There is also potential revenue from advertising, mobile phone companies, device makers and other music services that wish to have themselves incorporated into the network.

Supermarkets driving revenues down and stifling creativity

Another factor that many interviewees identify as influencing a downward trend in record music sales revenues relates to the entry of supermarkets into the arena of music retailing in the 1990s. Supermarket chains such as Walmart in the United States and Tesco in Britain and Ireland have significantly expanded their market share in music retailing in recent years. By 2008, such chains represented 65 per cent of all physical record sales in the United States (Nielssen Soundscan cited in *The New York Times*, 1 January 2009).

Beyond retailing CDs, supermarkets have also entered the realm of digital music services. Summer 2012 also saw Tesco extend its interests in this sphere by acquiring the We7 music streaming service.

As supermarket chain outlets have proliferated, so too has shelf-space for recorded music products. At the time of writing, Tesco operate in excess of 100 stores throughout the Republic of Ireland, all of which are licensed to carry music. On the surface, this appears to carry obvious benefits for record companies, given the added profile available for their recordings at retail level. According to Brian Rose, the commercial director of Universal Music United Kingdom and Ireland, supermarket music retailing:

> fits well with the music market's strongest growth demographic, the over-forties . . . They [supermarkets] make music easier to purchase for a mass market purely through convenience and the fact that fifteen million people who shop on Tesco each have music put in front of them. (cited in *The Guardian*, Thursday, 21 December 2006)

We might recall that when supermarket chains first stocked music in the 1990s, some music retailers retaliated by placing vegetables on their shelves as an act of protest at this new source of competition for music consumers. However, from a record industry perspective, interviewees point to supermarkets as an additional and valuable point of outlet for their products. Failing to do business with them would be effectively unthinkable, given the vast consumer base that is reachable via these retailers. Equally, many interviewees concede that supermarkets make for more difficult and challenging parties to negotiate with, given their sheer size. The ability of supermarket chains to engage in significant levels of bulk buying provides them with a high degree of leverage relative to other forms of retail such as dedicated music/entertainment stores.

Many other interviewees almost exclusively regarded the deals between music companies as damaging the long-term viability of their industry and levelled three main criticisms at the supermarket sector which they regard as contributing to the state of crisis:

1 The negotiating power of giant supermarket chains and their in-store pricing structures have forced down retail prices of recordings and consequently driven overall sales revenues downward.

2 Supermarket music retailing feeds a growing perception of music as a low-value (or no-value) product. In combination with a number of other factors, supermarkets contribute to recorded music being perceived as a product with little value in its own right, rather recorded music's value is seen as an 'add-on' to other associated products.

3 In addition to arguments around the effects of file-sharing on traditional recorded music retailers, some interviewees argue that by virtue of their pricing structures, supermarkets are hastening the decline of specialized music retailers.

Below I shall briefly examine each of these three factors that are seen as devaluing the recorded music market.

Supermarkets driving down recorded music sales revenues

Some interviewees see the deals between the record industry and supermarkets as a short-term panic-induced strategy on the part of the labels aimed at increasing unit sales and market share in a declining market, but with diminishing returns:

> With fewer records being bought, the record labels are doing whatever the can to try and get people to buy music, and this is what has driven them to the situation with the supermarkets. (Steve Lindsey, music publisher, personal interview)

As key bulk buyers of recorded music, supermarkets are perceived as having the negotiating power to acquire cheaper wholesale prices than specialized music/entertainment stores. For example, according to former London Records A&R man Jim Carroll:

> The supermarkets have become big powers in terms of pushing the price of the physical product down. They are happy to carry CDs as a loss leader because they need to have everything there. And they have got the power of the multiple buyer. They are so vast and massive, and they operate with the record labels the same way they operate with the people who are selling them milk or bread or cheese or whatever commodity they are buying in. So they are pushing wholesale prices down. (Jim Carroll, personal interview)

In a similar vein, John Kennedy argued that in most businesses people get volume discount from their suppliers. But what happens with supermarkets in particular is that they reduce their margins to next to zero. According to Kennedy, one of the key reasons that music is such a valuable commodity to the retail sector because of the vast amount of marketing and promotion there is in music, so 'it drives footfall in supermarkets' (personal interview).

Other interviewees regard the major record labels as being complicit in driving their own revenues downwards by agreeing to terms laid down by the supermarkets, who in turn sell on the records at reduced margins, or even as a loss-leader in order to attract consumers to their stores for other more traditional supermarket products and goods. According to Independent Records MD Dave O'Grady:

> The majors fucked up. I don't personally believe that their decline is specifically to do with digital. I think it is to do with the way they bent over for the supermarkets, and let the supermarkets sell their biggest sellers . . . For the labels it was just greed too. They wanted market share and units. They saw something and got greedy. They saw a million Westlife albums getting sold in a supermarket. They just bent over and took it. (Dave O'Grady, personal interview)

However, according to Steve Lindsey and John Williamson, the pricing structures and strategies of the supermarkets are in fact of little consequence to the major record companies as it is retail and not wholesale prices that are primarily affected:

> It is the supermarkets that are taking the hits on the profit margins, not the record labels. The record labels are certainly doing deals, they are doing deals for bulk that might not be as profitable as previous, but Tesco and the like will sell CDs at cost price or less than cost price in many instances just to attract shoppers. (John Williamson, personal interview)

The views of those who regard the deals between supermarkets and the record industry as ultimately hurting record labels are also reflected in the aforementioned Capgemini report examining declining revenues from sound recordings. As well as highlighting the decline of the album and proliferation of peer-to-peer file-sharing networks, this report highlights the ongoing deals between music companies and large supermarket chains such as Tesco and Sainsbury's as the third most significant factor in driving down revenues from record sales and reducing the value of recorded music products. The report found that supermarkets had succeeded in forcing the overall price of CDs and DVDs downwards. For Tesco, sales of such items as CDs, DVDs, books and electronics experienced double-digit growth during 2008 in the context of growing its overall sales revenues in Ireland by 5.2 per cent to €3.2 billion. In 2008, Tesco relaunched a revamped music download service, seeking to position itself as yet another challenger to Apple's iTunes. By early 2009, Tesco had licensed in excess of five million songs which it made available for download as MP3s. This is in contrast to its previous download store (www. tescodownloads.com) where songs were available in Windows Media format only.

Supermarkets narrow-casting and devaluing music

In addition to (economically) devaluing music, the second major criticism levelled at supermarkets is that they contribute to recorded music being perceived as a product with an ever-decreasing 'stand-alone' value. For music publisher and former Polygram executive Steve Lindsey, supermarket retailing combines with other contemporary circulation and distribution trends to generate a growing perception of recorded music as a free product, or a product that comes as a free add-on linked to other products or services:

> Supermarkets selling albums at the prices they are selling at, well that's just business. You also have the Sunday papers giving away albums. This doesn't help because it means the public perceives music as being either free or else not having much value at all. So a snapshot at this moment in time is that people can download it illegally where they just take what they want to take, they can get it for free from a newspaper or buy it cheaply in a supermarket. I think it is that devaluing of music that is the biggest problem. That's the main problem that the music business is now facing – finding

the ways and means of getting music bought and that it does have a value as it once had. (Steve Lindsey, personal interview)

Alison Wenham, the CEO of the AIM, the trade body representing independent labels in the United Kingdom and Ireland, argues that by only offering an extremely limited mainstream catalogue, supermarkets are driving society towards a conformist music scene where:

> the industry pursues 'sound-a-likes' for James Blunt in a market in derivatives . . . The stranglehold that supermarkets now have on the CD retail market is ultimately bad for music . . . The independents are the originators of all new trends and if you stifle the means with which they get into the market at an early stage, you will stifle the music market. (Alison Wenham, personal interview)

Thus by virtue of the fact that they only carry select Top 50 and classic hits recordings, supermarkets not only preclude vast catalogues of recorded music repertoire from access to an audience via their shop-shelves, such narrow-casting also hinders artistic and creative innovation which, ultimately will carry commercial consequences for the industry as a whole:

> The one thing to remember about the major record companies and the supermarkets is that they don't give a shit about what is on the records they sell. They don't care. That is another element that I am sorry to observe at the moment. The public are being sold very mediocre and very safe stuff and the record companies are trying to keep the accountants happy. (Steve Lindsey)

A number of interviewees also argue that while Tesco's digital service provides a vastly broader repertoire than the physical supermarkets that only carry Top 50 albums and select back catalogue, Tesco's digital store is almost exclusively licensed from the four major labels.

Even when independent labels gain access to supermarket shelves, a further problem comes to light. Tesco, for example, operate exclusively on a sale or return basis in terms of their dealings with record labels. Such agreements can carry the potential to be significantly more problematic for smaller labels rather than the majors:

> If Tesco want to stock that in all of their shops in the UK they might initially buy 50,000 copies of that album. If they only sell 20,000 copies then suddenly, six months down the road that label is finding itself being shipped back 30,000 copies. So this affects the way the record labels work because the supermarkets work in a totally different way. (Jim Carroll)

Supermarkets collapsing music retailing

One sector which has suffered significantly from the move by Tesco and other supermarket chains into music retailing is the traditional record store. According to Jim Carroll, supermarkets are most damaging to the independent retail sector. Price sensitive consumers, according to Carroll, no longer go to specialized music retailers who cannot compete with the supermarkets on retail prices. While the range of stock on the shelves of specialized stores usually far exceeds the narrow band of recordings retailed through supermarkets, outlets chains are losing a significant portion of their consumer base. We have seen the disappearance of Tower Records in New York and London and, at the time of writing, the potential close of HMV stores across Britain and Ireland. According to John Kennedy, price competition based on the volume discounts supermarkets can negotiate makes it increasingly for music stores to sustain themselves.

However, as former independent music retail chain owner Bruce Findlay emphasizes, it is smaller chains such as Golden Discs and Dolphin Discs as well as independent stores that are suffering most. As we noted earlier, independent retailer chain Fopp went out of business in the United Kingdom in 2007 and Road Records closed in Ireland in 2009. The loss of such stores also means the loss of a traditional means of acquiring knowledge and information about new music for music fans:

> What people forget about, and this is something that the independent retail sector hasn't been great at pushing is the fact that the independent sector was the place to go to get information about records, but that's gone now. (Bruce Findlay)

The demise of more traditional recorded music retail outlets must also be contextualized in the broader transition to digital, the emergence of new online outlets for physical such as Amazon and My Play, and rising high street rents.

Belle and Sebastian manager John Williamson questions a disparity between unit sales and falling revenues, and argues that declining revenues from sales at retail level does not imply that significantly less units of recorded music are being purchased. Williamson also highlights supermarkets as a key actor in reducing wholesale and retail revenues:

> Increasingly HMV are competing with Tesco on chart releases but keeping prices up on the kinds of releases that don't make it into Tesco. I'm sure it's the case that unit sales are not necessarily down as far as falling revenues suggest. The average price of a music unit is much lower than it was ten years ago. Looking at BPI statistics, they show that the actual decline in unit sales in the UK have held up pretty well. They have gone down, but not substantially, yet revenues have decreased substantially. (John Williamson, personal interview)

Williamson further argues that supermarkets are unfairly vilified by many over the decline of overall industry sales and the collapse of the traditional retail sector. He considers the actions of the supermarkets in 'playing hardball' to achieve greater volume discounts as 'no different from what Fopp or HMV or any of the music-specific retailers have actually done over the years' (personal interview). In negotiating lower wholesale prices, supermarkets have, as Williamson sees things, merely taken advantage of the fact that record companies are now in a weaker bargaining position.

However, alongside the decline of specialized music retail stores, new physical outlets for recorded music have emerged. While artist manager Ben Barrett explains that on one hand physical retailing has become 'so crunched up' in recent years 'that the margins are becoming smaller and smaller so its harder to make traditional retail work' (personal interview). On the other hand, she proceeds to outline how non-traditional 'bricks and mortar' retail outlets for physical recordings have become increasingly important to both artists and record industry. Supermarkets such as Tesco in the United Kingdom and Walmart in the United States form one example for Barrett. Starbucks coffee shops provide another: 'Starbuck's is becoming a massive retailer of music in America, and it's very important for people who want to sell records' (personal interview).

Chapter summary

Ultimately, the initial responses garnered from interviewees to questions of change in the music industry echo common-sense assumptions advanced in media, journalistic and other accounts referred to at the outset of the introduction to this thesis. For many, the record industry has seen its power fundamentally diminished as a result of technological change, primarily the proliferation of file-sharing software on the internet. Declining record industry sales statistics are taken as the key evidence of a crisis, alongside the consequent loss of jobs in the sector and the decline of physical retail outlets.

Interviewees advanced a variety of factors that they perceived as lying at the heart of these problems. Primarily, the widespread diffusion of digital distribution technologies as well as the development of cheaper and more powerful duplication and storage devices (the unauthorized copying and sharing of music that is associated with these developments). Beyond that, they highlighted consequences arising from shifting formats and changing consumption habits. Furthermore, some viewed the rise of supermarket music retailing in largely negative terms for the music industry. Others pointed to the record industry suffering through its own failure to act swiftly or effectively to developments in the digital realm, and other inefficiencies.

In the chapters that follow, the above accounts will come to be seen in a much broader context. It must be noted that while my initial questions asked for views and perspectives on change in the music industry as a whole, the vast majority of responses initially focused on the record industry. While the recording sector has been the most dominant sector within the music industry for many decades, it constitutes only part of the larger framework that is the music industry.

In addition to this, publishing, live performance and increasingly merchandise and other music services serve to form a network of business that increasingly generates revenues via the exploitation of rights from a broad, and increasing body of sources. As such, by focusing exclusively on recording, many other potentially significant revenue streams are precluded from consideration in the argument. As we shall see from the evolving trends across the broader music industries outlined by interviewees in subsequent chapters, arguing that there is a crisis in the record industry is distinctly different from arguing that there is a crisis in the music industry.

3

Response strategies of the music industry

Chapter 2 identified the key 'problems' currently being experienced by the record industry. In this chapter, we focus on some of the core strategies of the established music companies as they reposition themselves to respond to the challenges posed primarily by the disruptive potential of internet technologies. Initially, we will consider the ongoing roles of legislative and judicial systems in evolving and enforcing copyright law. In addition to their pursuit of file-sharing software suppliers and individual network users through the courts, this chapter outlines how trade bodies representing the interests of the major music companies have more recently switched their attention to ISPs. Concurrent with these developments is the rise of the digital music market. While authorized digital music stores have proliferated to grow the digital music sales market, the major companies have also been adept at engaging with social networks as avenues of both promotion for their products, and as a source of direct revenue through licensing agreements. These developments illustrate a trend where the major music copyright holders have successfully sued social media networks, and ultimately seen them evolve as licensed music services. The chapter then advances to consider the digital games sector as a site for the promotion of music and a potential source of revenue for the music industry. Finally, we discuss the opening up of new markets for music in the BRIC countries in recent years.

Copyright, ISPs and the courts

The rise and subsequent demise of platforms such as MP3.com, Napster, Grokster, Kazaa, Limewire and others illustrate how the major labels have taken recourse to the courts in their pursuits of internet 'pirates' for almost a decade and a half now. The pursuit of the suppliers of illicit file-sharing platforms and network users across the world continues to be a core response strategy of the major labels to the threats and challenges posed by such activities. For evidence of this we can visit the 'news' page on the IFPI's website, the contents of which, the major labels argue, highlight the scale of the problem facing music copyright holders. This site publishes a litany of accounts outlining the international pursuit through the courts of the suppliers of file-sharing technologies, individual network users and ISPs. Below are a handful of examples from the IFPI's archived stories over recent years. These cases illustrate how the IFPI, or more specifically its local partners are active in identifying and encouraging the prosecution of copyright infringers.

April 2011 saw the public prosecutor of Cagliari in Italy order local ISPs to block network users from access to the unlicensed torrent site BTJunkie (IFPI, 2011b). September 2010 saw a Finnish District Court sentence a peer-to-peer hub operator to a four-month suspended prison sentence and order him to pay €307,450 in compensation to music rights holders (IFPI, 2010b). Following an investigation by the Bulgarian police's cyber crime unit, August 2010 saw the closure of four illicit music sites in that country (IFPI, 2010c). July 2009 saw the IFPI achieve the shutdown of Qsound, a South American file-sharing network and Colombo-BT.org, the largest BitTorrent tracker site in Italy (IFPI, 2009b). In July 2008, the Sunnydale Hub which provided file-sharing services was shut down by authorities in Mexico (IFPI, 2008a). In May 2008, Zhongzou, a Chinese internet search engine, was found guilty of infringing recording copyright by the Copyright Bureau of Hebei Province and Cangzhou City following the lodgement of a complaint to the Copyright Bureau by the IFPI (IFPI, 2008e). In Prague, following an investigation and subsequent complaint by the IFPI Anti-Piracy Unit, Czech police shut down a computer server at the Academy of

Sciences of the Czech Republic that was being used to store and upload music onto the internet via a site called Blind Alley (IFPI, 2008b). December 2007 saw a landmark case in China where a Beijing court ruled that Yahoo China's music delivery service was in violation of Chinese law by facilitating mass copyright infringement (IFPI, 2007a). The initial claims filed in the No.2 Intermediate People's Court concerned infringement of key international artists such as U2 and Destiny's Child. November 2007 saw Dutch peer-to-peer file-sharing site Shareconnector.com closed by authorities following a successful case taken by BREIN, the Dutch anti-piracy watchdog, in the Civil Court of Appeal in Amsterdam (IFPI, 2007b).

These accounts offer a handful of representative samples of the type of story relayed via this source on a routine basis. one such story has garnered wider attention from industry pundits. The most high-profile copyright infringement case of recent years featured The Pirate Bay, a Swedish peer-to-peer service which enables users, provided they have downloaded a specific software application, to generate links to music, films etc. on other websites on the internet. According to David Sarno, writing in the *Los Angeles Times*, Pirate Bay operated as:

> one of the world's largest facilitators of illegal downloading . . . the most visible member of a bourgeoning anti-copyright – or pro-piracy – movement that is striking terror in the heart of an industry that seems ever less capable of stopping it. (*The Los Angeles Times,* Sunday, 29 April 2007)

However, in 2009 The Pirate Bay's four founders, Peter Sunde, Fredrik Neij, Gottfrid Svartholm and Carl Lundström were each found guilty of aiding and abetting copyright infringement and sentenced to a one-year prison term and a fine of US$3.6 million. June 2009 subsequently saw software company Global Gaming Factory X seek (ultimately unsuccessfully) to acquire The Pirate Bay. Similar to how Napster had attempted to 'go legitimate' almost a decade earlier (before the brand name was bought for a new authorized system), Global Gaming Factory X announced that they had devised 'a new business model' for The Pirate Bay which 'satisfies the needs of all parties, content providers, broadband operators, end users and the judiciary' (Global Gaming Factory X, press release, Monday, 30 June 2009). This new business plan centred on making the site 'legitimate' via licensing agreements with the four major music companies for the vending and streaming of their recorded music content. The music companies subsequently issued fresh proceedings against the former Pirate Bay owners, seeking a share from the proceeds of the sale of the site to Global Gaming Factory X on the grounds that the value of the website derived primarily from its 'illicit' use of their copyrighted material.

The pursuit of individual network users has also been a preoccupation of the record industry's individual trade bodies. Between 2003 and 2005 the Record Industry Association of America (RIAA) issued some 9,000 lawsuits against individuals across the United States for unauthorized file-sharing offences (Resnikoff, 2009). Sterk (2011) states that this figure subsequently rose to 35,000. Such accounts tend to imply the problems posed by digitalization to copyright owners to be many and widespread, but we recognize also that many of these stories are stories of success for the same copyright owners against 'infringers' in the courts. Thus, they advance another reality – the continued, successful and sometimes lucrative pursuit of 'pirates' by the record industry's various national trade bodies across the world.

Penalties handed down by courts for copyright infringement imposed by judicial systems have become increasingly severe (Lessig, 2001). This is perhaps most starkly illustrated by the widely publicized trial of Jammie Thomas-Rasset in 2009. She was ordered to pay the RIAA a total of US$1.92 million for uploading 24 songs to the file-sharing network Kazaa some four years earlier. While the RIAA had sought US$3.6 million in compensation, that is, US$150,000 per song, the fine imposed by the court amounted to US$80,000 for each of the 24 shared tracks. In a series of retrials and appeals, the amount was reduced to US$54,000, increased back up to US$1.5 million, and subsequently reduced to US$54,000 again. At the time of writing, a further appeal by the music companies against the reduction is ongoing. Ultimately, as Lessig (2001) had earlier argued, such cases illustrate how the penalty for file-sharing in cyberspace is typically much more burdensome than penalties meted out for the traditional form of theft of an item.

Here, we should also be mindful of the earlier work of Bakker (2005) and Hesmondhalgh (2007b) for whom file-sharing is associated with significant but nonetheless niche groupings. Also, the record industry's strategies for pursuing both software distributors and individual users serve to deter many from becoming involved in such sites (ibid.).

The pursuit of ISPs through the courts

As well as issuing lawsuits against the producers and suppliers of file-sharing technologies and individual network users, the major record companies have also turned their attention towards ISPs.

According to Willie Kavanagh, chairman of IRMA, the selective targeting of individual file-sharers is both time-consuming and costly. Kavanagh emphasizes how the company he works for and the industry he represents has suffered losses in revenue of approximately 30 per cent since 2001. He argues that the record industry is being 'savaged' and that ISPs must be placed under an obligation to filter traffic on their networks as to curb illegal file-sharing by their users. In a similar vein, a speech delivered to the Music Matters conference in Hong Kong in June 2008 by U2 manager Paul McGuinness saw him launch an assault on ISPs. McGuinness argues that recorded music is experiencing on going devaluation 'that has been anything but inexorable' since the advent of internet file-sharing:

> The record industry is in crisis, and there is crucial help available but not being provided by companies who should be providing that help . . . The real problem here, I believe, is the lack of willingness of ISPs to act. That is why legislation could well have to be the answer. (Paul McGuinness, Music Matters conference, Hong Kong, 4 June 2008)

According to McGuinness, 80 per cent of ISP network traffic is accounted for by peer-to-peer networks such as BitTorrent and Limewire. He argues that ISP revenues have soared from broadband subscriptions concomitant with the collapse of record sales. If we want an idea of just how much the expansion of broadband means to large ISPs, McGuinness urges us to consider that BT generated profits of ST£5.8 billion, 40 per cent of which came from broadband and IT services:

> Of course the champions of the ISP and technology industries spring from the internet free-thinking culture of California and Silicon Valley. Their passion for innovation and liberal hippy values in one sense sits well with the creativity of the music business. But at a deeper level there is a bigger problem and it's one those brilliant minds never resolved: I'm talking about the problem of paying for music . . . The music business once had to bear the accusation that it was full of dinosaurs who looked back to an old business model rather than embracing a new one . . . The visionaries and dinosaurs have perhaps changed places. If there are dinosaurs around today I think they are the internet free-thinkers of the past who believe that copyright is the great obstacle to progress, that the distributors of content should enjoy profits without responsibilities and that the creators and producers of music should simply subordinate their rights to the rights of everyone else. (ibid.)

As far back as May 2003 the RIAA succeeded in a case brought against the ISP Verizon, forcing it to reveal the names of four users suspected of offering unauthorized music downloads. In November 2005 Ireland was the site of a similar court decision when, following a round of lawsuits issued by IRMA, the High Court in Dublin set a new precedent for the region by forcing local internet access providers Eircom, BT Communications (Ireland) and Irish Broadband to reveal the identities of 49 suspected file-sharers. Cooperation from ISPs is what the record industry has been actively pursuing, and in many cases achieving since 2007. While some ISPs, such as Sky in the United Kingdom moved to enter into partnerships with the music companies to provide additional platforms for the sale of recorded music, the record industry has also been successful in obtaining legal judgements that hold ISPs responsible for activities that result in copyright infringement on their networks. Summer 2007 saw what appeared to be a landmark ruling delivered in a Brussels court when the Belgian society of authors, composers and publishers, SABAM, secured a court ruling stipulating that one of the country's ISPs must install a filter to prevent users from illegally sharing and downloading music. A brief overview is outlined below, as is an overview of the proposed solution – the application of the Audible Magic CopySense Network system.

SABAM versus Scarlet Extended, and the introduction of Audible Magic's CopySense Network system

On 29 June 2007, Belgium's Court of First Instance instructed Scarlet Extended SA to ensure that filtering technology was installed not later than six months from the date of the ruling or else face paying the IFPI compensation of €2,500 per day thereafter. The Brussels ruling was based on Belgium's interpretation of the European Union's Information Society Directive, otherwise known as the EU copyright directive. The ruling was welcomed by the IFPI as a measure that sets the mould for government policy in other countries around the world to act to ensure that ISPs operating in their jurisdiction acted to control copyright infringement.

In order to enable it to arrive at a decision in the SABAM versus Scarlet case, the court ordered an expert opinion on the feasibility of such filtering on an ISP network. The court ruling details that:

> In his report the judical expert has identified eleven (11) solutions 'technically pertinent in short term for filtering P2P' in which seven (7) are 'applicable to Scarlet's network' (p. 30 expert report; That among those seven (7) solutions, the expert concluded that only one (1), called 'Audible Magic' (CopySense Network Appliance) 'seeks to identify the protected music content in P2P flows'. (Brussels Court of First Instance, No.04/8975/A. Decision of 29 June 2007)

Audible Magic have in essence provided a filtering technology that enables networks to identify, track and monetize the flow of digital media moving through their networks.

During our interview in autumn 2007, EMI's Willie Kavanagh discussed the SABAM versus Scarlet case in detail, outlining that it held the potential to be hugely influential:

> The court listened to what the ISP had to say, it listened to what the copyright owners had to say, and it also commissioned independent research to assist the judge in coming to a conclusion. The independent research was delivered. The ruling that the judge made was that it is not the sole responsibility of the owner to chase somebody in breach of copyright. As gate-keepers of the internet, ISPs have a joint responsibility not to have their premises used, for want of better words, by people to set up shop and do things illegally. Here in Ireland we are in the process of negotiating with the ISPs to discontinue and disconnect people who are doing that. Since that ruling I have had communications with Eircom and BT Ireland to try to get them to put in place Audible Magic. (personal interview)

Kavanagh subsequently provided an overview of the Audible Magic CopySense Network system. It essentially connects into an ISP network via a 'monitor port' to which the ISP routes or sends all network traffic. As such, Kavanagh explains, it acts like 'a burglar alarm on your home' – an intrusion detection system that monitors IP flows. The Audible Magic system does this via three core functions:

1. It works to filter peer-to-peer traffic by blocking all peer-to-peer traffic on the network, or else by blocking specific works from being traded by peer-to-peer applications.

2. It can shape peer-to-peer bandwidth consumption by limiting peer-to-peer traffic to a specific level of bandwidth.

3. It can track violations using a point system and provide an escalated programmed series of communications and sanctions.

As such the CopySense Network system can identify and block the illegal sharing of copyrighted content without interfering with the circulation of sharing of other 'non-infringing' material.

However, the record industry subsequently suffered a major setback in this case when, in November 2011, the European Court of Justice upheld an appeal by Scarlet and deemed that ISPs cannot be required to filter content on their networks for the purposes of copyright enforcement. While acknowledging that intellectual property is enshrined in the Charter of Fundamental Rights of the European Union, the court concluded:

> Preventive monitoring of this kind would thus require active observation of all electronic communications conducted on the network of the ISP concerned and, consequently, would encompass all information to be transmitted and all customers using that network . . . [but] the protection of the fundamental right to property, which includes the rights linked to intellectual property, must be balanced against the protection of other fundamental rights. (European Court of Justice, *Judgement of the Court in Case C-70/10*, 24 November 2011)

Ultimately the court concluded that the injunction arising from the earlier ruling was not consistent with European Union law, infringing both the individual rights of EU citizens as well as contravening the 2004 EU directive on the enforcement of intellectual property rights (IPRs) which stipulates that measures to ensure the respect of IPRs 'should not be unnecessarily complicated or costly' (ibid.).

Other record industry-ISP court cases and negotiations

Since the latter half of the last decade a range of other developments have taken place between copyright owners, ISPs and governments.

For example in the United Kingdom, December 2006 saw the publication of the Gowers Report which recommended that the government request ISPs to 'cooperate' with creative industries in the interests of protecting copyright in cyberspace and, the drawing up of appropriate legislation in the event of the ISPs failing to cooperate. In February 2008, in the wake of the Gowers Report and the Belgian ruling, the UK government published a strategy paper on cooperation between ISPs and the record industry, and stated that it would introduce legislation in the event of an agreement failing to be reached. Subsequently, July 2008 saw the publication of a Memorandum of Understanding between ISPs and the BPI, representing all of the major players in the record industry in Britain. Both parties signed the agreement with the key stated aim of realizing a 'significant reduction' in the level of file-sharing on UK networks. As part of this agreement, six ISPs undertook to write letters of warning to network users suspected of peer-to-peer file-sharing.

Legislation in this sphere was subsequently drafted in the form of the Digital Economy Act that was enacted in 2010. This introduced provisions for initially warning online copyright infringers, then diminishing the quality of their network service, and ultimately disconnecting file-sharers who persist with their activities. In late 2011, Ofcom, the independent regulator and competitions authority for UK communications industries, announced its intention to distribute notification letters to illicit file-sharers. This marked the first step of the authority's graduated response actions as part of its obligations under the Digital Economy Act.

In France, the Olivennes Agreement of November 2007 marked a pact between French ISPs, copyright owners and government. The agreement was struck under the supervision of the Olivennes Commission, named after its chairman Denis Olivennes – President-Director General of FNAC, the largest French retailer of cultural and consumer electronics products. This pact essentially approved the adoption of a 'three strikes and you're out' approach to copyright infringement by network users. Users would receive a warning from the ISP for each illegal download made. In the event of the user doing this on three occasions, they would risk losing their internet access. Subsequent legislation came in the form of the HADOPI law which was introduced in France in 2009. This essentially refers to a law promoting the distribution and protection of creative works on the internet. With it came the setting up of a government agency charged with administering the three-strikes graduated response model against peer-to-peer file-sharers.

In 2008, IRMA instigated legal proceedings against Ireland's largest ISP, Eircom, in an attempt to force it to block peer-to-peer file-sharing by its users. February 2009 saw an out-of-court settlement reached where by Eircom agreed to implement a graduated response approach similar to the 'three-strikes' policy formulated in the Olivennes Agreement in France. Under the terms of this agreement, Eircom consented to remove network users who persist in file-sharing activities after two warnings have been issued. The ISP also consented to the sharing and exchange of information with IRMA regarding suspected file-sharers.

July 2009 saw IRMA issue legal proceedings against BT Ireland and United Pan-European Communications Ireland (UPC) on the grounds of aiding unauthorized file-sharing by, among other factors, wilfully neglecting to employ the means at their disposal (i.e. filtering technologies such as Audible Magic) to curb these activities. According to IRMA, approximately 45,000 copyright infringements per month occur on BT Ireland, while 75,000 such infringements take place on UPC (*Irish Times*, 7 July, 2009: 4).

While the Eircom settlement can be regarded as a significant victory for the major music labels, UPCs subsequent refusal to implement a 'three-strikes' policy and, their successful resistance to the imposition of such an arrangement upon them in the Irish High Court in late 2010 marked a setback for those same labels. While arguing that the 'scourge of internet piracy strongly affects Irish musicians' and 'the business of the recording companies is being devastated by internet piracy', presiding judge, Justice Peter Charleton ultimately found no legal basis upon which UPC could be compelled to disconnect network users who engaged in file-sharing activities. He effectively concluded that he could not stop UPC from allowing access to 'illicit' file-sharing sites because domestic law did not permit him to do so, and the EU directive on the enforcement of IPRs that would facilitate this had not been transposed into Irish law.

Since 2007, IRMA, BPI and IFPI publications and websites indicate ongoing developments in Japan, the Netherlands, New Zealand, Denmark, Spain among other countries between ISPs, governments and record industry trade bodies aimed at addressing copyright violations and making provisions for terminating the accounts of repeat infringers.

A simultaneous development worthy of mention in Ireland is the issuing of legal proceedings by PPI against the State on the grounds that it has failed to amend a law that exempts hotels from paying royalties for music played in hotel bedrooms. In 2010, the High Court in Dublin referred the matter to the European Court of Justice (ECJ) which, at the time of writing, remains before the ECJ.

Growing the digital market: Proliferating platforms for music in the digital era

Initial attempts at selling and distributing music via digital channels by companies such as Pressplay, Liquid Audio and Musicnet achieved little impact. These early models carried very limited catalogues and also fell victim to a series of licensing deals that saw different record companies sign exclusive deals with different services. Apple's iTunes, initially launched in late 2003, became the first such digital service to secure an agreement with all of the major labels. Since then, the volume of digital platforms for music has mushroomed with over 400 such licensed services operating around the world by 2012 offering 20 million tracks to music fans (IFPI, 2012). By 2010, major international digital music services were available in 23 countries worldwide. By the end of 2011, such services had been extended to 58 countries and, they combined to generate revenues of US$5.2, representing 32 per cent of overall global revenues for the industry that year (see Table 3.1 below).

iTunes and 7Digital represent the biggest actors in this sphere. iTunes, which launched in 28 new markets in 2011, is now available in more than 50 countries worldwide. In October 2011 it sold its sixteen billionth song. 7Digital is currently available in 37 countries. By early 2012 Ireland had 21 different 'legal' online services available to music consumers: 7Digital; ArtistXite; Bleep.com; CD World;

TABLE 3.1 Global digital recorded music sales market value 2003–11 (US$ billions)

	2003	2004	2005	2006	2007	2008	2009	2010	2011
Total	0.02	0.4	1.1	2.1	2.9	3.7	4.2	4.6	5.2

Source: Author based on various IFPI Digital Music Reports 2004–12.

Deezer; Eircom MusicHub; eMusic; Golden Discs; iLike; iTunes Ireland; Last.fm; Meteor Music Store; Music Unlimited; MUZU.TV; MySpace; Nokia Music; rara.com; Universal Music; Vodafone Music; We7; YouTube. Beyond digital music store models that offer a-la-carte and/or subscription services, a range of models has evolved including mobile services, streaming services, social networking sites, brand partnerships and other direct to consumer sites.

In recent years major music companies have evolved partnerships with ISPs in order to offer music services to end-users. Services such as Eircom (Music Hub) in Ireland and Sky (Sky Songs) in the United Kingdom are just two of the ISPs involved in such partnerships around the world. This is another manner in which the music industry has succeeded in growing the range of channels for the licensed distribution of its content. Former Sony Ireland chairman John Sheehan predicts a positive outcome for the big music companies as they negotiate the digital world arguing that copyright mechanisms will evolve to sufficiently protect musical works as to ensure that copyright owners can exercise control over them and exploit them. Regarding copyright infringement, Sheehan argues:

> There will always be a fix to that . . . We've had mechanisms in the past of embedding codes in the music to stop people making copies. There are now more advanced versions of that, that will be able to control the distribution of it. (John Sheehan, personal interview)

Furthermore, Sheehan sees recent digital platforms for the delivery of music providing significant new avenues for exploitation of new and, more importantly, established record industry catalogues:

> It [the record industry] got a second lease of life with the emergence of CD and DVD, and the back catalogue . . . That really sustained revenue growth. But that is slowing down now. However you have the new generation of formats and that'll give it another spurt. There'll be a huge release of back catalogue on those formats. (John Sheehan, personal interview)

The sheer extent of the spectrum of formats that Sheehan talks of is illustrated by Beyoncé's 2009 album *I Am Sasha Fierce* which was released across 260 different formats (IFPI, 2010a). Equally, the 2007 Justin Timberlake album *Future Sex/Love Sounds* was the biggest selling digital release of 2007, selling over 15 million digital units across 115 formats (IFPI, 2008c). The range of formats includes a host of online and mobile platforms including ringtones, full-track mobile downloads, video, online music store downloads and a plethora of others.

In the United States, the world's largest recorded music market, digital sales grew by 19 per cent in 2011 (to account for 52% of the overall recorded music market); in the United Kingdom the figure was 27 per cent; in France, an astonishing 71 per cent (IFPI, 2012). In South Korea, the single biggest digital music market in Asia, there was an estimated three million people subscribed to digital music services in 2011 where digital channels accounted for 53 per cent of overall record industry revenues. Globally, the IFPI estimate the number of paying subscribers to such services to have risen by 65 per cent in 2011 to a figure of 13.4 million people.

In 2004, the combined digital markets of the United States, United Kingdom and Germany accounted for 200 million licensed downloads (IFPI, 2005). The latter half of that decade saw this figure multiply phenomenally. In the United Kingdom alone, 77.6 million single tracks were purchased online throughout 2007, a 47 per cent increase on the previous year. This figure jumped to 110 million in 2008, with an additional 10.3 million full-length albums being downloaded (IFPI, 2009a). Single and album downloads in the German digital music market grew by 22 per cent and 57 per cent respectively over the same period (ibid.). In 2011, a combined total of 3.6 billion albums and singles were downloaded globally (IFPI, 2012). In the United Kingdom, propelled by the proliferation of download sales, the recorded music singles market has experienced rapid and enormous growth over the past few years. The total for 2005 was 48 million, rising to 115 million in 2008, and continuing in an onward upward trajectory to a record-breaking 162 million for 2011 (Smirke, 2011). All of this serves to emphasize the success of digital music service platforms, their massive and ongoing expansion, and their growing importance to the major companies.

In addition, Juniper Research's *Mobile Music Opportunities* report (2011) highlights the increasingly significant role of mobile music in overall digital music revenue streams and predicted that mobile music revenues would grow from the value of US$3.1 billion in 2010 to an estimated value of US$5.5 billion by 2015. This follows an earlier Juniper report (2008) that marked 2007 as a 'tipping point' for mobile adoption, driven primarily by rental music services, full-track downloads and growing consumer awareness of mobile music following the launch of the iPhone. This must also be considered in the context of a surging market for mobile music apps where, for example, the Apple App Store has seen the range of music apps balloon from less than 500 in early 2009 to almost 14,000 in 2011 (Informa Telecoms and Media, 2011). The synergistic possibilities of mobile music become apparent here. We can, for example, consider an individual at a concert or in a night club using the Shazam app to identify a particular song that they are hearing, and then going to the iTunes store to purchase it.

The volume of commercially released music is also increasing in the digital era. By 2008, well over 100,000 full-length new albums were released in the United States, marking a 400 per cent increase in 'output' in the space of less than a decade (Nielsen Soundscan, cited in *Digital Music News*, 8 July 2009). Over the same period in the United Kingdom, the quantity of annual releases had jumped by 30 per cent (ibid.).

Licensing revenue opportunities arising from new digital platforms

The major music companies have been actively forming alliances with online social networks and other internet and mobile content platforms from around 2007 onwards. Below we can see some of the key partnerships that have been formed. The starting point in the formation of such relationships has oftentimes been copyright infringement actions taken by the record industry against the online site. Ultimately doing deals with such platforms is important to the music industry as, aside from the promotional value they offer to music and artists, they offer significant opportunities for generating licensing revenues.

One of the first deals struck in this area saw Sony Music Entertainment enter a licensing arrangement with YouTube in 2006. A press release issued by the partners at the time announced that the video-sharing site would endeavour 'to expeditiously remove certain copyrighted materials which are not available for exhibition on the site' (Sony BMG Music Entertainment, 9 October 2006). Shortly after the deal with Sony, YouTube also signed a licensing deal with Warner.

As a result of such agreements, music companies benefit from different rights that are initiated by the use of their content on YouTube. In addition to revenue that derives from the use of the music companies recording, performance and synchronization rights, royalties are also arising from user-generated content that uses copyrighted music.

Royalty collection societies subsequently struck deals with YouTube. For example, in Britain, autumn 2007 saw YouTube obtain a blanket license from the MCPS-PRS alliance that allows the site to stream ten million pieces of music administered by the society in return for an undisclosed annual payment. According to music publisher Steve Lindsey:

> The MCPS-PRS alliance and YouTube will not disclose the terms of their agreement . . . Nobody knows anything about the deal. It is part of the deal that it remains utterly confidential. Nobody knows what the amount of money is that YouTube has paid over to PRS, and nobody knows what the nature of the license is. It's secretive for business reasons for both sides . . . There are all sorts of reasons. I would guess that they don't want to set any precedents for any other deals that are done in the future involving either party. Other societies around the world would see that PRS got a certain amount of money from YouTube so they will ask for same or better than that. So we might deduce from that that the PRS got a bloody good deal. It's a bit like asking a colleague what his salary is and then going to the boss for a raise. (Steve Lindsey, personal interview)

YouTube subsequently negotiated a range of similar deals with the American Society of Composers, Authors and Publishers (ASCAP), the Society of European Stage Authors and Composers (SESAC) and Japanese Rights Clearance (JRC).

In 2008, at the time of interview with music publisher Johnny Lappin, a similar arrangement was being negotiated between the Irish Music Rights Organisation (IMRO) and YouTube. Lappin, who also serves on the board of directors of IMRO argued that monitoring and processing such material on YouTube is extremely difficult given the vast amount of user-generated content on the site. In the United Kingdom, Cambridge University monitor user behaviour on the site and provide the PRS with an 'analogy' of which videos get played and how often they get played. Royalty payments are distributed to copyright owners on this basis. In 2010, YouTube signed a licensing deal with IMRO and the Mechanical Copyright Protection Society Ireland (MCPSI). IMRO subsequently pursued licensing deals with some of Ireland's most popular music blogs such as The Torture Garden and Nialler9.

Besides having separate agreements already in place with most of the music industry's major publishers (BMG Chrysalis being an exception), summer 2011 saw YouTube strike a licensing deal with the National Music Publishers Association (NMPA) in the United States. This agreement allows some 300,000 independent music publishers to receive royalties when their repertoires are used in videos on the site.

In addition to YouTube, December 2009 saw the launch of Vevo, a music video service in that sees two of the major music labels in collaboration with other partners. The site is jointly owned by Universal Music, Sony Music, the Abu Dhabi Media Company and E1 Entertainment, with Google/YouTube providing the technology. Users can access and play music videos for free, with revenue generated from advertizing being shared by the site's owners and Google. Within the first month of its launch in late 2009, the official Vevo blog boasted 30 million users for the site itself. In March 2011, just one month before the launch of the United Kingdom and Ireland Vevo site, Vevo boasted 52 million visits from US users, who spent an average of 80 minutes each watching music videos. Both YouTube and Vevo feature streamlines links to online stores such as iTunes where downloads of songs can be purchased.

September 2008 saw the recording and publishing arms of all four major music labels launch partnerships with social networking site MySpace, then owned by News Corporation. These partnerships involve MySpace providing on-demand and ad-supported streaming, music downloads, a subscription plan and a variety of other music-related features such as the sale of concert tickets and merchandise. In effect, these deals cover the entire 360-degree spectrum of potential revenue streams. Users are also enabled to assemble and share playlists using the cast catalogues of Universal, EMI, Warner's and Sony. The pay-for-download and music streaming aspects of this service directs users to purchase tracks and albums via Amazon. As part of this overall deal, the music companies received an equity stake in MySpace Music, which, according to the MySpace website boasted in excess of 68 million users in the United States alone by 2008. However, this figure had declined to just over 30 million by early 2012 by which time the site had been acquired by Specific Media. MySpace is no longer considered a major player in the social networking world having been surpassed by Facebook and other music-orientated platforms such as Soundcloud, Bandcamp and Reverb Nation.

As van Buskirk (2009) points out, the case of Imeem and the three above-mentioned platforms, Vevo, MySpace and YouTube, is illustrative of a trend where the major music companies have instituted legal proceedings against a social media network, then subsequently settled, licensed and ultimately developed an ownership interest in the service.

Also worthy of note here is that 2011 saw Skype founders Niklas Zennstrom and Janus Friis launch their online music subscription service called Rdio, with content licensed from all of the major labels and a host of independent record companies. Skype itself has been licensed to sell downloads and ringtones from the major music companies since 2006. Beyond these examples, there are numerous other cases of mobile and telecommunications operators and social media platforms entering alliances with major music companies (and sometimes independents too) to sell downloads, ringtones, ringback tones, mobile music videos, wallpapers and a host of other digital products and services.

According to artist manager John Williamson, the fact that many of these online and mobile platforms are recent means that they would not have been a consideration when many artists negotiated their recording and music publishing contracts:

> I know from the perspective of managing recording artists that if you take something like Facebook or Last FM or MySpace or some other such space . . . This is such a recent factor that it wasn't necessarily have been taken into account at the time many acts signed deals . . . so they won't really benefit from it yet via their recording or publishing contracts. From Universal's point of view, for example, it, I suspect, might well yield significant royalties. (John Williamson, personal interview)

As such this is one area where major music companies are benefiting significantly at the expense of the artist.

A range of ad-supported streaming and download services has also emerged to provide fresh avenues for revenue generation for music companies. For example, August 2008 saw the Warner Music Group became the first of the major music companies to license content to We7, an ad-supported music streaming service co-founded by musician Peter Gabriel. We7 subsequently entered licensing agreements with all of the major labels and by early 2012 offered a catalogue of approximately eight million tracks to some three million users, primarily in the United Kingdom and Ireland. Adverts are placed at the start of songs based on consumer demographics, and advertizing revenues are shared between the site and the music copyright owners. Such services as We7 operate on a similar principle to the earlier Spiralfrog model which offered a free download service to users. The major music labels also forged similar licensing agreements with lesser profile sites such as Amie Street, Sellaband and Magnatune.

Perhaps the most successful ad-supported streaming service of recent times is Spotify. Initially launched in late 2008, this service was available in 13 countries and claimed to have acquired over ten million users and 2.5 million subscribers by early 2012. Virgin Media have also recently announced an alliance with Spotify, offering this streaming service to its broadband and mobile customers. Deezer offers another notable example here. It is an online music streaming service that operates both ad-supported and subscription models. Available in 130 countries, it offers users access to approximately 15 million tracks licensed from major and independent record companies, operates both ad-supported and subscription models. We might also consider Last FM which provides free downloads, streaming audio and social networking, and Grooveshark which offers a streaming service and online radio.

AIM in the United Kingdom and Ireland, and the American Association of Independent Music are also pursuing similar deals for the independent music sector. From the perspective of independent labels, in addition to providing revenue from advertising, such platforms carry significant additional benefits. According to AIM CEO Alison Wenham they 'provide value as additional bandwidth providers to indies that can't afford to stream [music content] directly from their own sites' (personal interview). Furthermore, as Wenham and other interviewees from the independent sector point out, the rise of such portals and social networking sites can enable many independent labels to cut back on the amount of content they are offering on their own pages.

Gaming as a site of music revenue and promotion

Another relatively recent source of music industry revenue comes from the expanding games market.

The games industry itself has grown significantly across the early years of this century. By 2008, the US games market alone was defying the slowing broader economy and reaching record highs of more than US$21 billion (NPD cited in Parfitt, 2009). By 2011, IT research company Gartner had estimated that the combined global value of the gaming hardware, software and online games sectors had grown to US$74 billion, with further predicted gaming spending to reach US$112 billion by 2015 (Gartner, 2011). That same year, industry trade group the PC Gaming Alliance reported a new peak of US$18.6 billion in the PC games market (Marlowe, 2012). Elsewhere, other market research predicts that global revenues emanating from the video games software market alone will grow to US$70 billion by 2017 (DFC Intelligence, 2012).

While on one level we might consider digital games as a source of competition for the music industry in so far as it provides a rival form of entertainment for consumers, we must also consider that music is used widely within games themselves. As such, digital games offer valuable sources of licensing revenue to record and music publishing companies in return for the use of their recordings and songs. Beyond that, games also serve as sites of promotion for recording artists and their music as well as generating direct music sales by offering songs and artist-related content to users.

We must also be aware that music companies and digital games companies often exist as part of the same corporate family. For example, while Sony is a major actor in music recording and publishing, it is also a leading producer and supplier of consoles and games. Equally, while Universal Music is key music rights owner, its sister company Activision Blizzard is one of the most prominent publishers of digital games. Recent years have also seen Universal and Warner move into the mobile games sector. So, just as the economic interests behind some of the biggest actors in the music industry have substantial stakes in film, television and other media spheres, games are now very much part of that family.

Some games such as *Song Pro*, *Rock Band*, *Guitar Hero* and *Sing Star* are of particular relevance given that they are essentially music-based games. *Song Pro*, which operates on the Gameboy console comes complete with music management software and an internet interface to enable users to download songs, lyrics and artwork. *Rock Band* allows users to simulate performances of songs using controllers that effectively take the shape of musical instruments and has been made available for Microsoft Xbox, Sony Playstation and Nintendo wii. Each *Rock Band* game package comes with approximately 50 songs onboard, with access to approximately 3,000 others via digital download. *Guitar Hero* offers a similar such simulation experience using a guitar shaped controller via the Playstation platform. Karaoke style *Sing Star* is also available for Playstation. This game also has themed 'rooms' in the virtual social gaming platform – Playstation Home – where performances and virtual branded goods from established artists have been available to users.

By the final years of the last decade, the success and popularity of such music-based games and, their significance to the music industry was becoming clear. By late 2008 Microsoft claimed to be selling 3.8 million music downloads per month (more then 45 million over the course of a year) via the Xbox for *Rock Band* and *Guitar Hero* (IFPI, 2009a). This doesn't take into account downloads for these games on Sony Playstation format.

Also in October 2008, Harmonix, the company behind *Rock Band*, acquired licensing rights to The Beatles catalogue. Offering 45 of the band's songs as part of the basic package, additional single track and bundled collections of songs were made available for download via this format. According to Harmonix themselves, within the first three months of its release in late 2009, *The Beatles Rock Band* sold approximately 3 million units.

Beyond games that are based around music and recording artists, music content is widely licensed for use across a broad range of digital games. Preston and Rogers (2010) list a host of examples that illustrate how the relationship between music and games has grown closer and more complex. Some of these examples highlight how already popular back catalogue material is used in games such as *FIFA Soccer* and *Grand Theft Auto*. Elsewhere, record companies often license tracks or remixes for exclusive distribution through games consoles. For example, one version of the game *NFL Street* featured 11 previously unreleased tracks by various artists signed to the Sony label that can only be played on Sony Playstation 2, Microsoft Xbox or Nintendo GameCube consoles (ibid.). In other instances, games can focus exclusively on one particular artist or act. For example, 2010 saw US rock band Bon Jovi use a social gaming platform to sell digital download bundles of their *Greatest Hits*. The games *Happy Acquarium*, *Happy Island* and *It Girl* all of which are on Facebook, offer users Bon Jovi music, branded 'virtual' goods, and vouchers for the band's own online store.

Digital games have also given rise to the release of numerous soundtrack albums that feature countless established and emerging artists. The various versions of the games *Gran Tourismo* and *Grand Theft Auto* offer the most notable examples here, with both games giving rise to multiple soundtrack compilations since they were first launched in the late 1990s.

New possibilities (digital and other) in emerging markets

While global sales revenues have been falling, it should also be noted that fresh markets with fresh possibilities have been opening up for music. The potential for growth of 'legitimate' music sales in China and Russia has been flagged previously by authors such as David Hesmondhalgh (2007b, 2010). A number of interviewees in the research studies that this books draws upon identified these countries as well as their BRIC counterparts as territories that have shown immense promise as markets for music over recent years. The IFPI are fast to flag what they regard as a notoriously high level of piracy in those countries. For example, they placed the 2007 annual value of the digital music market in China at US$700 million, but argue that 95 per cent of this is accounted for by pirates (IFPI, 2008c). As Kennedy stated:

> You only need to look at the statistics for what is happening in the market, our statistics on the use of file-sharing, the statistics in the music industry . . . it's 95% piracy, and even if we've got it wrong, the film industry are quoting 99%. (John Kennedy, personal interview)

By 2012, the IFPI estimated the piracy rate in China to be at 99 per cent (IFPI, 2012).

The size of these markets is nevertheless considerable with, as Hesmondhalgh (2010) notes, China and Russia combining to account for over a quarter of the world's population, thus offering huge potential to the music industry.

In our interview, John Kennedy expressed disappointment that the 'Russian market has not achieved the potential everyone had expected' primarily as a result of what he regards as the failure of the Russian authorities to 'cooperate' more enthusiastically on copyright infringement. However, he advanced much greater optimism regarding the long term potential of the Chinese market, stating:

> The Chinese market will fulfil its potential, but it, like other markets, has to contend with the fact that if free is available then

consumers aren't going to pay. But based on my dealings with them I do think the Chinese government will get more engaged and will have instant success with litigation there as well. (John Kennedy, personal interview)

As another interviewee, Jim Carroll advances, the major music companies have, since the turn of the millennium, been developing their presence in China. Sony Music Entertainment also entered a partnership with Shanghai Audio and Visual Press; the Universal Music Group formed a partnership with the Shanghai Media Group; and the Warner Music Group set up Warner Music China.

By 2010, China's Internet Network Information Centre (CINIC) reported that broadband penetration in China reached 98 per cent (Higginbottom, 2011). This has occurred in the context of a booming national economy. According to the IMF, the Chinese economy has been experiencing year-on-year growth of approximately 10 per cent (IMF, 2011). The potential for growing the digital music market there is thus very significant and recent reports indicate that the established music industry has experienced significant success in this domain. Speaking in 2010, Ian Hogarth of Songkick, an online database for live music concerts, enthused over the rapidly growing market for Western artists in China:

China is experiencing the biggest growth in the entire world and if you're managing a band and you've got the opportunity to get in there early, when it's a fresh playing field, then you should definitely pursue it. (cited in Smirke, 2010)

In a speech delivered to the China International Forum on the Audio Visual Industry in Shanghai back in 2006, John Kennedy stated that in China, sales of music via mobile phone alone accounted for 15 per cent of industry revenues, some 5 per cent higher than the then global average for digital sales (Kennedy, 2006). He proceeded to note how China accounted for 'nearly half of all the broadband lines in Asia' and also boasts 'almost half a million mobile phone subscriptions' (ibid.). The IFPI (2011a) detailed how 'music services bundled with smartphones' were being targeted at developing economies, with China, as well as India and Brazil illustrating a 'very healthy uptake' on such services. By 2011, 71 per cent of record company revenues in China came from digital platforms (IFPI, 2012).

Another promising development for the major music companies came in the form of a partnership formed in 2011 between Universal, Sony, Warner's and Baidu, China's largest internet company. Under the terms of this agreement, Baidu closed its infringing 'deep-linking' music service, and saw a new, licensed ad-supported service called Ting will come into operation (IFPI, 2012). China presently has 14 licensed digital music services.

In an interview preceding the 2009–10 merger of Ticketmaster with Live Nation, Sean Moriarty, CEO of Ticketmaster stated that significant growth for the live industry in the near future would come not only from demand for 'high-end talent' in developed markets, but also from 'construction overseas', where he listed China as a key site for significant growth (Anderson, 2009: 4).

Like China, overall economic growth and investment has accelerated in Russia since the turn of millennium. Household consumption in Russia is 'bouyant' with improving access to credit fuelling demand (*The Economist*, 18 June 2007). According to the World Bank (2011), the Russian Federation weathered the storm of the global economic crisis 'well' and predicted continued growth of the domestic economy throughout 2012–13.

Interviewee Jim Carroll outlines how, since 2002, the major music companies have been developing their interest in the Russian market, primarily through the formation of the National Federation of Phonographic Producers (NFPP), a body that is backed by the IFPI and unites the major Russian and international companies. Sony, EMI, Universal and Warner's have all subsequently opened Russian offices. Between 2002 and 2006, the IFPI estimated that the value of the Russian recorded music market, grew from US$297.5 million to US$406.5 million (IFPI, 2007c).

In my interview with John Kennedy he pointed to a potential joint initiative involving the major record labels and leading Russian labels aimed at compiling an extensive database of file-sharing sites operating in the country. This alliance will also promote legal methods of accessing online music. To this end, Kennedy stated that copyright holders and major web portals were creating streaming services to provide for listening to music online without having the capacity to download it. One of Russia's biggest internet companies, Yantex, launched one of the first such services in the country following the signing of licensing agreements with all the major copyright owners. Fidel.ru provides a similar such streaming service. More recently Last.fm and Deezer have also launched Russian sites.

Overall, the sheer size of the potential markets in Russia and China and the opportunities that come with them, all serve to paint a more optimistic picture than the official IFPI statistics on piracy there portray (Hesmondhalgh, 2010). As we have seen, the IFPI are keen to emphasize how piracy is hindering the development of these markets for music, and how the effective enforcement of copyright regulations is central to the future of the music sector in these territories. However, as Hesmondhalgh also notes, arguments regarding poor or unreliable sales figures deriving from piracy boosts the lobbying power of the established music companies by strengthening arguments that domestic industries need government support in shaping legislation and administering copyright law (ibid.). To this end, success for the established music companies in legal actions regarding music piracy in Russia and China has also in evidence. January 2012 saw a widely reported case in which a Russian social networking site, vKontakte, found liable for copyright infringement at a St. Petersburg court. According to the IFPI (2012), vKontakte has a value somewhere between US$1.5 billion and US$3 billion and ranks as one of the Top 50 most visited sites in the world with over 33 million visitors each day. Thus, the potential benefits to the major companies from establishing a licensing agreement with such a platform are significant.

Significant growth has also happened in Brazil which by 2010, along with India and other Latin American markets, demonstrated strong growth (IFPI, 2011a). A range of online and mobile services have also launched in the Brazilian market recently including iTunes, Rdio and Ideas Musik bringing the total number of licensed music services in the country to 19.

The size and potential of the digital music market in India is illustrated by the fact that one telecommunications operator alone, Bharti Airtel, claimed 170 million mobile subscribers in the country during 2011 who made 150 million mobile music downloads (Joshi, 2012).

The Performing Rights Society in the United Kingdom cite Brazil, Russia, India and China as increasingly important target markets for British music as these economies continue to grow their music markets in recent years (PRS for Music, 2011).

While much depends on economic movement in those countries themselves over the years ahead, there remains great potential for the exploitation of music in these economies. As such, BRIC music markets remain a promising avenue for pursuit for Western music companies.

Chapter summary

The continuous pursuit of individuals, producers and suppliers of file-sharing technologies and ISPs emphasizes how copyright law is central to the strategy of the music industry in responding to the challenges posed by digital technological innovations.

The ongoing formation of alliances and agreements between the music industry and the technology sector indicates that music companies are creating business models and licensing systems that enable them to profit from the abundance of emerging and established digital outlets and services. Overall, the range of revenue streams open to artists and music companies has increased significantly with the proliferation of internet and mobile platforms. These developments have driven growth in the digital music economy. Equally, the potential for growing revenue streams within the evolving BRIC economies offers promise to the music industry.

In the next chapter we will examine how areas such as synchronization, live performance and more have evolved as sources of revenue for the music industry in recent years.

4

Developments beyond the digital realm

In this chapter we will consider the benefits for both the recording and music publishing sectors from synchronization fees arising from the use of music in film, television and, perhaps most significantly in the contemporary environment, royalties generated through the on going proliferation of advertising. In particular, the year-on-year growth in music publishing revenues suggests that more opportunities for the exploitation of music in public spaces now exists, and also that the royalty collection societies have intensified their efforts in tracking the usage of their members catalogues. Next, the chapter focuses on the growing live music industry and examines how processes of vertical integration and concentration are growing to characterize the evolution of this sector in recent times. Furthermore, it examines the convergence of the live industry with the other core industrial sectors, that is, recording, publishing and merchandising. The chapter then addresses a broader process of conglomeration whereby music recordings, music publishing repertoires, technological devices and the enabling software and services are all increasingly falling under the ownership of the same corporations. Such a convergence of interests between manufacturers and suppliers of technology and music companies enables the cross-promotion of products, services and content. Then, within the context of all of the above, a number of interviewees offer perspectives on the evolution of 360-degree deals for music artists. Here, the rights to all artist-generated revenues become centred on one corporate entity.

Proliferating revenue streams from secondary sources

'Performing rights' operate to ensure that music publishers and those owning copyrights to songs and music are compensated for the use of their repertoire. 'Neighbouring rights' operate to provide recompense for record companies and recording artists, as well as publishers and composers arising from the use of their recordings. Beyond income generated through the sale of physical recordings, these sets of rights also serve to provide revenue via numerous secondary sources. The sections below examine some recent trends regarding the trajectory of performing rights and neighbouring rights revenues for music publishers and record companies in the digital era.

The growing music publishing market

A number of interviewees highlight the fact that in the contemporary environment, new revenue streams are opening up for music publishing in particular. For example:

> I've studied the ins and outs of the deals that music companies have done with a lot of the new outlets and both record companies and publishing companies are in a strong position because there are more films and more TV opportunities now for music than ever before, and they've got their income from all these new internet sources. But while these are also sources of money for record labels, publishers don't have falling sales to contend with in the same way record companies do, so the spin-offs of all these changes have been much, much better for them. (John Williamson, personal interview)

Significantly, as Williamson, Jackie Hayden, Jim Carroll and other interviewees explain, while music publishing rights yield smaller returns than recording rights for the major music companies, the profit margins for publishing are far higher as music publishers only incur a fraction of the overheads that a record label must contend with.

Pointing out that the global music publishing market is dominated by the publishing arms of the major record labels, Williamson argues that Universal and EMI 'seem the most transparent' of the majors 'in terms of their business planning and shareholder briefings' and increasingly 'they are placing more and more eggs in the publishing basket' (John Williamson, personal interview). Music publisher Steve Lindsey reinforces Williamson's point on concentration in publishing industry:

> It is pretty much the same as recording. The major publishers collect the major amount of money by a long way . . . Non-major publishing companies will only make real money by picking up the publishing rights of an artist on a major (record) label. If you have an artist then with a very successful album then the non-major publisher will benefit . . . But it does tend to be the major that benefits most often and will turn over a big revenue just because of the massive catalogue they have. (Steve Lindsey, personal interview)

The vigour with which royalty collection agencies in the Republic of Ireland have acted since the mid-to-late 1990s is illustrated in table 4.1 that indicates how gross music publishing revenues gathered across the years have mushroomed. Statistics published in recent years by the IMRO show performing royalty collections more than doubling in the space of a decade to a figure of €40.4 million in 2009, before dropping back to €38.1 million in 2010. In addition, the net distributable income from combined music performing and mechanical copyrights in Ireland increased by almost 225 per cent in a decade.

TABLE 4.1 Gross performing royalties collected by the Irish Music Rights Organisation (IMRO) 1996–2010 (€ millions)

1996	1998	2000	2002	2004	2006	2008	2010
16.7	19.9	24.7	28.2	29.4	33.8	39.2	38.1

Source: Author, compiled from various IMRO Annual Financial Statements 1997–2011.

Similarly the Performing Rights Society's 'gross collections' of publishing royalties in the United Kingdom grew consistently for more than a decade to a value in excess of ST£500 million by 2009 (PRS for Music, 2010).

More promisingly for the music publishing industry on a global level, despite the extent of the broader economic crisis in recent years (and contrary to the slight dip of the fortunes of the music publishing sector in Ireland), the overall economic performance of the sector remains strong. In particular, global performing royalty collections are displaying significant growth (see Table 4.2 below). According to the International Confederation of Authors and Composers Societies (CISAC), such collections reached a new peak of US$7.5 billion in 2010 (CISAC, 2012). The French-based organization, which represents a plethora of collection societies in 120 different countries, boasts that this sector stands 'in striking contrast to the performance of other cultural sectors' (ibid.). Per head of population, this amounted to €3.90 in the United States, €8.40 in the United Kingdom and €5.50 in Ireland (ibid.). These figures reflect revenues collected from a broad array of music users that now include radio, television, film production, digital platforms, advertising agencies, night clubs, hotels, shops, restaurants, cinemas, sports arenas, buses and airlines among others, in fact, almost any public space within which music is heard. As radio and television broadcasters have proliferated across Europe since the early 1990s, this has brought with it a vast increase in music licensing revenues from this sector.

TABLE 4.2 Global copyright royalties collected by CISAC members 1995–2010 (€ billions)

1995	1998	2001	2004	2007	2010
3.6	4.9	6.5	6.5	7.1	7.5

Source: CISAC Global Economic Survey, 2012.

For former Lakota Records owner Jim Carroll:

This is making it look like very good shareholder value which is why you see a lot of investment in music publishing at the moment because there will always be revenue coming in from publishing sources. There will be money coming in from films, from ads, television, radio, all that sort of stuff. (Jim Carroll, personal interview)

What we must also note is that many of the sources of music publishing revenue also provide revenue for record companies as they involve the use of recordings. 2008 saw a reported rise of 16 per cent in such income with record companies taking US$1.5 billion in global recording performance rights payments (Informa Telecoms and Media, 2009). While relative to the EU countries, such payments to record companies within the United States remain relatively small, US performance rights payments still rose by 176 per cent during 2008 to in excess of US$100 million (ibid.).

Synchronization fees

Within the above picture of growing music publishing revenues, we must consider the revenues currently being generated through synchronization fees – the monies paid when movie and television production companies, advertisers, and the producers of computer games license the right to use songs and/or music from the repertoires of record and music publishing companies in their productions. These particular agreements are usually negotiated between a music company and the licensed user independently of any existing performing rights licensing agreement. According to one interviewee, Úna Johnston, the integration of recorded music with other media forms and products has increased in recent years with more media meaning more openings for the synchronization of recordings than ever before:

There are so many new outlets and platforms . . . It's become so much more sophisticated in recent years. So many other things sell using music. Music to sell a film. Music to sell television. Advertising. Music to sell a brand. You have advertisers migrating to link with bands and music brands more and more . . . Music revenues are more and more generated by the application of music in other things. It's music as a secondary factor. Music used as an emotional hook to attach you to other brands. There are just so many forms of media now for music. (Úna Johnston, personal interview)

The synchronization market is hugely lucrative for music companies. While the music industries are now competing with a broad range of media types and products for the attention of direct consumers, many of its competitors provide a significant source of income for both record and music publishing companies. We are thus reminded of Frith's definition of the music industry as a 'complex network of rights owners and licensed users' (Frith, 2004: 176).

Another interviewee, John Williamson argues that for both record companies and publishing companies, synchronization is:

definitely more important now than it was in times gone by. We (Belle & Sebastian) have never entered into any deals for ads but I know plenty for whom it is a source of income and quite a substantial one at different points in their career. (John Willamson, personal interview)

Williamson explains that the income generated through synchronization rights depends on a variety of factors. Sometimes advertisers and production companies will opt to pursue material by less well-known acts because it can be significantly cheaper than more popular catalogue. Furthermore:

Much can depend on how much they want a particular song. This is not necessarily artist-related, it just depends if there is a piece of music that suits a particular ad or programme or film. The other factor is where and when it's being used. If it's for use in Eastern Europe the amount can be small but if it's going out in the US or the UK it can be a lot. (John Williamson, personal interview)

Another interviewee, Steve Lindsey states that some record and publishing companies are better at this than others and 'have identified the need to be more aggressive in this area . . . as TV can yield a lot of money' (personal interview). According to some of the

Irish-based publishers I interviewed, the range for use of a popular song in an advert can run from €10,000 to well in excess of €250,000 depending on the context of its use.

Many interviewees emphasize the value of the US television market in particular to the major music companies. For Jim Lockhart:

> *The OC* is a good example. You get a fee for the original usage plus a fee for subsequent usage plus a fee for further exploitation on DVD and box sets and things like that. So you can gain further gain from all that. (Jim Lockhart, personal interview)

This view is echoed by Ben Barrett, manager of Lisa Hannigan, Damien Rice and others. Music from Rice's first two albums *O* and *9* was licensed to television productions in excess of 30 times, most notably to *Grey's Anatomy*, *The OC*, and *Scrubs*. Aside from the promotional benefits, Barrett states that the synchronization fees 'can be very lucrative . . . if you land the right shows' (Ben Barrett, personal interview). Such a comment is reinforced by the figures published by CISAC that indicate 15 per cent growth in music publishing royalties collected from audio-visual repertoire globally in 2010 (CISAC, 2012).

Referring to recent trends at the South by South West (SXSW) global music industries trade fair (of which she is UK and Ireland coordinator), Úna Johnston advances that the presence of music supervisors at this event has become more visible in recent years. She states that their role in television production 'has mushroomed in importance' as music brands become a more integral part of selling television productions internationally.

Some interviewees point to legislation recently formulated in the United States that will increase the benefits of such television exposure as well as radio airplay to music companies in the United States. During the summer of 2008, the House Judiciary Committee's Subcommittee on Courts, the Internet and Intellectual Property heard arguments for and against the updating of the Performance Rights Act. The RIAA was seeking broadcasters to pay increased royalty rates to its member companies for use of their records in radio and television broadcasts. June 2008 saw the US Department of Commerce issue a letter of support for the Performance Rights Act on the grounds that:

> Granting copyright owners of sound recordings a full performance right coupled with extending an existing statutory license is an appropriate and workable approach to providing compensation to recording artists and record labels for the transmission of their works in over the air broadcasts. (cited on FMQB [online], Wednesday, 11 June 2008)

The National Association of Broadcasters (NAB) opposed the act on the grounds that in addition to the statutory royalties being paid to the record companies by its members, broadcasters already play a significant role in promoting sales of recordings via airplay for records. However spring 2009 saw the House Judiciary Committee pass the bill.

Recent trends regarding music in advertising

Synchronization rights for music in advertising have also become increasingly lucrative for record labels and music publishers. For example, Steve Lindsey, publisher and a former catalogue manager at Universal Music states:

> Advertising is more lucrative now than even getting a track in a Hollywood movie. Advertising synchronisation fees have come down in general in the last ten years, but there are a lot more of them. I used to work for Polygram in London and even back in the early 1990s we could charge fifty thousand pounds for the use of a modestly successful tune in a national advertising campaign. Now there is satellite and cable that has really taken off in the last five or ten years. Now advertisers can really look at the demographic they are aiming for and just advertise on those particular channels that they know their target audience will be watching, and by doing so that means that they can go for a much shorter term licenses on fewer stations or channels and they are not obliged to buy a 12 month network TV license for the music anymore for the whole of the UK and Ireland. (Steve Lindsey, personal interview)

The significance of songs in advertising is illustrated through the increasing presence of music industry representatives at the Annual Cannes Lions International Advertising Festival. According to the festival website, entries for the best use of music category increased 23 per cent from 2007 to 2009, and 50 per cent over the five-year period up to 2009. The increasingly aggressive efforts of record labels and music publishers to licence their products to advertising agencies has increased the competition experienced by dedicated jingle-writing companies. According to Andy Bloch of New York–based music production company Human Worldwide, since 2007 there has been 'a palatial shift in the record and publishing industries to monetise their back and current catalogues, and for emerging artists to find an outlet for their music' (cited in Howard, 2008). As such, according to Bloch, his company is losing clients to the major music labels, clients who used to pay between US$10,000 and US$200,000 for advertising music, depending on the length of the music used and when and where the advert would run. According to Martin Bandier, chairman and CEO of Sony/ATV Music Publishing:

> If a brand is going to spend tens of millions of dollars for TV, radio or web time, they want a song that has immediate recognition and that can put you in a particular place or time . . . This is a good time to be in the music publishing industry. (ibid.)

A number of different interviewees point to US trade publication *Billboard's* practice of tracking when the use of a song on a commercial causes its sales to increase. According to *Billboard*, advertising is playing an increasing role in raising the profile of current releases. A cursory examination of recent commercial breaks on television channels broadcasting within Ireland provides numerous examples of major labels artists and catalogue used in this way.

At any given point in time, a host of current or recent releases from recording artists appear on high-profile television adverts either nationally or internationally. Some relatively recent examples include Dizzee Rascal and Armand Van Helden (T-Mobile), Justice (Adidas), Body Rockers (BMW), The Yeah Yeah Yeah's (Yves Saint-Laurent), Jonsi

(Ford), The Flaming Lips (Dell), Groove Armada (Marks & Spencer), Girl's Aloud (Homebase), The Plain White T's (Parker Pens), Craig Armstrong (Channel), Moby (Nokia), The Scratch Perverts (Lucozade Sports), Mis-teeq (Armani), Madonna (Motorola), Coldplay (Play.com), The Klaxons (Wrigley's), The Zombies (Bulmer's), Jay-Z (Chrysler), among a host of others. Examples from the back catalogue of the major music companies include Lionel Ritchie (Walkers Crisps), The Stone Roses (Vision Express), Sting (Jaguar), The Cranberries (Open University promo), The Rolling Stones (Bulmer's), Pink Floyd (Road Safety Authority), The The (M&Ms), Status Quo (Pimm's), Oasis (Sky Sports), Queen (Cadbury's), Guns 'n' Roses (EA Games), Iggy Pop (Carnival Cruises), and specifically in the United States, the music of Bob Dylan (Victoria's Secret), the music of The Beatles (Target), Meat Loaf (AT&T) among hosts of others. A choral version of The Beatles song *All You Need Is Love* has also been used in a 2011 advert for the Halifax Bank in the United Kingdom. While the use of popular songs in the Levi's adverts in the 1980s was almost novel for its time, the above examples offer a small selection of the vast repertoire of major music company catalogue material that is now commonly exploited across the medium of advertising.

Websites selling downloads from vast databases of songs in adverts also emerged in recent years. Some were short-lived, other more enduring. For example, tvadmusic.co.uk was initially launched back in 2001 and, in 2012 boasts 400,000 page views and 130,000 unique visitors each month, according to the site itself. It offers music tracks from just under 1,500 television adverts to view, listen to and buy (via iTunes and Amazon). Claiming to have a database of information on approximately 8,000 television adverts with music from almost 4,000 recording artists, www.uktvadverts.com also provides links to iTunes and amazon.com for numerous entries in its database. Adtunes.com, squidoo.com, splendid.com and songsofthesalesman.co.uk provide just a few additional examples of the host of sites that also list and link to a vast repertoire of songs used in both current and previous adverts, all of which are offered for sale through their respective sites (via licensed platforms). Commercialbreaksandbeats.co.uk and soundsfamiliar.info also provided similar such services in the recent past. Furthermore, established digital music stores such as 7Digital offer specific TV advert music sections.

The growing significance of ad synchronization to record and music publishing companies in breaking new artists is illustrated through English vocalist Natasha Bedingfield's 2006 debut album *Unwritten*. Bedingfield's record label (Epic) and publishers (SonyAV Music Publishing) achieved no fewer than 30 licenses for the album which contains 14 tracks. For example, songs from the album have been used internationally on TV promotion spots for the series *Ugly Betty*, on the soundtrack of the feature film *Flicka*, and in a number of different advertising campaigns, the most notable being a global campaign for Pantene shampoo onwards. In addition to generating revenue from each of the 30 licensing deals, its widespread exposure in promo spots spurred on both physical and digital sales of the album. It became a million selling album in the United States with the title track becoming one of the top ten most downloaded tracks on iTunes in 2006. The song also achieved top ten status in both the UK and US singles charts that year. Other acts such as Moby have also been extremely successful at leveraging their music into multiple licensing deals that have then had a knock-on effect on album sales.

All of the major record companies now actively promote the advertising synchronization services they provide on their company websites and, to a greater or lesser degree, enable to prospective clients to listen to song selections, carry out searches for 'easy to clear' copyrights, preview new and upcoming releases on their labels, and to create and compile project folders.

Late 2011 saw EMI launch a new enlarged synchronization and licensing division, as, according to its own website, the company 'looks to expand the music licensing service it offers to clients on behalf of artists and songwriters' (EMI, 2011). In January 2012, the 'licensing' link on emimusicpub.com, the company's music publishing website, pointed to a catalogue of 1.3 million songs being readily available to license for synchronization.

Steve Lindsey explains that such a drive towards advertisers increased momentum during his time as Creative Director at Island Music, a Universal company. He states:

I remember on the Universal [web]site seeing the description of the Thin Lizzy song *The Boys Are Back In Town* as being ideal for a 'lads night out drinking scene'. Quite a lot of work has gone into pushing that sort of thing, but it is logical that we are doing it and economic necessity is driving it. This is something that the record and publishing companies should have been working much harder on in years ago. (Steve Lindsey, personal interview)

Here, it is worth pausing to examine Universal Music Publishing's synchronization service. Until recently, this service was called SynchExpress and its website detailed the entire catalogue of new and existing tracks available for license from the company. Initially, the SynchExpress homepage categorized these tracks under a broad spectrum of musical genres. Then, the content under each of those genres was further subdivided into a range of different song 'types', each designed to relate to the specific needs of music supervisors or advertising creatives in different situations. For example, SynchExpress offered 'cooking/food songs', 'feeling better songs', 'clean/dirty songs', 'female empowerment songs', 'travel/road songs', 'sports songs', 'nature/earth/environment songs' and numerous other categories of songs aimed at matching the profile of the broadcast range of products, services and lifestyles. More recently, SynchExpress has been incorporated into the new Universal Music Publishing site (umusicpub.com) which provides a largely similar service.

In terms of the precise value of music license fees from advertising, it has proven extremely difficult to acquire data, and the accounts of different interviewees vary somewhat. However, their accounts, combined with the available data from music publishing royalty collection societies indicate that it is an extremely lucrative and growing market. As with television and film, many interviewees explain that the licensing fee with advertising companies depends on many variables. For example, the range of media across which the campaign will be issued, the geographical territories across which it will be broadcast and the duration of the advertising campaign and also the existing popularity or status of the music or song being pursued by an advertiser. John Williamson states:

For use within the UK, the ranges that I've seen for advertising can be as low as £10,000 and the highest is probably about £100,000. For global use it can be much bigger but you have to remember too that sometimes big gas-guzzling companies can extract a good deal from bands or record companies because the bands and companies might want to be associated with the product or get the publicity and the rest of it. (John Williamson, personal interview)

Steve Lindsey also offers a sample range:

At Island I represented the Bob Marley catalogue, and because Bob Marley's stature is such, you could ask way more, whereas for an unknown artist, for exactly the same amount of music over the same duration and terms, you might get one-fifth of what you would get for Bob Marley . . . You then might have a song that is familiar to people but isn't by a mega artist and a UK network campaign might get you forty or fifty thousand pounds, and if that's only for a UK campaign for just 3 months, then you might be down to twenty thousand pounds . . . Where as with a Bob Marley, or a Madonna, or a U2, you can be talking millions. For an artist that big for a global campaign, you would at least ask for millions. (Steve Lindsey, personal interview)

As the aforementioned CISAC report indicates, overall synchronization revenues are up, and all of the above accounts point to the contemporary relevance of Simon Frith's conceptualization of music as a 'basket of rights' where the use of music across proliferating synchronization and licensing platforms offer sites of promotion and revenue to music rights owners.

The live music industry

The value of the live music industry has increased significantly in recent years. For composer and producer Bill Whelan:

We see a major return to live music now. Many artists are going out performing live because it's the only way to have a connection to their audience; not just a physical connection but also a fiscal one. You pay your money to see, for instance, Sting. Sting gets so much, the hall gets so much, and the essential connection between performer and his remuneration is restored. In the world of free downloading, such a connection has been largely eroded. (Bill Whelan, personal interview)

For artist manager Peter Jenner:

People who are not really interested in buying The Rolling Stones latest album are still prepared to pay money to see them play live, or Genesis, or The Police. Have The Police put out a new album? No, nor does anyone care. But they do huge live business –a veritable goldmine. (Peter Jenner, personal interview)

Likewise, Jenner's fellow manager Bruce Findlay explains:

For years the price of a concert ticket and an album kind of remained the same . . . but the top price of a new album now is £13 or £14 or whatever the equivalent is in euro. But if you want to see the same band live it'll cost you £50 or £60 or more. The price of live tickets is astronomical. There are more festivals than ever, more concerts than ever, and it all means that more people are willing to pay more money than ever for music. (Bruce Findlay, personal interview)

Another interviewee, former Island Records representative Ross Graham argues that while less profit is being generated from record sales in recent years, the live industry has been booming:

A lot of artists are generating huge profits on the live circuits and the thing about that is that it's not just income direct from the tour, it's merchandising too. In fact some artists are making most of their money out of merchandising . . . Gigs make money and gigs let you sell other things. A ticket for a once-off live show for an hour and a half's entertainment can now often cost you two or three or four or five times as much as a product like a CD that would be a product for life. But that's the way the market is at present, for the industry's elite, live is where it's at for the big money, and the market is always right. (Ross Graham, personal interview)

Pollstar, a live music industry trade publication in operation since 1981, and Boxscore (published by *Billboard* magazine) collect, organize and publish data on concert ticket sales and concert tours. Over the past decade, both publications have published year-on-year record-breaking figures for global live concert revenues. They estimated the global value of the overall live music industry grew to US$19.4 billion in 2008, accounting for almost one-third of the revenue generated by the overall global music industries that year. According to Pollstar, the value of the US live concert industry more than doubled between 2002 and 2008. It generated approximately US$4.2 billion in 2008, demonstrating a rise of 7 per cent from 2007 (cited in *The Los Angeles Times*, Tuesday, 13 January 2009). These figures comprise of data collected regarding ticket sales, ticketing fees, venue ancillary, sponsorship and other miscellaneous related revenue streams. By 2009, US concert ticket revenues alone were generating US$3 billion (Levine, cited in Cabral, 2009).

The Performing Rights Society (PRS), the performing royalty collection society in the United Kingdom, published statistics indicating that music publishing royalties generated by UK concert revenues exceeded ST£400m for the first time ever in a single year in 2008 (PRS for Music, 2009a). That marked a 30 per cent increase on 2007 revenues. In addition to this, the PRS estimated that 2008 saw primary ticket sales grow by 13 per cent, secondary ticket revenues increase by 4 per cent and ancillary revenues increased by in excess of 18 per cent (PRS for Music, 2009b). Overall, they placed the value of live revenues in the United Kingdom at ST£1.4 billion for 2008. With the value of recorded music sales in the United Kingdom standing at ST£1.309 billion for 2008 (IFPI, 2009c), live revenues actually surpassed record sales revenues in the United Kingdom that year. Similar trends were also repeated elsewhere. In Australia, for example, ticketing agency receipts compiled by Live Performance Australia indicated that the live concert industry was experiencing year-on-year growth of approximately 12 per cent to the end of 2007, when it had an estimated value of AUS$503 million (cited in Mathieson, 2009).

However, 2010 saw widespread reports on a downturn in the live music industry. Similar to the media accounts of the decline or demise of the record industry, we read such headlines as 'Rock concert sales plunge as recession forces promoters into discounts' (*The Guardian*, Thursday, 30 December 2010). Such accounts were not without foundation with Pollstar reporting the worldwide concert industry's only decline in 15 years when gross profits for the Top 50 tours worldwide fell by 12 per cent to just under US$3 billion (Sisario, 2012). This drop was especially significant in North America where, according to *Billboard*, grosses fell by almost 26 per cent. In the United Kingdom, following over a decade of consistent growth, live revenues declined by 6.8 per cent to ST£1.46 billion (PRS for Music, cited in Sweney, 2011). Interestingly, within this overall picture of decline in 2010, the increasing significance of the live sector to the broader music industry is still emphasized by US rock band Bon Jovi who, with the top-grossing US tour of 2010, derived more than 90 per cent of their total income for that year in the United States from concerts (*Billboard*, 2011b).

Despite the reported downturn in the sector in 2010, the global revenues for live music were still estimated to be well in excess of US$20 billion. According to Dave Laing (2012), while the IFPI placed a value of US$21.6 billion on this industry, his own calculation of the economic value of live music in 2010 was US$25 billion.

Also, downturn in the sector was not uniform across the globe. For example, a national study of the value of live music in Australia in 2009–10 by Ernst & Young estimated that this figure had increased to AUS$653 million, with the live music industry benefitting the Australian economy to the value of AUS$1.21 billion and providing the equivalent of 15,000 full-time jobs (Australasian Performing Right Association, September 2011). Throughout that period of time, almost 42 million tickets were sold for 328,000 concerts at almost 4,000 venues across Australia.

Also, the market for smaller, non-mainstream concerts was performing admirably (Panay, 2011). According to Sonicbids, an online network connecting artists, live music promoters and labels internationally, such 'under the radar' gigs drive a US$10 billion global market with a growth rate of 11 per cent a year (ibid.).

2011 saw the worldwide live music industry demonstrating its resilience once again with an overall return to growth. The overall revenue from the Top 50 tours globally increasing by more than 11 per cent during the first half of that year (Pollstar cited in *The Los*

Angeles Times, Thursday, 7 July 2011). In the case of North America the increase in value of that period of time was markedly higher at 16.2 per cent. Globally, the Top 50 tours grossed in excess of US$3.07 billion across 2011, a rise of 3.7 per cent on 2010 (Pollstar cited in Sisario, 2012).

Former Polydor and CBS representative Jackie Hayden highlights how the large touring profits that have been generated in recent years have largely derived from older, established acts with extensive recording histories and catalogue. Many of these acts, Hayden states, were once defunct but have reformed primarily to avail of the 'concert cash cow'. Hayden cites superstar acts such as The Eagles, Yes and The Police as evidence, as do smaller acts like Orchestral Manoeuvres in the Dark. Hayden details how his role as a concert reviewer for *Hot Press* magazine has, in recent years, involved a 'never-ending string' of incoming major international artists such as Bruce Springsteen, Bob Dylan, Leonard Cohen, Barbara Streisand, Neil Diamond, U2, Ry Cooder and a host of others. Hayden notes how acts such as Dylan, The Eagles and Springsteen are effectively on 'a never-ending tour', travelling the globe annually including visits to Ireland for (often multiple) stadium or arena shows. Acknowledging that the annual volume of live concerts by touring international acts has proliferated over recent years, Hayden is doubtful of the sustainability of this in the long term, arguing that the music industry will 'pay the price' for banking on established acts to the detriment of investing sufficiently in newer emerging acts over the past decade. However, as Ben Barrett explains, touring is not just profitable for older superstar acts. In the case of her artist, Damien Rice, who has released two albums through the Warner Music Group, touring revenues form an important part of the artists overall annual income:

> You can tour and make money, but it's about being clever in the first place and not exceeding your means. There is a certain investment of time and money and then touring becomes lucrative. When it works it also brings income from merchandise and income from increased record sales, and if all of the stars align then it financially makes sense . . . Looking at it over a year, we'll come out at the end making good money. (Ben Barrett, personal interview)

The Irish Times music columnist Jim Carroll outlines how in decades gone by, outdoor concerts were occasional events, with no more than 'two or three' major international touring acts visiting each year. This, according to Carroll, has evolved into a plethora of stadium concerts and outdoor festivals occurring from late spring until autumn and, 'near nightly' performances by major international acts in Dublin's main indoor concert arena, the O2 arena, as well as 'medium-size gigs' in theatre venues such as Dublin's Olympia. This, for Carroll, marks as 'quantum leap' in the profitability of touring, which, in former times, according a number of interviewees, was primarily a vehicle for promoting records and selling merchandise, without being necessarily profitable in its own right.

Another interviewee, RTE Radio 2 producer Ian Wilson advances:

> You can see from the proliferation of live music events in Ireland, there is certainly something going on . . . There must be a festival, or live music event every day throughout the summer in Ireland, and they are all big business. So there is obviously something going on out there, the music industry is not just necessarily related record companies. (Ian Wilson, personal interview)

Crashed Music MD Shay Hennessy concurs, stating that artists and music companies now view touring and live performance in a new light:

> There is much money in live performance. I think there is. Look at all of the international acts that come. There are very few international acts who come to this side of the Atlantic who don't have Dublin on their gig dates. Yet we are frequently told by the big acts and big labels that touring doesn't pay? Well Westlife don't do five nights in the O2 to please a record company and sell records. They do it because it works in its own right. Dolly Parton doesn't come to Millstreet because it doesn't make money. It's more than just promoting a record. Absolutely. There are very few people who will perform of it's not making money. (Shay Hennessy, personal interview)

A number of interviewees question the sustainability of this 'cash cow' in the context of an overall economic downturn. However, artist managers Bruce Findlay, John Williamson and Gerry Harford all point to the continuation of a decade-long trend regarding increases in advance ticket sales for major acts. Many other interviewees highlight the growing age range of concert-going audiences as a factor contributing to the sectors continuing growth, with many established artists attracting a 'seven to seventy' patronage. Others cite social networking platforms and other similar sites in the digital domain as another factor driving increased attendances at concerts and resultant growing revenues from the sector. They detail how there is no longer a time lag between hearing about a band and hearing a band. Social networks such as Facebook, YouTube, artists own websites and other online sites mean that audiences are 'primed' for seeing artists live much earlier now than was previously the case. Most interviewees who commented on the live industry emphasize, however, that this development is more usually the case with new acts reaching peripheral markets. Nevertheless, Peter Jenner advances that the 'grassroots' live industry needs to be strong to facilitate success further up the chain, and that it is a significant contributor to overall revenues in the sector, primarily through the generation of performing royalties in the multitudes of small venues throughout the country.

Secondary revenue streams generated by the live music industry

Beyond the generation of revenue for agents, promoters and artists directly by the sale of concert tickets, live sponsorship and other related ancillary activities, live concerts also generate significant income for the music publishing industry courtesy of both primary and secondary performance sources. Music publisher Johnny Lappin cites the live music industry as a key area within which music publishing companies have benefited in recent years with 'more and more people going to see live concerts than ever before' (personal interview). The live performance itself generates publishing 'performing' royalties based on every song or piece of music performed in a concert venue. These license fees, calculated on the basis of gross (primary) ticket revenues, are collected from the promoter and administered by performing rights collection societies on behalf of publishing copyright owners. In cases where copyrighted music recordings are used as part of a live performance, as is the case in many rap and hip-hop acts, a licence fee is also collected on behalf of the recording rights owners by the local phonographic performance royalty collection society. Performing royalties generated through live concerts in the United Kingdom in 2008 totalled almost ST£1.3 billion (PRS, 2009a).

Live concert performances by recording artists have long-since been produced and distributed across a range of video and audio formats. In addition to issuing live releases via DVD and a host of physical and digital audio platforms, YouTube has, in recent years, evolved as a site for the where acts make recordings of concerts available in their entirety. This, combined with the seemingly inexhaustible array of user-generated concert footage courtesy of concert-goers uploading their own footage from their mobile phones makes YouTube a valuable resource, both in terms of promotion for artists and, the licensing revenues it generates for music copyright owners.

Another relatively new activity that has evolved in the live music sphere relates to the recording of concerts for direct sale to the audience at the event itself. Shows are recorded, duplicated onto memory sticks and then sold to the audience at the end of the performance before they have even left the concert venue. Recent tours by established acts such as Elton John, Kiss and Simple Minds offer examples here. In the case of Simple Minds, recordings of these shows were subsequently distributed via MP3 download as well as sold on MP3 Players and USB 'Concert Stick' formats from the bands website.

Production costs, in these instances, are extremely low as it merely involves recording the live itself in real time. As such, the range of personnel and resources often associated with the recording studio do not apply. So, while the consumer-base at which such products are targeted is relatively low – that is, concert-goers and/or fans who are sufficiently dedicated to visit and peruse an artist's website – the profit margin on each unit sold is large.

Secondary ticketing

Another indication of an expanding live music industry is the increase in traffic relating to secondary ticketing. According to its *Concert Ticket Revenue Report* (2009), StubHub – the eBay-owned online ticket market – grew its business by 91 per cent during 2007 and a further 40 per cent throughout 2008. Ticketmaster offer three secondary ticketing services: TicketsNow (in the United States and Canada), GET ME IN! (in the United Kingdom), and TicketExchange which operates across Europe and North America. Seatwave has also evolved as a significant ticket exchange service in recent years.

In 2007, the UK Music Managers Forum, with the support of major recording artists such as Radiohead, The Verve and over 200 British recording artists launched the 'Re-sale Rights Society' – an industry group seeking to regulate the secondary sale of concert tickets and collect a levy from resellers on behalf of artists and concert promoters. The Re-sale Rights Society estimated the value of the online secondary ticketing market to be in excess of ST£200 million in 2007. According to interviewee Johnny Lappin, the sale of concert tickets is effectively a contract between the seller and the consumer. Lappin argues that the seller should be able to dictate the terms of use of the ticket, including the right to resell the ticket in territories where such activities are legal.

Live Nation Entertainment: Growing concentration and vertical integration in the live music industry

The live music industry, internationally, is becoming increasingly concentrated and vertically integrated. This is most vividly illustrated by the merger announced in February 2009 between Live Nation and Ticketmaster. This marked the alliance of the world's largest touring agency with the world's largest ticketing retailer under the banner of Live Nation Entertainment. The merger was approved by the US Justice Department in early 2010.

In many instances, local promoters are engaged in exclusive agreements with Ticketmaster, whereby Ticketmaster have exclusive retailing rights regarding primary ticketing. Furthermore Live Nation, formerly the live entertainment arm of Clear Channel Communications, has in recent years acquired numerous live music promotion companies internationally. Examples include Milano Concerti (Italy) and Gunnar Eide Concerts (Norway) among a multitude of others. The case of MCD (McCann-Desmond) in Ireland provides an example of how concentrated power has become in this area. MCD delivers live music events through approximately 40 venues that it either owns or operates across Ireland. These include The Olympia, The Academy and The Ambassador in Dublin. Through its joint acquisition of London-based promotions company Mean Fiddler (rebranded Festival Republic) MCD also promotes and manages some of the biggest music festivals in Ireland, the United Kingdom and Europe on an annual basis. These include Oxygen (Ireland), Heineken Green Energy (Ireland), Electric Picnic (Ireland), T in the Park (Scotland), the Reading and Leeds festivals (England). From 2005 until 2007 its partner in Festival Republic was Live Nation, at which point Live Nation was reportedly seeking to acquire MCD. Subsequently Live Nation also acquired a 50 per cent stake in Dublin's largest indoor concert arena, the O2.

Live Nation already owns and/or operates hundreds of venues, predominantly in the United States but with a growing international portfolio consisting of amphitheatres, arenas, theatres, clubs and festival sites. They radically increased this aspect of their business in 2008 with the formation of a strategic alliance with the American Capital–owned venue operator SMG, bringing a further 216 venues under their management. Live Nation Entertainment is thus the predominant player in the global market regarding the sale of tours, concert promotion, primary and secondary ticket sales. In the case of artists signed to 360-degree contracts with the company, it enjoys the additional ownership of recording rights, music publishing rights, merchandising rights, artist image rights and all other artist-related licensable rights.

With 360-degree deals providing Live Nation Entertainment with the rights to new recordings from some of the most established artists in the world, users visiting Ticketmaster sites are now, in some cases, offered the option of buying music recordings or merchandise as an alternative to paying the booking fees added to concert ticket prices.

By 2008, Ticketmaster had itself acquired Front Line Management, one of the world's most prominent artist management companies. This means that in addition to owning 360-degree rights relating to artists like Madonna, Shakira and Jay-Z and 180-degree rights to U2, Live Nation Entertainment now manage The Eagles, Aerosmith, Christina Aguilera, Guns'n'Roses among a myriad of other major artists. Live Nation Entertainment's 2011 annual report indicates that Front Line Management represents in excess of 250 music acts internationally.

By early 2012, the Live Nation Entertainment (LNE) website boasted ticketmaster.com as one of the world's top five e-commerce websites with 26 million monthly unique visitors. Moreover, LNE estimates over 200 million consumers annually. Live Nation concerts produce well over 20,000 concerts for over 2,000 acts internationally each year. For example, 2010 saw LNE's concerts business promote 21,000 live music events and sell 232 million tickets (Live Nation Entertainment, *Annual Report* [Form 10-K], 28 February 2011). Concerts generated revenues of US$3.4 billion for LNE that year, which amounted to 67.6 per cent, of the company's total revenue with an additional US$1 billion derived from the ticketing services aspects of the business.

Peter Jenner argues that it is becoming harder for independent touring agents and promoters to sustain themselves:

> Anyone with a brain knows that with this merger you are reducing competition across the entire industry. They'll probably have investigations for two years to try and work out how they can pretend it's not reducing competition. But it is self evident. The prime reason for merging is to reduce competition. Operators in the free market know that the best thing for their business is to get rid of the competition. Monopoly is the ideal position for any company to be in. (Peter Jenner, personal interview)

Likewise for AIM chair Alison Wenham, this merger marks the further consolidation of the established music industries and the continued evolution of a trend that is 'detrimental to smaller operators in all areas of the business'. That said, we must be mindful of the Sonicbids research (detailed earlier) that points to a very healthy non-mainstream live market.

Overall, the live music industry has expanded very considerably over the past decade and a half and it carries significantly greater benefits for its stakeholders in terms of direct revenues for agents, promoters, ticket retailers, merchandise companies and artists accruing from live events. It also produces indirect benefits in terms of performing royalties for music publishers and secondary ticketing revenues for outlets facilitating these activities. Live concerts also remain a vehicle for promoting records and stimulating sales. Power within this sector is becoming more centralized as the sector is evolving into a more vertically integrated structure, with many of the core stakeholders falling under the umbrella of LNE.

The content-technology relationship

A further matter for consideration in examining the apparent crisis in the record industry relates to conglomeration of music and electronics companies. For artist manager Bruce Findlay, alliances between content providers and technology providers serve the continuing interests of both sectors:

> This idea about free music pisses me off a wee bit. I'm going to sound old-fashioned here, but we don't get music for free, we buy computers, we pay for software, we pay for connections, we buy iPods and lots of us subscribe to music services. They say it's free. It's never free. Even when the content doesn't cost you anything, you buy the machinery from the same fucking people, so there is always a cost to the end user. (Bruce Findlay, personal interview)

Findlay proceeds to argue the 'add-on' value of music to technological devices, where music is used to attract consumers or entice them to purchase devices, and 'telecommunications licence music and the payments go into a kitty for intellectual property rights owners' (ibid.). He further compares the present environment with that of the

1970s when he owned an independent chain of recorded music retail outlets across Scotland. He argues:

> All that's changed is the means of receiving music . . . with the internet and iPods all of the stuff that goes with it, they've just found another way of cutting out old record shop men like me. (Bruce Findlay, personal interview)

Some interviewees point to technology companies from the same corporate families as the major music labels gaining from internet downloading and CD-burning activities as they produce and supply electronic devices and software programmes used for these activities.

Some of those with interests in the major music labels have also acquired holdings in other areas associated with media entertainment and electronics. Here we must consider that major music companies form part of larger conglomerates that, through different aspects of their operations produce and/or supply hardware, software and content across a variety of media formats. For example, aside from music, the Sony Corporation has interests in movies, television and digital games as well as consumer electronics, computer hardware, CD manufacturing, and telecommunications (including mobile phones). Vivendi, the owners of the Universal Music Group, has interests in film, television, digital games and telecommunications. The Warner Music Group is owned by Access Industries who, among other things, has interests across various media and telecommunications. Prior to the sale of its recording and music publishing operations to Universal and (a consortium led by) Sony respectively in 2011, Electrical and Musical Industries (EMI) had been the largest stand-alone music company in the world and, until relatively recently had held interests in consumer electronics and information technology. As such, music companies are closely related to a plethora of other media and communication related spheres.

Given the level of attention that has been paid to the 'unauthorized' duplication of music down the years, it is worth noting some of close links between actors in the content and technology arenas. While the record industry has undoubtedly lost money through CD-burning technologies enabling users to duplicate recordings quickly and easily, some of its 'relations' have profited from producing and supplying a combination of hardware enabling CD copying, blank CDs or software for CD duplication.

Equally, the convergence of interests between actors in the technology sector and music companies also enables the cross-marketing of products, services and content. For example, Research In Motion, the company that makes Blackberry products, sponsored the world tour to promote U2's *No Line on the Horizon* album. This coincided with the launch of an application for Blackberry smartphone users called the U2 Mobile Album. The application, which was promoted by the 'Blackberry Loves U2' commercial, enabled users to access photos, videos, music and streaming news relating to the band. Similarly U2 went into a partnership with Apple to release a U2 branded iPod that included the band's back catalogue on it. Another relatively recent example saw Hewlett Packard offer consumers album art from a range of Universal recording artists in the form of digital tattoos. Such cross-promotional strategies are not necessarily new. Back in the early 1990s the Dire Straits album *On Every Street* (and the world tour that promoted it) was used as the platform for launching Philip's unsuccessful Digital Compact Cassette (DCC) format. Philips also owned Polygram, the label that the band was signed to at that point in time.

360-degree artist deals

In recent years the major music companies have executed broader, all-encompassing deals with the artists on the respective rosters. The emphasis has been on growth through diversification. Not only have the spheres of recording, publishing, live music services and merchandising grown more concentrated, they have also become more integrated. The four major recording and music publishing companies have become more aggressive in securing touring rights for both new and established acts on their rosters. Many of the artist managers that I interviewed advanced that while record labels have traditionally applied pressure to sign to their publishing arm, recent years has seen them increasingly push for touring rights in recording negotiations. Equally companies that have traditionally focused on live aspects of the industry are now moving into the terrains of recording, publishing and associated marketing and promotion of recordings and repertoire. As one such manager, Ben Barrett, explains:

> From our dealings with Warner's, the labels are obviously very keen to get their share of every aspect of an artist's income, from recording to publishing to merchandising to live to whatever. That's very much one way that they look at the future, one sort of big umbrella organisation with everything under the same roof. (Ben Barrett, personal interview)

360-degree deals, thus, see artists sign contracts with one company, assigning to them the handling of all facets of the artists career including recording, publishing, live performance, primary and secondary ticketing for tours, merchandising, endorsements, all aspects of image rights, and all other artists related rights. For Ross Graham, CEO of NIMIC:

> The majors will not be on the ropes if they can more readily access merchandising and live incomes. Merchandising incomes are more important than they ever were and live incomes are certainly much more important than they ever were. (Ross Graham, personal interview)

The most significant and high-profile 360-degree signings include acts such as Madonna, Jay-Z and Shakira who departed from their respective music labels to sign deals with Live Nation, the hitherto (almost) exclusive live touring agency. U2 also signed a 180-degree deal with Live Nation, giving them rights to touring and merchandising, while retaining a licensing agreement with the Universal Music Group in relation to recording and publishing.

For artists with the stature and (current) selling power such as these, such deals mean greater revenues can be generated and greater economies of scale achieved through such consolidation. Dedicated online and print music publications have carried numerous accounts of music companies across the recording, publishing, merchandising and live music spheres staffing increasingly broader levels of expertise. Examples include the Warner Music Group's acquisition of a majority stake in Spanish artists management firm Get In. This company oversees the career of Spanish chart-topping group La Oreja de Van Gogh, a band that has also achieved significant commercial success in Mexico and other Latin American countries. Similarly Warner's carry a majority stake in Japanese management company Taisuke as well as substantial investments in online properties Lala and (the now defunct) Imeem.

While the Paradigm booking agency has traditionally functioned as a touring agency, recent years saw the company develop a marketing and branding operation. Paradigm have forged alliances with major music companies to source additional avenues for revenue on its roster via endorsements, sponsorship, merchandising and branding deals as well as integrating artists such as Aerosmith, Coldplay, Pharrell Williams and Lily Allen into television and film projects being managed by the agencies sister Paradigm divisions, and beyond. Such alliances between companies from different strands of the music business also means more muscle within bigger negotiations, especially in the areas of non-traditional/ancilliary revenue streams such as endorsements, merchandising, sponsorships, acting or book deals.

As interviewee John Williamson stated, it is no longer about how many units of an album a band can sell, rather it is 'how much profit can be made across various sectors or earnings and revenue' (personal interview). As such, a more holistic structure encompasses all aspects of an artistic career and all potential sources of revenue deriving from that career, and the fruits of artistic labour.

A number of interviewees point to such developments leaving recording artists at a distinct disadvantage. International music industry conference organizer Úna Johnston argues that it has always been in an artist's best interest to ensure that the administration of each discrete activity is kept in the hands of separate actors. For example, she outlines the drawbacks associated with artists signing a 'cross-collateralization' clause in a recording contract. Under the terms of this clause, the artist signs their repertoire over to the publishing arm of the same record company. Johnston describes a scenario whereby a band or artist might generate a profit through publishing, but make a loss on a recording. If this artist has signed 'independent' publishing and recording deals, then they will receive their agreed share of publishing profits. However if they have signed to the same record and publishing company, then cross-collateralization means that the record company are entitled to recoup their loss from any publishing profits before the artist qualifies for any payment. For Johnston, cross-collateralization is 'rarely a good deal for a band' (personal interview).

As Johnston and others argue, 360-degree makes such scenarios the norm for artists in their dealings with all music industry sub-sectors, and removes any autonomy to engage with actors outside the one company. As many interviewees advance, already 'superstar' acts are rewarded with huge advances in exchange for handing over all rights, however smaller or new acts are increasingly only offered an 'all or nothing' deal when it comes to negotiating with major labels. In these cases, without the 'clout' of a successful catalogue or established artist brand behind them, they have little leverage in these negotiations. Furthermore these deals also include management services. Thus, having all eggs in the one basket means that very significant power lies with one source.

Chapter summary

When we also consider the expansion of outlets for music content through already existing intermediaries such as radio, television and advertising and the significant growth of the live music industry, the broader music industries landscape paints a significantly healthier picture than the digitally induced Armageddon suggested by record sales data and popular media reports. Continuing processes of convergence and conglomeration and the evolution of 360-degree artist contracts points to a growing centralization of power within the music industries.

Given the emphasis placed on declining record sales in much media and industry discourse surrounding the relationship between the internet and the music industry, Chapter 5 will now proceed to examine the organization and structure of the contemporary record industry over a decade after the internet emerged as a conduit for recordings. In doing so, the chapter will focus on the disruption caused to established distribution and promotion practices, and, given the proliferating range of platforms for music to reach an audience, examine the potential of new technological platforms to enhance the ability of independent artists or smaller record labels to get to market.

5

New rules for the new music economy? [Part one]

Chapter 2 outlined arguments contending that the music industry has been experiencing a state of crisis as digital technologies for the dissemination of music have rapidly and widely diffused. Chapters 3 and 4 placed this crisis, predominantly associated with the recording sector, in the context of the broader music industry. In doing this, copyright has been highlighted as central to the sustenance of the industry, particularly with the development of new digital platforms for licensed music as well as the expansion of more traditional licensing revenue streams. Combined with the overall picture of growth in the live music industry over the past decade and a half, all of this serves to illustrate a different reality to the picture of a music industry in crisis as illustrated commonly in media accounts. This chapter primarily concerns itself with another aspect of the internet music 'revolution' – the promise of disintermediation and the potential for digital distribution and internet promotion to provide creative artists with the necessary machinery to access and succeed in the marketplace, independent of the intervention of the major record labels. Here, we are reminded of Simon Napier-Bell's declaration that for 'artists and managers, this is the moment to take things into their own hands' (2008: 41). It is useful also to recall the extent of internet-induced disruption predicted to the 'rules of the economic game' by Kelly and Negroponte, the two foremost 'information-age gurus'. Such predictions around the collapse of organizations and the disintegration of copyright keep suit with Toffler's (1970, 1980) theme of a break with the old relations of industrial capitalism. They ultimately suggest a much more level-playing field upon which cultural corporations can no longer hold advantage or power over the individual, independent artist or content producer. This chapter thus draws upon the accounts of a number of the interviewees to examine the extent to which a 'do-it-yourself' approach to the promotion and distribution of music has been enhanced by evolving digital technologies.

To meet this end, this chapter first examines the composition of the contemporary recorded music market, and proceeds to consider the roles of and relationships between major and independent actors. Interviewees were asked to reflect upon earlier techno-centric predictions to the effect that more independent artists and companies would achieve increased and easier access to the marketplace and offer their perspectives on, and experience of the current relationship between major and independent actors. Beyond this, drawing significantly on the contributions of the artist managers who participated in interviews, the chapter will examine contemporary routes for getting new music to market and the role and implications of internet technologies in evolving these processes. A number of interviewees outline what they perceive as the current working model for breaking an artist into the mass market. Ultimately, as we shall see, their accounts highlight the ongoing significance of the major companies in shaping these developments.

The composition of the contemporary recorded music market

Since its origins, the music industry has experienced a situation where production and distribution channels fall under the ownership and control of a small number of companies. By the early 1990s, six major companies controlled over 70 per cent of the global market and approaching 80 per cent of the American market. By the early 2000s this number had reduced to just four companies. By late 2011, this had reduced to three, namely, Sony, Warner's and Universal. In 2007, the combined market share of the then four major record companies stood at approximately 74 per cent of the global market (IFPI, 2007c). Consistent with its labelling as one of the most globalized states in the world during the 2000s, the market share of these four companies in Ireland stood at 92 per cent in 2007 (ibid.).

Alison Wenham, president of the Worldwide Independent Network (WIN) – a body representing over 20 independent music trade associations globally – argues that the recorded music market is 'a market that is suffering from the features of collective dominance'. While, according to Wenham, the record industry operated on a 'relatively territorial' basis up until the early 1980s, it has subsequently evolved to experience increasing consolidation of control. This affects artist and repertoire acquisition, sets increasingly global/international priorities for majors operating in national territories, and raises the cost of entry into markets for independent companies. Such 'massive concentration' has created 'a vicious circle where the larger you get the larger you need to be' (Alison Wenham, personal interview).

Another interviewee, Úna Johnston echoes Wenham's statements, advancing that, in the Irish context, while the ease with which recordings can be produced these days means that there are many more independent labels in existence, those of 'any [commercial] significance are being subsumed more quickly into the major labels in 'an ongoing process of takeovers, mergers and consolidation' (personal interview).

As the existence of WIN indicates, there has also been a strong international coagulation of independent music companies in recent years. IMPALA in Europe, A2IM in the United States, Cirpa in Canada and AIR in Australia all provide examples of independent music company trade associations. In 2006 these national/international associations formed into a global coalition that is WIN. The AIM, of which Alison Wenham is also chair, represents various sizes of independent companies in the United Kingdom and Ireland. The only criterion for membership is that a major company cannot own more than a 50 per cent stake in the independent company. Wenham detailed how the size of independent companies relative to major companies has diminished significantly in recent decades. Her comments here were focused particularly on the Beggars Group. Beggars is one of the largest independent labels in the world consisting of 4AD, Matador, Rough Trade and XL Recordings. It has headquarters in London and five additional offices in North America, Europe and Japan.

> If you look back fifteen to twenty years you will find that the market was populated by dozens of larger companies – the largest independent was only half the size of the smallest major. Now, after the acquisition of those companies by the majors and the ongoing concentration which the industry has experienced over the last ten years you will find that there is not one of our member companies in Europe that has more than 1 per cent of the market. So they are all small players, even if in comparative terms the size of a company of Beggars stature versus many of our new members is also staggering. But the point is that the size of someone like Universal compared to Beggars is also staggering. (Alison Wenham, personal interview)

The new millennium has seen some of the largest independent music companies in the world move under the umbrella of the major labels. For example, 2002 saw BMG purchase Zomba, what was then the world's largest independent company for a reported US$3 billion. It is now a division of Sony Music Entertainment. Mute was acquired by EMI. Rykodisc, the company once owned by former Island Records founder Chris Blackwell, was bought by the Warner Music Group in 2006. V2, the label started in the 1990s by Richard Branson following the sale of Virgin to EMI is now owned by Universal. Until July 2007 Sanctuary Records was the largest independent record label in the United Kingdom until it too was acquired by Universal. For the four major companies, the corporate structures are global, so they have global marketing initiatives and global distribution networks. Even for an independent company the size of Beggars, they remain reliant on separate independent distribution systems in different territories. Former Island Records representative Ross Graham argues that beyond the issue of distribution, 'the majors also have a stranglehold on media control for pushing their artists'. All of this, according to artist manager Peter Jenner combines to make it increasingly difficult for smaller independent labels to access the market:

> They're pretty hostile towards each other because the majors make it very hard for the independents to get to market. What they do, in

effect, is to drive up the price of admission to the market. Whether it's the price of bribing a DJ, or the price of getting your record displayed in the shops, the price of bribing a journalist – they have a lot of power and they use that power to make it harder for the indies. (Peter Jenner, personal interview)

Prior to the advent of the internet as a technology of mass communication, digital had long since established itself in the spheres of music production and consumption and provided a key tool that enabled and facilitated this increased concentration – the compact disc or CD. Among my interviewees, the accounts of (primarily) independent record company owners and personnel indicate that the independent recording sector was unable to make significant gain from the premium profit market in CD sales from the late 1980s onwards. The shift in format from cassette to digital saw the major labels employ their extensive back catalogues to grow the market and their market share. The potential for rehashing former releases as 'digital remasters' explained, in part at least, the willingness of the major labels to acquire the catalogue of the larger, more established independent companies in the late 1980s – Motown, Island and Virgin provide examples. However, the absence of significant (or in many cases, any) back catalogue material places newer and emerging independent companies at a disadvantage. Interviewee Jackie Hayden emphasizes this point:

> If you take a small company, say Setanta for example, they might need to sell 20,000 or 30,000 copies of a CD to have any kind of income from a record. But for a small label like that, generating the equivalent return from what are largely going to be individual single track downloads is very, very difficult . . . So *they* suffer in a way that the bigger companies don't . . . So I see the internet as a much bigger threat to smaller companies than it is for the majors. The majors have vast back catalogues to exploit at little or no additional cost to themselves, and they have the resources to market newer artists and records and the Justin Timberlake's of this world through which they can sell millions in a way that the Setanta's of this world can't. (personal interview)

Likewise, other interviewees see the vast catalogues under the ownership of the major labels as buffering them against potentially harmful effects of technological change and bolstering their dominant position in the marketplace. According to Steve Lindsey, 'the actual medium through which people receive their music is academic' once a company has ownership of a sizeable repertoire. Lindsey emphasizes that the larger the catalogue of recordings under the ownership of a company, the greater the opportunities for exploiting it across a variety of media and platforms. Successful back catalogues are perennial 'cash cows' for the major labels so one key strategy for maintaining dominance is to 'batten down the hatches' on spending on new acts and divert funds to the further marketing and promotion of already popular repertoire.

In 2008, UK Culture secretary, Andy Burnham, recommended the extension of copyright term in sound recording from 50 to 70 years. This was in the wake of EC Internal Markets commissioner Charlie McCreevy's proposal to increase the term of protection to 95 years in order to bring Europe into line with the United States. This proposal was subsequently amended to 70 years and the European Parliament voted in favour of the amendment on 23 April 2009. On 12 September 2011, the EU Council of Ministers passed this copyright term extension. A number of my interviewees point to the success the major music companies have had in lobbying for the extension and expansion of copyright laws in recent years. While they acknowledge that such changes carry potential economic benefits for all copyright owners, the consensus is that such developments as an extension to copyright term will further enable major labels to weather the 'digital storm' by allowing them to retain control over established catalogues of music for a much longer period of time. Lindsey describes the marketing budgets for rereleased and remastered back catalogue as sometimes 'astronomical' and 'quite obscene' but based on the reality that 'millions of people are still buying *Hotel California*' (personal interview).

According to Alison Wenham, in a territory like Ireland it is almost impossible for an independent company to survive unless it is attached to a major label. For Wenham, the ability of a record label to sustain itself in a local market is largely a matter of geography and a matter of local market practice. Despite the evolution of internet music markets with the ability to transcend physical boundaries, Wenham contends that 'local' remains a huge feature of the independent sector. She states that the United States recorded music market is approximately five times the size of the United Kingdom market and 'many, many times bigger' than the Irish market. Wenham explains that there are hundreds of local independent companies who serve local markets within the United States and 'survive very happily on their local reach' (personal interview). These companies rarely generate national or international chart successes and tend to shift volumes of recordings in tens of thousands rather than hundreds of thousands or millions, but economies of scale enable them to turn a profit. As Wenham explains:

> By 'local' I might be talking about Nashville, or Miami, or West Coast. There are plenty of consumers within any given constituency that create an eco-system upon which you can run a successful business. The same applies but to a lesser extent in the UK where local geography would see, for example, the North-West sector being particularly strong and Scotland maintaining a relatively decent industry around what is essentially locally-produced music. London and South-East is another one. (personal interview)

Outlining how the UK and Irish markets have seen high-street retailers and key tastemakers like radio consolidate, many interviewees argue that there is less choice for the consumer on the shelves. As Wenham continues, supermarkets in particular are adept at 'taking the cream' by selling recordings at low prices and thus upsetting the retail economy.

The evidence gleaned from Wenham and the independent label operators interviewed points to a decrease in the number of independent record distribution companies in existence that serve the UK and Irish markets. Again, they relate this to issues of consolidation and the aggressive entry of supermarkets into music retailing from the 1990s onwards. Given that much independent recorded music product is unsuitable for supermarket shelves, they regard a whole hinterland of independent music as operating increasingly beyond mainstream margins. While many of the independent label owners and artist managers interviewed point to the potential of the internet to bypass these processes, they predominantly argue that it has not transpired to transform the retail of independent music.

Despite its significant growth up until 2007, the overall size of the Irish market is relatively small. In such a market, where the four major companies dominate, many of my interviewees argue that it is extremely difficult for an independent label, indigenous or other, to have a commercial life.

As a number of interviewees explained, the distinction between major and independent companies has become increasingly blurred and, the ability of an independent label to enjoy a commercial life increasingly relies on a relationship with one or more of the major corporate actors. Fachtna O'Ceallaigh advances that independent record labels that have 'any substance to them or any longevity to them or any capacity to sell records' would of necessity have 'some kind of relationship with a major' (personal interview). This point is reinforced by Bruce Findlay who states that independent labels face only two possible fates: they either 'get swallowed up' by the majors, or 'go bust' (personal interview). Findlay explains that those labels showing promise will almost without exception move under the umbrella of a major if they are to enjoy a commercial life over time. He outlines how this relationship may involve one or more factors including distribution, marketing and promotion, licensing rights for a variety of purposes. O'Ceallaigh points to a number of cases where one of the major labels is the minority or majority stakeholder in a given independent label. In other cases, an independent label may be solely funded by a major label. This latter scenario as forwarded by O'Ceallaigh is exemplified by Lakota Records, the label formerly operated by another interviewee Jim Carroll.

> You could call us a 'mindy' label – a major-indie. To all intents and purposes we were an independent label in Ireland and the UK and were distributed by an independent distribution company, but we were entirely bankrolled by Sony. It was two incredibly bright people at the distribution and marketing end of Sony who basically did deals with labels . . . Lakota was owned by Sony but all our records in the UK came out through Vital because we needed to *look* independent. We had to because there is an awful lot of kudos involved. (Jim Carroll, personal interview)

Sony had other deals in operation with Setanta Records and Creation Records at different times. Similarly there are companies such as Loog and Be Unique who are tied to the Universal Music Group. These, as Carroll explains, are all labels that effectively carry an 'independent tag' but are funded by majors.

In some cases, the impetus behind the formation of the indie label comes from the major. In others, an independent entity already exists and it is usurped by a major. Other independent labels find themselves simultaneously engaged with more than one major label. This scenario is perhaps best illustrated through the case of Petr Pandula's County Clare–based independent label Magnetic Music. Two of the most significant deals signed by Magnetic in recent years saw them contracted to provide promotion and distribution services in the German and Irish markets for new releases by Moya Brennan and Carlos Nunes, signed to Universal and Sony respectively.

Such processes as described above illustrate how the independent sector increasingly exists as a shopfront for majors, taking them into sections of the market that were once the preserve of niche suppliers. As evidenced from the account of Jim Carroll in particular, major companies 'need the kudos' of independent labels and will place bands on the rosters of those labels that they know will benefit from an indie gloss.

Carroll proceeds to point out that even in the case of larger independent labels such as Domino and the Beggars Group (both of whom remain independently owned), they have entered into distribution deals with major actors Columbia and Epic (both Sony companies). Thus, while they may have 'no obvious allegiance' to those companies, 'Domino and Beggars are nevertheless reliant on the machinery of major companies distribution networks' (Jim Carroll, personal interview).

For Steve Lindsey, the process of majors 'bank-rolling what you and I might otherwise perceive as independent labels' is nothing new, but has accelerated since the latter part of the 1990s. As Lindsey advances:

Genuine independent labels are very, very few and far between now . . . [In the UK] majors will put aside several million quid as seed money for any independent labels they like the sound of . . .

Independents with any degree of success will, to one degree or another have support from a major. It might just be distribution, or it might be marketing and distribution, or the independent label might be in effect the A&R office of the major. (personal interview)

The sum of the above accounts is that for many independent companies, survival is still dependent upon being fundamentally linked to a major company. For those indies existing outside of this loop, sustaining a commercial life is extremely difficult. Access to effective distribution, marketing and promotion resources remains relatively limited. The opportunities and challenges around accessing the marketplace independently of major companies are examined in much greater detail in the following sections.

Getting new music to market in the internet era

Many interviewees highlight the advantages of digital in terms of production, promotion and distribution for independent artists and labels. They emphasize the growing potential for adopting a do-it-yourself approach in terms of the production of recordings and the promotion of artists and their wares. In addition to highlighting digital platforms for the circulation of music such as online streaming and video-sharing sites, a number of interviewees point to the emergence of new digital intermediaries such as social networking sites, blogs and online music magazines as new key tools in helping to break a new artist. Other interviewees also point to the emergence of various public and privately funded information and training initiatives which, they argue, makes for a much broader awareness of the music industries and enhances the do-it-yourself approach to producing recordings and the marketing and networking involved in launching artists. Crucially, interviewees also point to the limits of an independent, do-it-yourself approach, arguing that for successful acts, access to mainstream markets remains almost exclusively the preserve of major music companies. The remainder of this section looks at each of these factors in turn.

Digitalization enhancing the do-it-yourself approach

As with many of my interviewees, Independent Records owner Dave O'Grady and Magnetic Music's Petr Pandula point to cost reductions in making recordings and the increasing ease with which they can be produced as a primary benefit accruing to artists and 'small operators' associated with digitalization. O'Grady also proceeds to explain that many artistic and administrative functions surrounding the production of recordings are now more efficiently executed than in the predigital environment:

> There was always someone who would charge you *more* for something very simple, but something you couldn't do without. There were all these little ancillary industries that were built around the production of CDs, or film for artwork or other stuff where you always had to pay a little more than you thought. You can do that stuff yourself now. You don't have to pay to get an MP3 encoded anymore. You don't have to pay to adjust and look at your own artwork. You don't have to pay to burn a CD-R. It's become a lot faster and cheaper to do these things and disseminate stuff . . . From a small independent labels point of view, you can definitely run an operation with less staff and less costs than you might have needed in the eighties and nineties. (Dave O'Grady, personal interview)

For another interviewee, SXSW's Úna Johnston, digitalization has produced a significant level of independence for Irish acts and labels in particular. Johnston argues that the digital era means that Irish acts and labels are no longer bounded by geography and tied to majors in the United Kingdom or elsewhere. The fact that digital bypasses many traditional manufacturing costs and provides independent platforms for distribution and promotion means, according to Johnston (speaking in 2009), that:

> bands are empowered to have direct access to the market and to have direct access to an audience who can be anywhere. The fifth member of the band is the webmaster . . . We're talking ten years really since the internet happened and because of its viral nature

it's changed in ten years what would have taken a hundred years to change before. Artists don't need record companies the way the used to. (personal interview)

Johnston proceeds to explain that the internet has bred 'a culture of entrepreneurial spirit' that has hitherto been poor in an Irish context:

Bands doing it for themselves? That culture of entrepreneurial spirit or business development has been poor in Ireland in the past. Bands setting up businesses and actually being their own business would be at odds with the current model of the way the majority of people work in Ireland. Eighty or ninety per cent of people don't set up their own businesses here, they go and work for somebody else . . . We've got the major labels in the music industry the same way we've got multi-nationals in other industries . . . Our model has always been to bring in the multi-nationals and let them pay us wages . . . Now, with a new internet-based approach we can set up labels and companies to run the music industry here. There is a real, real opportunity now for a band as a business if you are clued in. (personal interview)

In the mid-to-late 1990s, the potential for disintermediation in the music industry was widely discussed as the internet emerged as a new and potentially transformative player in the music distribution sphere. While acknowledging that the digital distribution of music held the potential to serve the interests of the major music labels and give them 'even more control and larger profits', Robert Burnett also made the point that it 'could open a Pandora's box that could ultimately destroy their own control of popular music' (1996: 148). In the latter half of the 1990s, much commentary and analysis pointed to the advent of digital distribution technologies inducing a process of disintermediation – removing the 'corporate middlemen' from the distribution process. It was widely predicted that such a process would ultimately lead to the collapse of the traditional music industry. Burnett suggested that the internet could, in theory, ensure that 'a small group of users spread out geographically, could generate sufficient demand to sustain the product of small independent producers' (1996: 144). During the course of our interview, artist manager Fachtna O'Ceallaigh sought to explain the extent to which this potential has been achieved or not. For O'Ceallaigh, two key factors combine to enhance 'do-it-yourself' opportunities for breaking new music in the contemporary environment: first, the proliferation of social networks and other online avenues for self-promotion combined with relatively cheap and reliable digital recording technologies for the home computer; and second, O'Ceallaigh points to 'the spread of knowledge' about how to put out records, make them digitally available and promote them (primarily) via the internet. Beyond this, he emphasizes that while the do-it-yourself approach to promoting and distributing artists and music has been enhanced by digitalization, such an approach has limits that can generally only be surpassed by engaging the support and resources of a major company. Drawing initially on the account of O'Ceallaigh, and subsequently on other interviewees, the remainder of this section outlines the changes and continuities that have evolved over the past decade in respect to breaking new artists and promoting independent music content.

Using digital platforms and new digital tastemakers to break an artist

At the time of interview, Fachtna O'Ceallaigh was working with an emerging US singer-songwriter called Lissy Trullie. A range of blogs, online social networks and video-sharing sites were being drawn upon to promote this unsigned artist that made music content, videos, photographs available to users. For O'Ceallaigh, mass-user platforms such as Facebook, MySpace, YouTube and Last.fm are all potentially useful for growing the profile of an emerging artist. However, he sees the benefits associated with such sites a relatively limited, primarily due to the fact that they are colonized by many of the music industry's already established and popular acts. This, combined with the sheer volume of new artists vying for attention through these platforms means achieving visibility can prove challenging. Other niche or underground online platforms can be more rewarding when it comes to growing a local fan base.

Regarding the usefulness of blogs, O'Ceallaigh talks of his collaboration with US media firm Big Hassle in the marketing and promotion of Lissy Trullie:

> When I was in New York two weeks ago I had a meeting with this woman [from Big Hassle] and she produced an outline of how they saw things developing with Lissy . . . There were all the usual kind of print things like *Rolling Stone*, *Spin*, *The New York Times* etc. Then there were the various digital publications but first, before any of these, there were blogs. Now I said I wanted to have a t-shirt that said 'Kill All Blogs' because I just hate them. She said she knew what I meant, *but*, when I asked if they had any impact she said that they definitely have an impact and that their research shows how people will sit there religiously and absorb what's being said . . . They [Big Hassle] are pushing this as an important form of dissemination and enthusiasm and excitement for breaking new acts . . . Back in the olden days, when I was trying to break The [Boomtown] Rats, we had *NME*, we had *Melody Maker*, we had *Sounds* and *Disc* and *Record Mirror*. And that was it. Full stop. You only got in *NME* if you got in *Sounds* first, and you only got in *Sounds* if you got in *Melody Maker* first, and they only wrote about you if they wanted to say they hated you. At least this [blogs] opens that up a little bit. (Fachtna O'Ceallaigh, personal interview)

O'Ceallaigh proceeds to state that he finds it difficult to quantify the 'precise extent' to which 'the promise of the internet has been realised', but argues that using these recent and new online spaces to generate a sufficient 'buzz' about a new artist in order to achieve synchronization licenses, a bigger live audience, more music press coverage and digital sales is 'a scenario that is perfectly valid and feasible'.

The emergence of public and private funded training initiatives

O'Ceallaigh's point regarding the 'spread of knowledge' is also taken up by various other interviewees who highlight the emergence of a number of music industry information, training and education initiatives, both state-sponsored and private that evolved from the early 1990s onwards. For example, music management and technology programmes are delivered by the City of Dublin Vocational Education Committee (CDVEC). During our interview, record producer P. J. Curtis took time to describe his involvement in designing and delivering the initial CDVEC programmes at Ballyfermot College of Further Education. The 1990s also saw the evolution of Musicbase, an Arts Council of Ireland–funded popular music information and education resource of which musician and current IMRO chair Keith Donald was director. Beyond that, there is First Music Contact – a free information and advice service for musicians and bands funded by the Arts Council of Ireland since the mid-1990s. *Hot Press* general manager Jackie Hayden also points to the FAS Music Training Programme, an initiative co-funded and co-delivered by FAS (Ireland's state training agency and the Catholic Youth Council in Dublin throughout the 1990s). Festival organizer Úna Johnston argues that such initiatives have provided artists and prospective industry professionals with an awareness of the mechanics of the music industries and enhanced the do-it-yourself approach to developing a career in different areas of the business. As Jackie Hayden argues:

> Those initiatives are hugely valuable in a way that is almost impossible to quantify. If you have government money put into that area, and even if it never produces a single hit record, it still is a huge input into education in Ireland, never mind culture or music or anything fanciful like that. But it *is* teaching people basic skills. There are a whole range of social skills, technical skills and business skills . . . simple things that some people might not have any other way of learning. (Jackie Hayden, personal interview)

In addition, *Hot Press* magazine publish an annual music industries directory and have, over the past 15 years organized numerous music business seminars and workshops.

Some of these interviewees also point to the many private training courses offering technical tuition and training for business that evolved. It is worth noting that a small number of the industry professionals interviewed during the primary research phase of this thesis participated as trainees in some of the above-mentioned initiatives. For example, Ben Barrett attended a music management programme at Ballyfermot College of Further Education in Dublin.

Limits of the do-it-yourself approach in the contemporary environment

All of the factors considered above combine to provide for, or comprise essential resources for an artist or small label taking significant steps towards commercial success without the finance and resources of a major music company behind them. As many interviewees stated, major record companies are now more reluctant than ever to invest in the early stage development of recording acts. While the independent recording sector has long since been regarded as the research and development arm of the industry, artists and their managers are increasingly adopting a do-it-yourself approach. As Fachtna O'Ceallaigh argues:

> You're going to wait and you're going to hold on to your ownership of your copyright, make your music available, develop your audience, because you've nothing to lose. (Fachtna O'Ceallaigh, personal interview)

However, he immediately proceeds to emphasize that this approach has limits that can only be surpassed by using the support and resources of a major music company:

> It's all in this relatively small little box. You might even kind of permeate out of Ireland and the UK and across into Europe until you are at the point where you have been doing this for two or three years and . . . somebody comes along and says: 'Now that you are selling 100,000 records in the UK or whatever and so many more in the US, do you want to change that to one million in the UK and five million in the US? Well the only way you'll do that is by having our [major label] machine behind you'. (Fachtna O'Ceallaigh, personal interview)

Speaking in 2008, artist manager John Williamson offered a similar argument, stating that smaller labels and artists are more empowered and independently capable of going much further than before, but 'while more and more people become more competent and knowledgeable' it still remains to be seen if there are individuals or companies in the industry, beyond the major labels, that are 'actually capable of seeing it through to its conclusion' and breaking into a mainstream market (personal interview). Such sentiments resonate with the accounts of other interviewees. So, while digitalization greatly enhances the potential for successfully adopting an independent, do-it-yourself approach, this only works up to a certain point.

The marketing, promotion and distribution benefits that being allied to a major label brings, still remain attractive to many artists and managers. Many interviewees argue that it is not necessary to commit to a major at an early stage, but equally concede that moving from a peripheral market, where record sales may reach tens of thousands, to a mainstream market where they move into hundreds of thousands or millions, still requires the 'clout' of one of the major industry players. As O'Ceallaigh concludes:

> Musically, the majors don't know what's going on, so the minute you come up with something that is a little different, or is different to what they've heard before, and you can show that your MySpace page has eight thousand friends, they are going to buy you up immediately if they can possibly buy you. (Fachtna O'Ceallaigh, personal interview)

Employing recent and emerging digital platforms and new types of intermediaries ultimately forms part of a strategy to increase the stature of the artist, engage the interest of a major label and enhance the bargaining power of the artist or independent label when it comes to dealing with the major. Below we will proceed to further examine the role of the major record companies in the contemporary environment.

So why has disintermediation not occurred?

Other authors have addressed the potential of the internet to greatly enhance the ability of artists to produce, market and distribute their own work independently. From the mid-1990s, many commentators predicted that digital distribution technologies would induce a process of disintermediation – the removal the middle layers of distribution channels. Producers of music would be able to directly access their public without a major label acting as middleman. Yet, as the responses advanced above indicate, much of this potential has not been realized. Here, we draw upon the interview material to examine why, and to what extent the major labels remain key record industry 'middlemen'.

In his keynote address to the 2008 *Music Matters* conference, U2 manager Paul McGuinness stated that international record labels remain crucial to the future of the music industry:

> They [record companies] bring to the mix unique and valuable skills: A&R, marketing, financial management and career building. The truth is that there is always a long list of artists who are either succeeding with their record deal, or desperate to get one. (Paul McGuinness, manager U2, keynote speech delivered at *Music Matters* conference, Hong Kong, 8 June 2008)

Such sentiments were echoed by the majority of interviewees, many of whom still perceive the major music companies as crucial to the present and future of the industry. While many interviewees regard digitalization as greatly enhancing and democratizing the production process and providing the potential for artists and independent music labels to market, promote and distribute their recordings, the level of success achievable without the aid of a major label is seen as limited. As Gerry Harford, manager of Therapy and Nina Hynes explains:

> If you want to sell records which is what we all want to do . . . you need to be connected to a big label to put the money behind you to tour and to pay for the advertising, the press, the video etc. The people with the infrastructure and the way of doing that are the big record labels. You need to have that clout . . . You *do* need to sign to a major label. (Gerry Harford, personal interview)

Some of the smaller label owners interviewed argue that while the internet arrived with undeniable potential, it has worked best primarily for established mainstream recorded music markets or labels that serve very narrow niche markets. Smaller pop labels in particular possess difficulties here. If it not possible for such a label to brand itself as niche or alternative, then becoming 'signal' above the 'noise' of the internet proves especially challenging. According to Jim Carroll:

> Those who bought into the idea of the internet taking the major companies out of the picture were wrong from the start. That has *not* happened and is *not* going to happen. (personal interview)

He proceeds to highlight the ongoing dominance of a small number of corporate players in maintaining a stranglehold over the channels of distribution. Beyond this, Carroll sees the same major actors as being best placed to exploit the potential of new and emerging media:

> He who pays the piper calls the tune . . . Sure you can use MySpace to create a bit of a buzz about your band or your label, but in terms of record labels the majors dominate that arena too because they have the money to spend on bumping up the amount of MySpace friends they have and all that. (ibid.)

The interview with Carroll indicates the potential the internet holds for the promotion of independent artists and labels. As with other interviewees, he outlines various online platforms through which artists can generate a public profile. However, in terms of labels using these platforms to sell significant quantities of recordings independently, Carroll acknowledges that this potential remains largely theoretical. While he regards independent distributors such as ADA in the United States and City Slang in Europe as:

> viable ways of getting your music out [and] being in the game, the market they serve is . . . peripheral . . . removed from the main centres of activity . . . You have got to be realistic about it. It ain't going to happen just because you think the internet is where everyone's playing on the same playing field . . . You still need a distributor, you still need a marketer, you still need a big promoter. (ibid.)

Carroll argues that the seed capital needed to market and promote an artist or independent label can be acquired from sources other than major record labels:

> But you will probably take a major labels money at some stage, because, to use a football analogy, the major labels are like the Real Madrid's of this world, they will buy up talent when it reaches a certain stage as they are the primary means of getting it to the next level. (ibid.)

Music publisher Steve Lindsey advances a similar perspective stating that the major labels:

> are still the only ones that can bring into force large promo budgets to push the artists they want to push . . . So if you're not signed to a major label it's extremely difficult to make yourself known . . . In many ways this picture is exactly the same as it was pre-internet. In fact it's exactly the same as it was even thirty years ago. That hasn't changed at all. (Steve Lindsey, personal interview)

He proceeds to qualify this by outlining that majors most readily possess the infrastructure and experience necessary to generate a profile at mass-market level for recording artists. This, according to Jim Carroll, is primarily achieved through the established relationships that the major labels have fostered with broadcasters, print media and other key tastemakers.

It is these companies that still most readily possess the necessary contacts and alliances to achieve broadcast exposure for recordings and music videos, press coverage and synchronization licensing deals. Further, a primary source of funding for the necessary marketing and promotion to make a hit lies with the major music labels. For Gerry Harford, without this finance the opportunities for recording artists to gain profile are very limited:

> What you need to break an act internationally is a bank, and that's what the major labels still are. My artist Nina Hynes is a good example. We did a Nina Hynes album on Reverb [independent label]. It was a very good album, but there was nothing behind it.

Reverb had no money . . . and they didn't have anybody to take it up and market it. Marketing is expensive. It's a big investment. To make your band leap out at people you are going to need some sort of finance behind you. (Gerry Harford, personal interview)

Steve Lindsey further emphasizes this point stating that an independent recording artist might:

bring things up to forty miles an hour by themselves, but a major will cone in and say 'we'll take it up to a hundred miles an hour'. And to be honest, that is still the only way forward beyond a certain point for any artist. (Steve Lindsey, personal interview)

Furthermore, many interviewees state that when it comes to new or emerging acts, major music companies are oftentimes a crucial source of financial support for promotional touring. Beyond new and emerging acts, some interviewees also point to established acts still needing the machinery of a major label. As studio owner John D'Ardis advances:

It all still relies on the big companies. If the record companies promote you, you'll be okay. But if they want to kill you, you'll be dead. (John D'Ardis, personal interview)

This ongoing significance of the major record labels as industry gatekeepers is perhaps most succinctly outlined by Ben Barrett in her account of the career trajectory of one of the artists she manages, singer-songwriter Damien Rice. According to Barrett, the key to independently breaking Rice into peripheral markets was a broad combination of factors. She outlines in detail how, over a two-year period following the release of his self-recorded debut album *O*, Rice achieved sales of 15,000 copies in Ireland and approximately 50,000 in the United Kingdom. This, according to Barrett, was achieved through their formulation of a 'whole plan' of promotional activities aimed at specialized music press, specialized music radio and television shows, and word of mouth in physical and digital realms, as well as constant and extensive touring through small venues. Having negotiated with independent distribution networks such as Pinnacle and Vital, Barrett initially secured distribution for Rice with 3MB, a small independent company. She defines this process not as an end in itself, but rather as a 'plot' to convince a major label to:

> back a horse that's going to win . . . You just present them with the whole plan as something that has already proven itself somewhere, however small. (Ben Barrett, personal interview)

Barrett's 'plot' ultimately resulted in Rice's album *O* subsequently being licensed to Warner's for international release. The blueprint for launching Damien Rice internationally was the earlier marketing and promotion plan used to promote David Gray, also signed to the same management company, Mondo Management and released through Warner. Barrett states that within 12 month's of Warner issuing *O*, sales jumped to two million copies internationally. She concludes:

> It's really all about who is spending the money, and increasingly about who is spending the money at the very top level, with the power to get promotion and distribution in all its forms sorted out at a global level . . . To cut a very, very long story short, this is the way that that it's increasingly going. (Ben Barrett, personal interview)

Another interviewee, Bruce Findlay, advances a similar approach in his attempt to break Scottish act Aberfeldy. Findlay places more emphasis than Barrett on the role of internet platforms on this process stating:

> In terms of getting your music to would-be labels, agents, promoters, distributors who might want you – they can look at you, see what you're doing, hear what you're doing, see live concert footage, read what people are saying about you, read fans reviews and all in an instant on their computer screen. (Bruce Findlay, personal interview)

As such, while serving to heighten the public profile of an emerging act, social networks and other platforms are also tools for engaging the interest of, and gaining leverage in potential negotiations with an established record label, music publisher or promoter. To this end, we might thus consider such platforms as key artist and repertoire (A&R) devices in the digital era [A&R is the department in the music company charged with finding new talent].

What this implies is that while technology has evolved to place a new range of media at the disposal or new artists, the process of breaking an artist on a wider stage remains largely filtered through many of the same channels as in the pre-internet era.

Akin to Barrett's account of Damien Rice, US band Arcade Fire offer a similar example. Having achieved moderate success with two independent releases on the Merge record label in North Carolina, the band subsequently signed to Universal through which they achieved a major international breakthrough.

At the time of interview, Fachtna O'Ceallaigh was plotting a similar course of action with singer-songwriter Lissy Trullie. For O'Ceallaigh:

> Because, in my opinion her music has that cross-generational spread to it, there is a good reason for me to talk to majors. At a certain point there *is* still a very good reason to have that big machine by your side. (personal interview)

Further emphasizing the ongoing importance of engaging with a major label, O'Ceallaigh proceeds to state that there are:

> two different layers to this industry – one huge, and the other one, this gritty underbelly who don't generate articles in the paper about what it's like to sit in a van going from Cork to Ballybofey overnight to play to 75 people and then getting in the van again and driving back down to Waterford to play to 150 people and keeping your dream alive. It's all well and good doing it once, or doing it twice, or maybe even doing it three times, but when it's three years later and you're sitting in the same van playing to the same people, even if the material is new . . . That's the reality of the thing. All of this talk about touring and internet sales and merchandising making it possible to do it yourself is fine, but no more than theoretical in a lot of cases . . . The reality is that there's a well-established path. (ibid.)

These accounts suggest that using the internet as the primary means for launching or promoting a recording is of limited benefit to independent artists. However, an example frequently cited in the media as exemplifying the transformative affects of the internet on the sphere of music distribution is the album *In Rainbows* by the band Radiohead. Following the expiration of their recording contract with EMI, Radiohead initially released the record in late 2007 for 60 days only as an exclusive digital download that customers could order for whatever price they saw fit. Echoing the sentiments of a variety of media reports, *The New York Times* labelled this as 'the most audacious experiment in years' to increase the misery of 'the beleaguered recording business' (*New York Times* online, 9 December 2007).

During the course of our interviews, the various artist managers were asked if this independent, digital-only release provided evidence of the ability of the internet to enable an act to bypass corporate machinery when seeking to access a mass audience. Their combined responses imply that such a ploy can really only effectively work for an already established act. Radiohead had previously issued six albums over a 13-year period on EMI labels Parlophone and Capitol records. This included hit singles and chart-topping albums on both sides of the Atlantic and reputed overall album sales of approximately 30 million units. As such, by the time they departed their record label and released *In Rainbows* independently, Radiohead were a hugely successful international act. As such, the successful independent launch of an album akin to the *In Rainbows* model requires the act concerned to be an established brand with significant marketing and promotional support behind them. As Therapy manager Gerry Harford argues:

> Smaller bands can't do what Radiohead did. Internet or not, you still need the same package that you always needed. Everything is still fairly traditional in that respect. (Gerry Harford, personal interview)

At the time, neither Radiohead nor its management made public statistics or information relating to the number of downloads achieved or revenues generated from this experiment. Its launch, however, generated widespread media coverage and earned them exposure as a mainstream news story. *In Rainbows* was subsequently released for retail across a variety of physical and digital formats via licensing agreements with various major and independent companies in different territories.

Chapter summary

This chapter has highlighted a number of key characteristics of the contemporary record industry. There remains a high concentration of power in the recorded music market where a small handful of major labels continue to dominate. For independent record companies, access to this marketplace is still largely mediated through the major companies, with the distinction between indie and major becoming more blurred.

Recent and emerging digital technologies and internet spaces provide new opportunities for unsigned artists and wholly independent labels (i.e. those that have no connection to or relationship to the major labels) to generate a profile at retail level. However, this access is largely restricted to 'peripheral' markets as the resources and relationships vital to accessing mainstream or mass markets remains under the control of the main corporate actors. This is most vividly illustrated through Ben Barrett's account of the career of Damien Rice, where this artist sold tens of thousands or records by utilizing both traditional and new promotional tools. However successfully moving this artist into a mass market with sales of hundreds of thousands or millions of units required of necessity, the distribution links, marketing resources and access to key tastemakers (predominantly daytime radio) provided by a major label.

The various interviews indicate that internet platforms for the promotion of music essentially work on two levels: on one hand, they function as platforms through which already established artists access their fanbase; on the other hand, they serve as a platform through which independent artists and labels compete not only for the attention of an audience, but also for the notice of a major music company that can provide them with the resources to access a larger, mass market. What is key to note here is that the research findings indicate that while digital technologies have provided a new range of platforms for the promotion of music, the process of breaking an artist internationally remains largely filtered through the same corporate structures and channels as before.

Chapter 6 will proceed to consider the evolving role of music tastemakers in the digital age as well as examining the perspectives of interviewees on the music industry's end-users – fans.

6

New rules for the new music economy? [Part two]

In Chapter 5, arguments were advanced regarding the potential usefulness of blogs, online audio- and video-streaming services, social networking sites and other online music discussion and review platforms in assisting an emerging artist to independently generate a public profile. This chapter draws upon the accounts of various interviewees from across the spectrum of music industry sub-sectors and related spheres of activity to examine the key ways in which mass-market audiences are reached, and big-selling hits achieved.

A fundamental question posed to interviewees related to the form and extent of the internet's role in music 'tastemaking' and, what the implications of this might be for more traditional intermediaries in this area. While highlighting some potential benefits associated with social networking sites and other online platforms, interviewees almost invariably switched the conversation to the medium of (terrestrial) radio as crucial tastemaker. Television and music press were also highlighted, but only to signal their limited and diminishing effectiveness in the contemporary environment. These issues and related findings are elaborated on in the remainder of this section.

Leading on from this, interviewees were asked to reflect upon and advance their concepts of the contemporary music consumer and the consumer bands that constitute the music consumer market. The evidence gleaned from this aspect of the primary research interviews serves to problematize accounts indicating that file-sharing activities are having a detrimental effect on recorded music sales.

Making 'hits' in the internet era

The role of internet tastemakers

As was outlined in Chapter 3, music companies are generating revenues directly from licensing agreements with social networking sites, among other online and mobile platforms for music. However, these same social networking sites also form an important constituent element in the music company's marketing plans for new artists or fresh recordings. A range of interviewees all explain that there are different routes to launching and promoting different types of acts. As one interviewee, Peter Jenner advances, managing an artist or label 'is a bit like horses for courses'. While mainstream pop acts often leave the recording studio 'ready-made' for launching directly at a mass audience through radio, television and other elements of the popular press, acts in other genres (such as singer-songwriters or alternative rock) can require a more long-term plan of action. Traditionally, such a strategy has involved drawing upon such resources as the specialized music press, specialized 'off-peak' radio shows and working to gain a billing at relevant live music festivals in order to develop a fan base. While such activities are still regarded as important, interviewees outline how this process is increasingly linked to online social networks. Jim Carroll states that such platforms have developed into 'crucial word-of-mouth' mechanisms for growing the public's awareness of an act. While word-of-mouth once referred primarily to those peers in the music fan's immediate social environment, the internet potentially makes this a more widespread and larger social grouping.

These sites have evolved as important mechanisms through which to reach and mobilize those music enthusiasts that will actively seek out new music – the 'early adopters'. At the time of interview in late 2007, Willie Kavanagh of EMI Ireland stated that his company had one member of staff dedicated to promoting the company's catalogue of music and artists across such social networking platforms. According to Kavanagh:

> It's about getting the message to the small group, who then take the responsibility, because they become fans of the band, to expand that and get it to the next layer. It's like an onion, and we're only at the inner layer. (personal interview)

In essence, we might regard such developments as the commodification of friendship.

Kavanagh forwards the band Thirty Seconds to Mars as an example of an act that was successfully promoted in this way by his label. While at the outset the band had an extremely small fan base, he outlines how EMI used profiles on social networking sites to 'increase the whole community base and try to broaden it as much as we could' (ibid.). This process, according to Kavanagh, grew the bands fan base exponentially and provided his labels 'pluggers' with significant leverage in promoting the band's debut album to daytime music radio programmers and producers.

However, while online social networks and other internet platforms have evolved as a key tools in the promotion and marketing of music, the generation of mass-market sales still (usually) requires the intervention of a more traditional and long-established medium – radio.

The contemporary role of radio

As one interviewee states:

> In our rush to believe in communications revolutions and digital revolutions we can overlook the importance of radio . . . It has certainly maintained itself in the contemporary music world. (Ross Graham, personal interview)

The extent to which radio may be measured as a contemporary active promoter of music is elaborated on by Fachtna O'Ceallaigh who states:

> There is huge evidence to suggest that radio sells records . . . The only way that a [artist's] first single is going to succeed is if BBC

Radio 1 puts it on their playlist . . . played thirty-five times a week for six weeks or so – hit record. Second single, played thirty-five times a week – hit record. Put out the album – hit album. So there is a specific pattern . . . They release a record to radio and they desperately hope radio will play it and if they don't their record is buried. (Fachtna O'Ceallaigh, personal interview)

O'Ceallaigh has managed different acts that have broken internationally in the 1970s, 1980s and also in the new millennium. He contends that the significance of radio to breaking an artist and selling records is common to all periods. He views online-streaming sites as an extension of traditional radio and, while individuals may exercise control over the content they choose to listen to on these sites, he argues that they form useful tastemakers.

In his earlier comments regarding the trajectory of Thirty Seconds to Mars, EMI's Willie Kavanagh advanced that creating a 'buzz' about an artist on social networking sites and other internet spaces provides significant ammunition to major labels in when it comes to promoting recordings. Likewise, according to a number of other interviewees, these new and recent online tastemaking sites are effective as tools for engaging the interest of daytime radio programmers. Thus radio, one of the oldest mediators between record industry and audience, remains hugely significant to achieving commercial success. Based on his experience of working in and reporting on the record industry, Jim Carroll explains:

You can quantify radio. Listenership surveys [are] . . . goldmine data . . . Radio is still the most important medium for the major labels. They die where radio is concerned. It's radio, print, television, carrier pigeon and the internet. And it's in that order with radio leading by a mile . . . As far as the permanent establishment are concerned, radio is vital. That's it. (Jim Carroll, personal interview)

John Sheehan, former chairman of Sony Music Ireland, illustrates Carroll's point during the course of our interview:

This is very simple. If you don't get it on the radio you're not going to sell it. I don't care how good it is . . . One of the things you talk about when you're in the studio and they're mixing a track is a radio mix. You're looking for a radio mix. You're looking for three minutes twenty-five seconds, and as you're listening you're asking 'will this work on contemporary radio' . . . And it's always been the same. That's not changed. (John Sheehan, personal interview)

The evidence from interviews essentially describes a pool of intermediaries/tastemakers that has become more cluttered and complicated over the years. The positive within this for Sheehan is that there are now many more outlets, both traditional and new, through which music can be promoted and exposed than in former times. However, Sheehan validates Ben Barrett's claim that radio remains central by stating: 'Without radio, the others [intermediaries] don't work . . . It is fundamental to the whole marketing mix' (personal interview). This point is further emphasized by other interviewees who effectively state that music magazines that serve a larger, less specialized audience essentially follow the lead of radio regarding the acts that their editors choose to feature. It is likewise for other lifestyle and celebrity-centred publications. According to artist manager Peter Jenner:

Why will magazine editors know that they should write about an artist? Because they've heard a record on the radio or in a club. That's how it works. Radio play marks your output as being from someone who is *in the game*. (Peter Jenner, personal interview)

Jenner continues:

Radio is still a pretty crucial thing . . . Look at the results . . . I mean nobody takes seriously a book that is released straight to paperback or a film that goes straight to dvd. Likewise, radio is a sort of badge of honour in commercial terms which in turn drives the whole promotion game through print, TV, retail displays, interest from promoters etc. (ibid.)

Willie Kavanagh advances a similar sentiment: 'Radio is crucial. Absolutely crucial in breaking any new artist or selling any established one'. Kavanagh explains how his label, EMI, also expend resources on marketing and promotion through various new and recent digital platforms such as social networking sites and blogs, and entering into cross-promotional alliances with online music stores and outlets. He describes the promotional process as a synergy of radio, television, press, touring and all of the available online spaces, however he concludes that, of all of these intermediary spaces: 'Radio is number one by a landslide'. For supporting evidence, Kavanagh outlines the trajectory of The Plain White Tees, an act signed in recent years to a distribution deal on the EMI label:

> We had a huge hit with a band called The Plain White Tees who have a track called *Delilah*. It is disproportionately successful here [Ireland] compared to the UK or elsewhere. Two months ago, nobody here had ever heard of The Plain White Tees, now they've had a number one single and a number two album, and all on the back of their very first single which is very unusual . . . That's the power of radio . . . So still to this day, in any country in the world, and I'm including America very much in this, and the UK, there is nowhere in the world that I can think of where radio isn't the number one way to get your music heard and sold. (Willie Kavanagh, personal interview)

For another interviewee, music journalist and broadcaster Stuart Bailie, the plethora of radio formats for a daytime audience may essentially be broken down into stations that fit two broad categories: 'those for the housewives market with DJs that grow old with their audience . . . or else they'll be much more youth orientated' (personal interview). In the case of either, from a station manager's point of view, 'the persona of a daytime DJ is a lot more important than the musical content' in communicating the 'identity' of the station, so record companies will 'invest heavily' in accommodating radio programmers with records that fit 'the orientation' of the station (ibid.).

Radio also remains a key priority for independent artists and music labels. For the vast majority of interviewees who work, or who have worked in the independent music sector, the core problem they advance in this respect is the difficulty in accessing the airwaves. For labels other than those operating under the major labels, lack of radio play is widely regarded as hindering their development. The evidence of their accounts suggests that while there might be more music infrastructure and outlets for music now, the situation has not become particularly easier for alternative or independent music as the market has shrunk with the dominance of the major labels. For many, the crucial factor in getting to an audience is broadcasting, but the problem of getting broadcast is more difficult than the problem of getting distribution.

For Crashed Music owner Shay Hennessy, launching and promoting an artist in the contemporary environment can be a 'nightmare' because there are:

> so many angles that you have to hit. You've got the local radio stations, the national radio stations, television stations, the mass of print media that now exists, and all of the internet spaces. It's great in that you have so many opportunities, plenty of opportunities, but . . . radio is important . . . The big record companies take the approach that they have to get airplay and they go out and try to demand it . . . For a small company, this stuff breaks your heart, it really does. The number of artists that we've got and that we can't get played, just can't get played at all. (Shay Hennessy, personal interview)

Hennessy states that for the artists on his label, the pursuit of a music career remains a part-time activity due to their inability to generate sufficient revenues to sustain themselves through music.

The success of radio as a promotional tool relates to the fact that it is both pervasive and invasive, as many interviewees emphasize. Beyond the role of specialized music shows in helping to introduce new music to niche audiences, many interviewees highlight how the public are exposed to mainstream daytime radio in a range of both voluntary and involuntary settings. We experience radio in our homes, our cars, our places of work and various public and social settings. As Sony's John Sheehan puts it: 'Radio is everywhere' (personal interview).

The account of Ben Barrett regarding the success of Damien Rice is again highly pertinent here. Barrett attributes his success to one primary factor: the increased radio exposure gained following Rice's alliance to the Warner Records:

> I still fully believe that radio is the thing that did it for us. There is no way that we would have sold two million records without the singles that we had on the radio. It just wouldn't have happened . . . Radio is crucial . . . yeah, radio is essential. (Ben Barrett, personal interview)

Barrett proceeds to detail how having a presence on 'certain new media outlets' help in gaining access to a 'younger MySpace generation', but for the broad mass of 'people like us working in offices, commuting to work, shopping, driving or whatever, radio is absolutely key, because radio is everywhere' (ibid.).

Barrett describes the 'before' and 'after' of radio for Rice on an imaginary graph illustrating Damien Rice's record sales trajectory. Prior to gaining access to mainstream daytime radio, she traces a slight gradual incline over a lengthy period of time. Post-mainstream radio playlisting, she traces a sharp, steep incline. She subsequently outlines how mainstream radio exposure opened the door to key television appearances and areas of print press beyond specialized music publications that would not have been available previously. As such, Barrett's testimony validates John Sheehan's claim that radio opens the door to other gatekeepers and tastemakers.

Aside from the promotional aspect of airplay for recordings as evidenced by these accounts from my interviewees, we must note that radio is also a direct source of revenue for both recording and music publishing companies. As noted in Chapter 4, music publishing market has experienced significant overall growth over the last two decades, and performing royalties from radio-play feature as one of a number of core revenue streams. Equally, record companies benefit from the broadcast of their copyrighted recordings through licensing arrangements between broadcasters and phonographic royalty collection societies such as PPI and the BPI. As John Williamson explains:

> If you get onto the A-list of a BBC station you are getting paid £80–90 per play and you are getting played forty to fifty times per week over a number of weeks, then this does add up to a lot

of money. The publishers and the record companies get money which is possibly why they still pursue radio more vigorously than proportionately they should. (John Wiliamson, personal interview)

Remixing for radio

While, in the case of the album *O*, Damien Rice initially, independently recorded the songs for the album, many of these tracks were returned to the recording studio on a number of occasions for modifying and remixing for different platforms and markets, but primarily for radio exposure:

> When we sat down with Warner's, there was absolutely nothing on Damien's record that would work on radio, no matter how good it was, so we had to remix the tracks for radio . . . They argued that people want to hear something with a beat, something with a pulse. They want to hear something that is a bit fluffy. So yeah, radio does dictate . . . And you know, even with the edits that we give them [Warner's], they'll shorten it, take bits out or whatever. (Ben Barrett, personal interview)

Barrett then outlines how these initial remixes only met with limited success:

> Radio pretty much still said no, and said no to many, many things. So away we went and did other remixes of the tracks. If they say no, you've just got to go back to the drawing board again . . . We had *Cannonball* [promotional single] released for the first time, and we had certain friends in BBC Radio 1 and Radio 2 that played it, but that didn't take it over the tipping point. So we had to go back and do another remix, and that one flew, it really took off on Radio 1, and then the other stations. In all of these cases it was the same songs we were working with, the very same ones we had started out with but were doing and re-doing . . . so I guess it's all a big game really. (ibid.)

Barrett argues that the more formats, both physical and digital, through which a single or album is released these days, the greater chance of commercial success. It is important to 'cover all angles', and this frequently involves remixing and/or editing Rice's tracks primarily for radio, but subsequently for use by DJs in nightclubs, for specialized genre-specific radio shows, for pitching at specific television and films productions, and also for a variety of different internet and mobile platforms.

The producer of the international release of *O* was David Arnold. Arnold is the long-established producer of global, multimillion selling acts such as Bjork, George Michael, Tina Turner, Joe Satriani, and other European-wide successful rock acts as The Kaiser Chiefs and Cast as well as artists such as Natacha Atlas, and Propellerheads. He is also a successful producer and composer of film and television scores and soundtracks, most notably the James Bond movies since the 1990s. The willingness of Arnold to work on Rice's album, and his contribution in remixing various tracks proved crucial in engaging radio producers and other intermediaries. In Barrett's account, all of this constituted 'the drawing board' they returned to for constructing a successful international release.

While possessing little musical similarity, in many ways US band The Plain White Tees trajectory resembles that of Damien Rice. The band, from Illinois, self-released two albums, *Come On Over* and *Stop* before the latter album was licensed to Warner label, Fearless, in the United States, and subsequently remixed and relaunched. Their album *Every Second Counts* was recorded on the Walt Disney Company's Hollywood Records and distributed via Universal in the United States and, in the case of Ireland, Willie Kavanagh's label, EMI. The track *Hey There Delilah* had originally been released in 2005 but failed to make an impression on the charts. The track was remixed by Ariel Rechtshaid, producer of such acts as The Hippos (for Universal's Interscope label), We Are Scientists (for EMI's Capitol Records), Taking Back Sunday (for the Warner Music Group) and Valencia (for Sony Music Entertainment's Columbia Records). Rechtstaid's remix became a global chart hit.

Ultimately, according to Ben Barrett, amidst proliferating avenues for promotion and exposure, many established practices and continuities remain. When it comes to generating 'serious' revenues from music:

> It's about hearing somebody on the radio . . . it's radio that really makes the difference . . . It helps you cross over to an audience

that might not as individuals buy a whole lot of records, and it's access to a big new market. That's what radio is to us. (Ben Barrett, personal interview).

The contemporary role of television as a promoter of recorded music

In general, various accounts of interviewees point to contemporary television as a less helpful medium for the promotion of music than it was in the final decades of the twentieth century. Clearly, television generates revenues from licensing fees for music companies (courtesy of synchronization rights) as noted in Chapter 4. Yet, many interviewees argue that the use of specialized music television output has long since been decreasing in its significance to the marketing and sale of records.

Within an Irish context, the popular primetime RTE television show *The Late Late Show* forms a key target in the marketing strategies of both major and indie labels. Julian Vignoles, a deputy commissioning editor at RTE, states that this represents one of the few 'real' opportunities for music on television in Ireland as it broadcasts to a large audience that encompasses the 'broadest possible' demographic (personal interview). Vignoles advances that the audience the show commands makes these slots lucrative for record company executives. Along with the exposure gained through having songs used in internationally distributed dramas such as *Grey's Anatomy*, he contends that this is the one of the few areas where television works to promote music. Vignoles states that specialized music programming for television has 'had its day' and 'doesn't really work' in terms of audience:

> Music just doesn't work on television. Radio is still the king for music, compared to television. Even with Jools Holland on BBC2, they'll never chance it before half-eleven, and it has a tiny audience. It's a cool audience . . . but it's tiny. (Julian Vignoles, personal interview)

Vignoles proceeds to outline how audience research conducted by RTE indicates that the teenage audience–base categories that constituted the main target group of such output have largely migrated to YouTube and various internet sites where videos are streamed to access music video. He states that beyond this, the broad mass of potential viewership has little interest in music television.

Vignoles views are shared by many working within the record industry. Artist manager John Williamson advances that specialized music stations and output has been continually decreasing in importance over the past decade as its audience has 'rediscovered social networking . . . a more interesting way of finding out about music and sharing it with your friends' (personal interview). Ross Graham, Johnny Lappin, Jim Carroll and Jim Lockhart advance similar perspectives. Jim Lockhart states that the 'MTV generation . . . has stopped picking up stuff on television anymore' (personal interview). Stating that the 1980s and early 1990s saw specialized music television stations become prominent as sites for the promotion of music, their effect has long since dissipated as the output of such stations as MTV and VH1 increasingly veers towards reality and lifestyle programmes.

Senior management at major record labels further emphasize many of the above perspectives. EMI's Willie Kavanagh states that in the late 1980s getting promotional videos aired on MTV was crucial to breaking a record, particularly in America. Once it broke America, MTV Europe picked it up and 'then the whole ball started rolling' (personal interview). However Kavanagh and Sony's former chair John Sheehan, advance that the influence of music television has waned considerably. While its effectiveness as a promotional vehicle for recorded music was confined to a specific period in time, it also produced limited results in terms of generating sales. As Kavanagh states:

> The whole message of video-play, because it was a great form of entertainment for a period of time, but it only produced relatively shorts spurts of consumption. Like, there was a programme here in the 80s called *MT USA* with Vincent Hanley. That was enormous, but only enormous with teen audiences. It was hugely influential in what sold across record shop counters to them. But they are only one part of the picture . . . Television just doesn't have the same punch as it used to. So it is absolutely radio. (personal interview)

In short, television is perceived by my interviewees as possessing limited potential for the promotion of recorded music. While limited 'prize' slots on primetime chat shows and drama can bring artists and repertoire to mass audiences, specialized music programming output enjoyed a significant but very short-lived appeal before seeing its importance largely dissipate. Many interviewees perceive one-time specialized music television audiences to have gravitated to internet platforms.

The contemporary role of the music press

For some interviewees, the music press is viewed as having a limited and diminishing reach, but this, they contend, was not always the case. Many point to the 1970s and 1980s as a period when gaining exposure through the music press was hugely important for artists and labels, particularly when it came to breaking a new act. While radio was also cited as the most influential tastemaker in making hits back then, Peter Jenner, Fachtna O'Ceallaigh, Bruce Findlay and others advance that the music press was a key mechanism for building an initial fan base and bringing an act to the attention of radio. As Findlay advances, making the cover of the *NME* was once 'a big statement', but that this is much less the case in the contemporary environment (personal interview). Findlay and others outline how significant record company investment was once directed towards securing 'cover story' status in such magazines. However, the dwindling size of the market for such publications is a reflection on how this section of the music consumer market has gravitated elsewhere and the interest of the record companies has accordingly dwindled. Some interviewees point out that blogs and online publications have replaced the dedicated music magazine for many consumers. This was noted earlier in Fachtna O'Ceallaigh's contemporary experience of working to break Lissy Trullie.

Former deputy editor of *New Music Express*, Stuart Bailie, describes a 'then' and 'now' scenario relating to specialized music press:

> You had these dedicated music organs like the *NME* around the late seventies and eighties selling 300,000 copies a week. It was

almost absurd. That was incredible. It was called the music business bible and it almost had that authority about it, to make and break reputations . . . When I arrived in London [in the mid-1980s] there were *New Musical Express*, *Record Mirror*, *Melody Maker* and *Sounds* . . . The turnover was immense in those days . . . The *NME* do about 30,000 per issue these days. That used to be 300,000. (Stuart Bailie, personal interview)

Bailie then proceeds to outline the demise of *Melody Maker* and *Sounds*, as well as pop magazines like *Record Mirror* and *Smash Hits* and hard rock publications like *Metal Hammer*. Bailie highlights how all of these changes have occurred since the arrival of the internet. While not laying the blame for the demise of these once-significant tastemakers solely with the internet, he advances:

In an environment where they were increasingly under threat, the music press have done a very bad job of safe-guarding their own reputation. Tabloids, pop and lifestyle magazines were all taking slices of their market, and then the internet came. And that was that. So by and large, that era of the rock bible has been over since the 1990s. (Stuart Bailie, personal interview)

Music magazines with a viable commercial life in the contemporary world are perceived, by some interviewees, more as lifestyle magazines pitched at an over-thirties market than specialized music publications. While these magazines are hugely important sites in terms of advertising and promotion, they write about already successful artists and material. As Bailie again states:

Magazines like *Uncut* and *Mojo* are about re-selling the sixties and the seventies to a new audience, so they service the major record labels in that respect. All very consumer-orientated. They tend to service that retro market. They fall into a cluster of broader print publications that follow that demographic, that older consumer. Many of the artists on their covers died a long time ago. *Q* magazine started that trend in the eighties with sympathetic profiles of Phil Collins etc, but these days they tend to cover the kind of safe rock bands that are stocked in Tesco. It's a comfortable home for Coldplay and Kasabian. (Stuart Bailie, personal interview)

When it comes to newer acts, as a number of interviewees advance, these magazines will follow radio.

In the case of *Hot Press*, Jackie Hayden points to significant coverage given to new or unsigned acts, particularly Irish acts. However he also states that the 'cover' of the magazine is vital to generating sales, therefore the face on the cover must be already familiar to a potential readership. As with many of the UK publications, this magazine now has a reduced but hardcore readership and also sustains itself by the fact that it is available online only through paid subscription.

In summary, while interviewees point to the dedicated music press as having once been of immense importance to both established and emerging artists, and major and independent labels alike, their significance has now diminished considerably. The music press retains significance in terms of the overall 'plot' outlined by some artist managers to bring new acts to the attention of an audience, as well as potential distributors or major labels. However regarding its overall effectiveness, the role and potential of dedicated music press is now quite limited compared to previous decades.

Concepts of the consumer in the internet era

Within the context of a highly concentrated recorded music market it is worth considering the contemporary consumer base. Accounts in Chapter 2 detailing various causal factors producing the decline in recorded music sales over the past decade raise issues around evolving consumer practices and trends. Arguments in particular around the proliferation of file-sharing and the illicit circulation and duplication of recordings as well as shifting formats imply important changes in the realm of consumption. The remainder of this section is dedicated to examining concepts of the contemporary music consumer based primarily on the accounts of key informants within and around the music industries.

The record-buying public can be seen to comprise of 'actives' and 'passives' according to some of my interviewees such as former music retail executive Dermot Hanrahan. From his experience in the record industry and in music radio, Hanrahan argues that the 'actives' tend to be predominantly male in the 15–35 age bracket, highly literate, 'disproportionately well educated', heavy readers and heavy consumers of movies. Hanrahan is at pains to point out that the 'actives' represent a small minority of the overall music consumer market and they largely move in homogenous circles:

> There are people who comment on the industry, who are interested in the industry, or work in or around the industry like myself, who *do* collect music, who *are* interested in music, who *read* about music, who want to know the names of band members. But *most* people don't. *Most* people aren't like that. *Most* people couldn't give a flying fuck. (Dermot Hanrahan, personal interview)

Hanrahan describes the market for recorded music as a 'consumer pyramid', of which 'a small wedge' at the thin end is populated by the small minority of actives, while the bulk of the pyramid is occupied by 'occasional-to-rare' purchasers of music. He continues:

> A typical Irish home has a chipped Sanyo sitting in the corner that was bought ten years ago on hire purchase with seven or eight CDs leaning up against it. There's probably Phil Spector's Christmas album, a U2 album, probably a Michael Jackson album, a *Now That's What I Call Music* album, and the little brothers Arctic Monkeys album. That's a typical Irish home. These are typical music consumers. They have no interest in who produced the album. They don't even know there's such a thing as a producer on the album. They have no interest in that kind of stuff, but they are a much bigger force to be reckoned with than the 'actives'. (Dermot Hanrahan, personal interview)

Hanrahan qualifies the latter part of that comment by highlighting how the occasional-to-rare purchaser constitutes by far the greatest share of the consumer pyramid. By their sheer numbers, this consumer group are hugely significant to the record industry.

> Most Irish people visit a record store twice a year. Usually both visits are within 10 days of Christmas. 50% of those two visits are

to buy something for somebody else. This is far more typical of how the record business works, than the *Hot Press* reader or the *NME* reader or *Q* reader who knows their music and is in on the day of release. These people are *not* the public. The twice a year guys are. (Dermot Hanrahan, personal interview)

Hanrahan further argues that radio stations that 'kowtow to actives' will win critical acclaim, but will quickly go out of business as such a policy only serves to alienate the greater percentage of the potential music-listening audience. The key point, however, to be gleaned from Hanrahan's evidence is that the music-buying public comprises of a consumer base that extends far beyond the boundaries of the 'music fan'.

The music consumer scenario outlined by Hanrahan is repeated elsewhere by other key interviewees. George Ergatoudis, Head of Music at BBC Radio 1, describes a 'music industry cone model' operating on a similar basis. This cone model is divided into three distinct segments. Ergatoudis defines the thin narrow end of the cone as the 'scenester' segment. This, according to Ergatoudis is a group of up to ten thousand people in the United Kingdom that effectively shape the domestic music scene – that is, tastemakers. Within this group he places artists; music industry professionals across recording, publishing and live sectors, as well as other related fields; people that edit or work on music magazines and online sites; and music broadcasters. This is the group that Radio 1 define as creating, nurturing and driving music consumption and consumer scenes across the United Kingdom. According to Ergatoudis:

> This group is definitely about carefully balanced reflection, and leading . . . There is no question that there is an element of subjectivity to this, about who are the most exciting, innovative, relevant, interesting new acts, and then gauge that and follow it and work with it. (George Ergatoudis, personal interview)

Beyond 'the scenester' end of this cone model, we move into what BBC Radio 1 define as 'the restless' segment. They place 'a few' million people in this category. This group represents the segment of the music consumer base that is actively interested in finding music, that is, the active music fan:

> They are the ones that listen to Zane Lowe. They are the ones who read the NME, Q Magazine or whatever. They are active music fans. They go out to gigs. They like telling their mates about new bands or new artists but they are not people initially driving or nurturing the scene rather they are the next wave . . . Now those are the people who listen to BBC Radio 1 to some degree in daytime, and enormously so in our specialist night-time output. (George Ergatoudis, personal interview)

For Ergatoudis, this group represents a significant, but relatively small minority of the overall music radio listenership / music consumer market.

The final segment of the cone model consists of what Ergatoudis terms as 'the contented'. This segment, at the broad end of the cone, represents the mass market and covers by far the greatest section of the music listening / consumer base. According to Ergatoudis:

> Many of these will probably never listen to the new Radio 1 . . . They will find Radio 1 ultimately too challenging because we cover too many genres, play too much new music, and they will find us a difficult listen. (George Ergatoudis, personal interview)

However, for Ergatoudis, this segment of the music consumer market is 'most representative' of the record-buying public. They are most likely to choose a classic hits / top 40 format radio station to listen to, and will occasionally purchase recordings. Again, as Ergatoudis explains, it is the sheer size of this market segment that makes them so significant to the music industry and also the commercial radio sector.

EMI Ireland MD Willie Kavanagh outlines a slightly more complex consumer pyramid within which there exists a variety of different levels of consumer categories. The broadest consumer category, situated at the base of the pyramid that Kavanagh describes consists of the once- or twice-a-year purchaser. These consumers, almost exclusively purchase an already popular recording, oftentimes compilations released for the Christmas market, 'Greatest Hits' or 'Best of' packages, or current chart albums.

Towards the tip of the pyramid, EMI place the 'early adopters' who are 'heavy users' of music that purchase regularly (i.e. on a weekly basis, or more). This group acquire music, both new and old, across a wide variety of record genres. The methods of consumption employed by this group include physical music stores, second-hand music shops, digital music stores (e.g. iTunes) and electronic mail order stores (e.g. Amazon). Consistent with the accounts given by Dermot Hanrahan and George Ergatoudis, they are heavy consumers of music-based media in print, broadcast and electronic forms. Kavanagh further states that this sector of 'active' music fans incorporates an increasingly wide age range. Although significant in the process of breaking new acts and making certain types of new acts accessible to a broader market, this group do, however, represent a small minority of the overall music buying population.

However, a range of consumer categories gradually expands outwards from early adopter / heavy users to the once- or twice-a-year purchasers. As Kavanagh proceeds to explain:

> It's not just divided into two. It's not just early adopters and the rest, or music "heads" and the rest. That "rest" is made up of quite a few parts (personal interview).

Below the frequent heavy purchasers of music come the intermittent heavy purchasers, that is, individuals that buy music on a regular but 'relative infrequent' basis (i.e. approximately monthly). It is not unusual for consumers within this band to acquire two to three items each time they purchase. Below this in the pyramid there exists a significantly larger grouping who make multiple purchasers on an occasional-to-rare basis. According to Kavanagh, this consumer band represents:

> a more recent phenomenon . . . and [an] interesting bunch of people out there right now who might only buy records twice a year, but they do a multiple purchase thing where they might walk in and buy ten albums . . . I'm one of them myself. They mightn't buy music for two or three months or more, but when they walk in they buy everything they meant to buy for the last three months . . . We do research on a regular basis as to who is buying what,

what influences them and how to get to them. The way to get to the multiple purchasers is to somehow encourage them to get into the shop every now and again, and when they do they'll buy around them. (Willie Kavanagh, personal interview)

Once again, below this group in the pyramid lie a variety of types of occasional purchasers including those who visit physical and/or digital retail outlets occasionally and purchase (often multiple items) on each visit; those who visit occasionally and sometimes purchase; and those who visit occasionally but rarely purchase. Then at the bottom of the pyramid lies the broad mass of people who buy an album once or twice a year. So, as Kavanagh concludes:

It doesn't hold true that there are just two types of consumer, it's a multi-layered thing, and there are multi-layered awareness levels (personal interview).

In the views of the above interviewees, the general rule of thumb regarding methods of purchase is that the further down the pyramid you go towards the broader consumer bands, the less likely digital (i.e. online or mobile) purchases become.

Other interviewees also offer similar conceptions of the early twenty-first-century music consumer ranging from a narrow band of heavy music users at one end of the spectrum, to a broad mass of occasional-to-rare purchasers at the other. This latter group, given their sheer size, are hugely significant for the music business. As former independent record label owner and retailer Bruce Findlay puts it:

I've been in the business all of my life . . . Who is most important? The guy with the big stack of records? *Personally*, yes, I'm a lover of music junkies. But who is most important to my *business*? . . . There is culture, and then there are the cultural industries, the business of culture. Now, the business of culture can fuck it up big-time, but equally the business of culture can get the music spread . . . So the business of culture needs the biggest audience possible. (Bruce Findlay, personal interview)

However, the core point gleaned from interviewees is that the mainstay of the record industry has most often been ephemeral pop acts that sell to a mass market of occasional buyers. This consumer band is largely uncritical and by virtue of the fact that the people within it only purchase music on very rare occasions, it is the easiest market for record executives to satisfy. While it is not essential to sell to this mass market in order to achieve commercial success, it is this segment of the consumer base that generates the biggest hits, essential to sustaining the major labels.

Such a picture of the recorded music consumer market complicates the view of a market decimated by illicit downloading. If the implication from many media and industry accounts is that file-sharing is widespread and thus having a detrimental effect on record sales, the suggestion from the above consumer profiles is that it is *most likely* the preserve of niche or minority groupings located towards the narrow end of the models illustrated where 'actives', 'early adopters' and 'the restless' are located.

Chapter summary

The accounts of interviewees reveal not only changes, but also very significant continuities within the process of marketing music. Despite the expansion of a more complicated field of tastemakers and gatekeepers in which many more sites for the promotion of music now exist, terrestrial radio is still the most potent force when it comes to influencing the consumption habits of a mass audience. We might also consider that in many respects, the role of new platforms regarding tastemaking and gatekeeping may be seen as extensions of, or the electronic equivalents of already existing functions based on older technical platforms.

The accounts detailed in this chapter also emphasize the changing perception of the role of the record producer, and the pivotal role a producer can now play in branding a record.

This chapter also advanced the perception of the contemporary music consumer market held by those working within and around the record industry. Most interestingly, the findings here suggest that the largest and most significant band of consumers as identified by my interviewees (i.e. those who make rare or occasional purchases) are among those least likely to engage in file-sharing.

7

Evolution,
not revolution . . .

This book is about the popular music industry. However, as we noted in the opening pages, examining this industry in the early twenty-first century can also tell us something about how we understand our relationship with technology. As the sum of the preceding chapters indicates, conventional wisdom pertaining to digital technologies as the primary force driving change in the music industry tends to over simplify the story somewhat.

That change has occurred, and is occurring in the music industry is unquestionable. And that much of this change is closely related to technology is not in doubt either. Music gets produced, distributed and consumed in all kinds of new ways. Cheaper and ever more powerful sequencing and digital recording technologies mean that more people can more readily produce and store musical works than ever before. The proliferating range of digital platforms for the marketing, promotion and distribution of music offers seemingly endless possibilities for creative artists (both established and aspiring) to access an audience to a level that would have been inconceivable less than a generation ago. The opportunities to 'do-it-yourself' have never been greater with aspiring musicians having a veritable arsenal of digital resources upon which to draw. Equally, as consumers or fans of popular music, the opportunities for experiencing it in daily lives have proliferated in recent years. There is a plethora of new devices and platforms across which we can access and share quantities of music far exceeding earlier generations.

Also, we absorb music as a private or public experience in all sorts of ways that would not have been possible in previous times. Popular music has become more pervasive and invasive. As previous authors (e.g. Kassabian 2001, 2002, 2004) have indicated, music has become ubiquitous. We find it everywhere, whether we are looking for it or not. And we can find it instantly. If there is a space, music will fill it. It embeds itself within and attaches itself to all kinds of spaces in our social and media worlds. Perhaps the most fundamental change arising from the transition to digital is that there is more music produced and circulated, and more ways of accessing it.

Despite all of this, it would be wrong to assume that the popular music industry has undergone fundamental structural upheaval in the wake of digitalization. As we have seen, the radical innovations that have occurred in the realm of technology have been met by a diverse set of matching innovations in other areas. Forces of change have been diluted by forces of continuity.

Let us briefly summarize some of the key developments outlined in the earlier chapters of this book.

Chapter 2 pointed to accounts and evidence of some of the fundamental problems and challenges being experienced by the music industry (or more specifically, the record industry) since the late 1990s. While the much-cited issue of unauthorized internet 'piracy' (leading to a significant fall in profits for the record industry) is perceived as inducing a 'crisis' for the industry, a number of other key challenges for the music industry are also flagged. Beyond illicit file-sharing, the industry has been contending with the proliferation of CD duplication technologies and the development of cheaper and larger portable storage devices. While single-track download sales have been thriving, the process of 'unbundling' is also seen by many as having a negative impact on overall sales revenues by encouraging consumers away from the more traditional habit of purchasing whole albums of music. Thus, shifting formats and associated changes in the consumption habits of end-users is a factor in shaping the fortunes of the industry in recent years. So, the ongoing 'legitimate' transition from physical to digital worlds, as well as the 'illicit' online distribution of music have both been challenges facing the record industry in the twenty-first century. The increased role of supermarkets in music retailing is also a threat to record industry profitability because, as bulk buyers of a relatively narrow range of recordings, supermarkets are better positioned to negotiate lower wholesale prices than more traditional music stores. Digital formats in tandem with supermarket-based discount music retailing and mail order sales of CDs and DVDs can also be seen as hastening the decline of 'bricks and mortar' music stores.

Chapters 3 and 4 outlined some of the response strategies of the music industry to the challenges arising within the recording sector. The major music companies have engaged in intense lobbying for the extension of music copyright control mechanisms. Since the later 1990s they have (in many cases successfully) pursued the producers and suppliers of file-sharing technologies and platforms through the courts, as well as individual music consumers, and more recently ISPs. While revenues from physical record sales have dipped considerably since 1999, the market for digital music has also shown remarkable growth with the range of online and mobile platforms for the licensing and distribution of music expanding significantly in recent years. Digital games have also emerged as a useful site for the promotion and licensing of music. Potential also exists for the continued growth of a legitimate record industry in the BRIC countries and other developing economies. Beyond the growth of the digital music economy, the music publishing sector and live music sector have also performed strongly in the new millennium, with growing healthily throughout the period despite the economic downturn post-2007. So, despite the discourse of crisis that evolved around the music industry from the late 1990s onwards, the overall performance of the music industry has been strong. Other sectors have not suffered the decline in fortunes experienced by the record industry, and even at that, the record industry continues to be a profitable and very significant component of the broader music business.

Chapter 5 considered the recent evolution of the music industry in light of the utopian prophesies around internet technologies diminishing the power of the major music companies and creating a more level-playing field for smaller independent artists and labels. While new technologies and platforms have greatly enhanced the 'do-it-yourself' approach to the recording, distribution and promotion of music, access to mass markets is still largely mediated through many of the same industry actors as before. Digital technologies have not lived up to their promises and potential in terms of dismantling many established industry structures and mechanisms. The record industry, as with other music industry sub-sectors, remains highly concentrated. Overall the music industry is also more highly integrated in terms of ownership.

As Chapter 6 indicates, despite the proliferating range of intermediaries or 'tastemakers' in the digital world, terrestrial radio is still generally perceived as the most influential medium for shaping the habits of the music consumer. The concepts of the various categories of music consumers that are identified by interviewees in Chapter 6 also support the contention of earlier authors (e.g. Bakker, 2005; Hesmondhalgh, 2007b) that file-sharing activities are predominantly associated with niche groups of heavy music users. At any rate, legitimate digital sales appear to be in rude health (as we saw in Chapter 3).

The findings and trends advanced in the preceding chapters are based largely on perspectives and tacit knowledge volunteered by my interviewees – all of them current or recent actors from across the spectrum of music economy sectors or related spheres of activity. Some have been active over a number of decades, thus providing historical context to the insight and perspectives they offer. Many have been actively involved in more than one sphere of music industry–related activity throughout their career, thus the perspectives advanced are frequently shaped by a 'cross-sectoral' experience. Overall their combined accounts suggest that the evolution of the music industry in the internet era is a much less straightforward process than the mere story of decline in the face of novel file-sharing technologies that has been circulated so frequently via popular media and by other, often highly partial, sources.

Ultimately this book contends that the music industry has indeed undergone a complex set of significant restructuring processes during the past decade. These changes primarily stem from the diffusion of internet technologies and other digital applications that have evolved to produce both threats and opportunities, particularly with regard to the record industry. However, the evidence collected posits that the changes that have occurred are not determined by technological developments. Rather they represent a restructuring and reconfiguration of the broader music industry based on strategies designed to 'manage' the outcome of technological innovations or negate their potentially harmful effects on the established industry's core centres of power.

The remaining sections of this final chapter are dedicated to outlining some of the most significant trends and implications arising from the above findings.

Continuing and increased integration of music industry sub-sectors

Music industry consolidation has resulted in the increased convergence of the various music sub-sectors, as will be shown throughout this section. Despite the promises and potential of digital technologies, there remains an intense concentration of power across all of the music industry's sub-sectors. What were until recently largely discrete but related music industry sub-sectors have now become much more synergized.

The research that forms the basis of this book underlines the value of reframing the music industry as a horizontally integrated chain of sub-sectors where record companies, publishing companies, live industry actors and music merchandise companies all fall increasingly under the umbrella of a small handful of transnational entities. In this light we can see a different picture of the music economy than that commonly illustrated in media reports that focus purely on the fortunes of the recorded music sector. It indicates how the largest players in the music industry draw revenues from an increasing variety of streams across diverse sub-sectors and how such shifts allow them to spread losses incurred from any downturn in record sales across a broad line of activities. It also brings profits from a much wider range of sources increasingly under the roofs of a small handful of superpowers. While traditionally, record and music publishing companies have existed under the one roof, the merging of these sectors with the live sector as well as merchandising has accelerated and intensified over the past decade. In addition to the major record labels having sister companies that dominate the music publishing marketplace, these companies have continued to evolve interests in the live and merchandising sectors. Given the rapid expansion of the world's largest live music actor, LNE, into the spheres of recording, publishing and artist management, this book describes a situation where a small number of corporate entities continue to dominate all spheres of music industry activity globally. Furthermore, the evidence gleaned from the research interviews clearly points to the increasing blurring of lines between major and independent recording companies. Indeed the evidence gathered in the research study underpinning this book suggests that it is almost impossible for an independent label to enjoy a commercial life without being allied to or supported by one of the major labels and that many apparent independent labels are in fact 'majors in disguise'. This, in turn, clearly implies an ongoing centralization of power in the music industry over a decade into the realization of the internet as a mechanism for distributing and promoting music.

In essence, the findings outlined in the preceding chapters highlight the major limits of techno-centric analytical frames when it comes to understanding the evolving structures of the music industry. A decade after Kevin Kelly predicted 'new rules for the new economy' and 14 years beyond Nicholas Negroponte's assertion that the media corporation would no longer hold dominance in the marketplace, all music sectors have grown more concentrated. Far from the diminishing of corporate power and the dismantling of corporate structures, the dominance of the few has expanded and intensified. Such an outcome resonates much more intensely with the approach of Brian Winston's model for the nature of change in media technologies that argues that the 'great corporation as the primary institution of our society' countervails the disruptive potential of technology on existing power structures.

The integrating live music value chain

Very similar trends have been unfolding in the live music sector – the one sub-sector of the music industry that traditionally has not experienced the same level of vertical integration as the record industry or music publishing industry.

While a small handful of global touring agents dominated the international touring sphere, and live music promotion was dominated by a small number of players in each country or territory, from the point of view of ownership these specific activities remained unrelated. As such, the live music industry chain comprised of separate and discrete actors at the various stages of the process linking artist to audience. While this sector has grown its economic value, the live industry has also experienced rapid vertical integration over the past half decade. While, in terms of revenue, the live industry has become more and more lucrative, the various stages in the vertical chain have rapidly integrated. This is illustrated most vividly by the merger of Live Nation and Ticketmaster to form LNE, which was approved by the US Justice Department in 2010, thus providing one dominant actor with control over touring rights, promotion, ticketing, venue operation and all other ancillary revenue streams surrounding the live industry. We must also consider this in the context of music industry convergence where all sectors and services including artist management, recording, publishing, live, merchandise and other rights are controlled and administered from the one source. In this light, the live music industry has developed a more integral role in the activities of the music industry's largest actors and can be seen to have increased its economic value significantly throughout the first decade of this century.

Re-conceptualizing the recording artist

In light of the restructuring processes outlined above, the recording artist has been repositioned or re-conceptualized as a universal source of revenue for one central rights holder. This is best exemplified through the evolution of 360-degree deals whereby all revenues generated through the exploitation of artist copyrights, trademarks, patents and other are funnelled back to the same corporate entity.

In essence, the major corporation's embrace of 360-degree deals effectively serves to mitigate any downturn in recorded music sales revenues. For copyright owners, recorded music sales now form the source of one set of potential revenue streams alongside music publishing, touring, merchandising, sponsorship and other. The fact that touring agents and live concert promoters have been moving into the spheres of recording and publishing, and that record companies have moved into touring and merchandising illustrates the evolution of a new industrial paradigm for the early twenty-first century.

The processes described in earlier chapters point to how the ongoing pursuit of strategies of vertical and horizontal integration in the music industry have facilitated the evolution of artist-label deals that involve studio recordings, music publishing, touring, television and film projects, merchandise and, essentially, anything that is licensable from the brand of the artist. As such, the twenty-first-century recording artist is now conceived as all-encompassing bundle of rights where all artist-related exploitation ultimately channels all revenue streams back to one overall rights owner. While recording and music publishing have long since been siblings, live rights, merchandising, management services and other artist-related rights are recent introductions to the same family. This illustrates a significant change in the approach of music companies to underwriting the artists on their roster. With a sole actor in charge of all aspects of rights, risks on investment are now being hedged against the entire range of a recording artist's activities rather than different actors controlling each discrete industrial strand of activity. This can be seen as a trend undermining the utopian notion of the internet as a facilitator of autonomy for the recording artist.

With many established recording artists signing all rights over to one of the major industry companies for hugely lucrative lump sums up front, their long-term income from copyright exploitation and other sources is guaranteed to either LNE or one of the four major record labels. The significant growth of the live music market in recent years means that Live Nation, the core actor in this sector, can offer huge advances to established artists to encourage them to surrender their 360-degree rights. However such activities are not just the preserve of already established hit-making artists. These 360-degree developments make smaller acts increasingly lucrative to major labels. While, for smaller acts, no single revenue stream may be sufficiently significant to attract the attention of a major company, the potential for an act's combined revenue streams to generate profit makes them a more tempting proposition.

Equally, while top-tier artists such as U2, Madonna, Jay-Z and Prince have all reportedly been able to command advances of up to US$100 million for handing over their 360-degree (or 180-degree in the case of U2) rights to Live Nation, smaller, less well-established acts may well lose out as royalties and incomes from the spectrum of music industry revenue streams can now be used by rights-owners to offset losses in the recording sector. Here, we are also mindful of the process of cross-collateralization (outlined by interviewee Úna Johnston in Chapter 4) where revenues that were once beyond the reach of record companies (such as publishing) are now readily accessible to these labels. Previously, artists who made a loss with their record releases may have generated profit through the publishing of their music, merchandise or through live performance. Now any profits in those areas can be diverted away from the artist to recoup investment at the recording end. Furthermore, with the same entity controlling all aspects of an artist's rights, the potential exists for conflicts of interest to arise that may hinder the potential of an artist.

The sheer size of the widely reported advances offered to some of the world's top revenue generating artists signals that LNE possesses the financial clout to attract superstar acts and to prise them away from their traditional home with one of the major established music labels. While this means that hugely lucrative recording and publishing revenues are now being diverted away from their traditional 'big four' owner, the underlying oligopolistic power structures are nevertheless being strengthened, not diminished.

In addition to copyright, 360-degree deals means that trademarks and patents now play an increasingly significant role in overall revenue generation, because when any company in the industrial chain enters a 360-degree business agreement with any recording artist, the entire *brand* of that artist becomes a potential source of revenue for that company. All artist-related rights are then owned by the one entity, and can thus be exploited.

A new music industry model

In essence, such developments as described through the various accounts of the interviewees in this book indicate a reconfiguration of the music industry towards a more thoroughly integrated and networked model. While on one level, the record industry remains highly concentrated and the distinctions between independent and major companies have become more and more blurred, equally the lines of distinction between the different sub-sectors that constitute the broader music industry have become less clear.

The various music industry sub-sectors have long since been intrinsically linked and are, in many respects, co-dependent. Investments made by record companies in the production, marketing and promotion of recording artists have produced the big-name acts that have in turn formed the financial mainstay of the live music industry. For its part, the live music industry has returned the favour by being a vehicle for the promotion of artists and recordings, thus serving to drive record sales. Equally the live industry has provided a platform for the sale of merchandise for artists, and the generation of performing royalties for music publishers. The record industry has been a source of revenue for the music publishing industry in so far as it pays 'mechanical' royalties to publishers for the use of copyrighted songs and music on the records they make and sell. Also, music publishers have promoted and licensed the catalogues they administer to a range of users and platforms that in turn generated licensing revenues and also sales for record companies. In the midst of such processes, various royalty collection societies have sustained themselves by administering and distributing the various rights and royalties among the different actors in the chain.

The symbiosis outlined above remains largely the same, if a little more complex given the range of platforms that have emerged for music in the digital era. What has changed, however, is that the various music industry sub-sectors have become more integrated. As illustrated by the evolution of 360-degree deals for recording artists, we are now dealing with 360-degree music companies, as opposed to related, but nonetheless discrete actors operating across the range of sub-sectors. Consequently, revenues derived from activities across all sub-sectors are increasingly channelled back to one corporate interest/entity.

This development carries with it potential ramifications for recording artists, and in particular new or emerging acts. While it can be potentially advantageous for artists to have rights relating to the different aspects of their activities administered by different, unrelated (i.e. not owned by the same corporate entity) companies, it can be potentially disadvantageous for an artist to have all such rights administered from under the one corporate roof. In a situation where all roles and functions relating to the artist are administered by the same company (or different arms of the same company), the potential for the artist's interests to be (albeit incidentally) promoted by independently standing industry actors applying pressure to each other in their own self-interest, has evaporated. For example, a music publishing company that stands independently from an artist's record company is potentially more likely to pressure that record company to act as quickly and effectively as possible to market and distribute recordings as the publishing company's scope for generating royalties is directly linked to the circulation of the recording. Equally, a record company's interests are best served when the live music industry most effectively promotes the artists that they record and distribute. Clearly it is always the case that the various actors share a large degree of dependency, however when all aspects of the artist's activities are administered 'in-house', a greater potential exists for an artist to be under-represented within the company, or even 'undersold'.

Within these processes, the artist has traditionally been represented by a manager who is charged with getting the best return possible for his client in dealing with all of the other actors in the chain. However, in cases where artists sign management clauses in 360-degree deals, management service duties are then administered by the same company that owns all other rights. As such, the traditional marriage between artist and manager is undergoing separation with the evolution of this more convergent music industry model. This is most starkly illustrated by the fact that LNE's Front Line Management provides management services for approximately 250 major international recording artists.

This research has further highlighted the increased tendency of media corporations towards synergy. With music, opportunities to simultaneously market and license and sell the same product across a variety of platforms have expanded. We considered how the parent companies of major music companies own holdings in other areas of media. Alongside these processes, we outlined how music companies are engaged in an ongoing process of forging alliances and indeed gaining a stake in the ownership of online and mobile content platforms. What must be noted here is how copyright law has been used as the mechanism to incorporate new digital platforms that have emerged into this synergy. As was illuminated in Chapter 3, in the cases of many of the new digital platforms that have evolved, the majors have used copyright law to pursue digital music start-ups through the courts. Resulting settlements are followed by licensing agreements, and in some cases the music company gains an ownership interest in the site.

The internet and mobile music value chains consist of a wide range of companies and the industry trends show that the actors are converging in order to compete for a larger share of the value chain. However the recorded music distribution chain is less than transparent given the constant development of new digital distribution partnerships and business models. As noted, initiatives such as Nokia *Comes with Music*, Orange-Sony Ericsson's *Let's Go Mobile* music partnership, EMI-SendMe's mobile music alliance in the United States and other partnerships serve to highlight music as a key enabler within the mobile entertainment sphere. More intense alliances have formed between music companies and the technology companies that in many instances supply the consumer electronics and hardware that the record industry claims are a primary cause of damage to its economic welfare. Arguments that digital technologies are killing the record industry might thus be more accurately defined as successful attempts at appropriating these technological platforms as distributors of the major music companies' copyrighted content.

Again, the fact that it is now increasingly converged music companies that form part of this synergic network means that more of the benefits accruing from the exploitation of copyrights, patents and trademarks via these proliferating media channels are directed to an increasingly concentrated group of companies.

Also, we must consider how potential sources of revenue for the music industry have expanded with, for example, the increase in terrestrial broadcast space and the proliferation of cable, satellite and digital radio and television channels over recent years. This means first, more dedicated airtime for music, second more television programmes licensing music, and third, more advertising that licenses music from the industry's major suppliers. 'Suppliers' here, as we have earlier noted, means two core music industry sub-sectors: recording and publishing. Beyond this we have seen how the film industry, the digital games industry and a multitude of online platforms of various natures increasingly license recorded music from copyright owners. All of these sites serve to actively promote music and artists while also providing sources of revenue for music labels. As we have established, the most significant owners of recording and publishing copyrights have now become evermore industrious and assiduous in marketing their wares for license to all of the aforementioned users of music. These developments also point to an increased centralization of marketing, where major 'hits' are produced through the simultaneous promotion of artists and music across an increasing number of platforms, each of which also pays licensing fees to music companies for the use of their repertoire. Within this context, the Top Forty singles charts in Ireland / United Kingdom / United States appear increasingly indistinct from one another.

One further implication of this research is worthy of note here. Given the emphasis placed on the increasingly intense relationship between recorded music and advertising by many interviewees, we observe a change in attitude towards the interface between music and advertising/marketing functions. When we consider the range of established and new artists and repertoire that are used in advertising campaigns, and how aggressively they are promoted to advertising executives by the major labels and publishers, this trend effectively goes against traditional notions of authenticity in rock/critical music culture. While this is something of an aside from the core points being addressed in this book, it serves to emphasize the increased commodification of this cultural form. The broader proliferation of media has produced a multifold increase in advertising space that has in turn produced rich new soil for the exploitation of music copyrights. Such arguments also lend themselves to the music industry's appropriation of internet spaces and platforms courtesy of the extension of copyright control mechanisms into cyberspace which has seen them wrestle control of social networking sites, streaming services and others.

All of the above serve to refine the logic of the contemporary music industry as a growing network of marketing/promotion activities and revenue generating activities. It is no longer the case that marketing and promotion occur purely in order to sell music recordings or music products. Rather, marketing and promotion sites are increasingly treated as potential sources of revenue in their own right for the music industry. While in the case of broadcast and film, we can argue that this has been the case for many decades, the evidence here suggests that their significance as direct revenue streams to record and music publishing companies has increased in recent years. As this has occurred, many new platforms and outlets (social networks, digital games etc.) that simultaneously use and promote music have evolved. This is one of the factors that make music so unique as a product and a cultural and media form. It is ubiquitous. It possesses the ability to be easily embedded in other media forms. It can colonize spaces that are inaccessible to other media forms. All of this lends to the potential licensing of music to almost any space we can think of in our social and media worlds.

This is the logic of the contemporary music industry, a logic within which the notion of the industry revolving around the 'basket of rights' advanced by Simon Frith over two decades ago is ever more pertinent. Music publishing deserves particular note here. The strategies of the music industry over recent years illustrate the continuation and intensification of their capacity to act as exploiters of copyright. Unlike recording, music publishing is a low cost activity for music labels. The expansion of sites for the use of repertoire and growth in the live music industry as described in this book seem to suggest that publishing copyright will continue to grow in importance to the overall music economy in years to come.

Unfolding record industry trends

As we have established, the 'crisis' rhetoric commonly circulated regarding the music industry is primarily based on perceptions of one of its sub-sectors, that is, the recording industry. Beyond the decline in record sales, the evidence presented in many interviews tells us something of other processes of change and continuity in the record industry since the internet emerged as a medium for the distribution and promotion of music. The remainder of this sub-section will consider some of these processes that characterize the evolution of the record industry over the past decade.

The record industry has long since established the infrastructure for the promotion and distribution of music on a global scale. Many prior authors have addressed how the industry has traditionally comprised a series or chain of vertically integrated processes that encompass the production, manufacture, marketing and distribution of recorded music. The dominant role or position of the major record labels derived from maintaining a stranglehold over these processes. While digital technological innovations (primarily the internet) hold the potential to fundamentally undermine the established order here, the power and role of the major music companies is nevertheless bolstered by the ongoing need of recording artists and smaller record labels for their services. This is particularly the case in terms of marketing, promotion and distribution functions.

Contemporary 'music-to-market' model

Based on the various accounts described and discussed throughout Chapter 6, let us consider the path music must travel in order to achieve a mass-market audience in the contemporary era.

One key change arising from the advent of the internet as a medium for the promotion and circulation of music is that a more dense and complex field of tastemakers has evolved. Beyond offering music fans access to recordings via a plethora of licensed and illicit platforms, the internet has provided the basis for the emergence of blogs and online social networking that offer a range of marketing and promotion mechanisms to music companies and artists.

As we discovered in Chapter 5, the proliferation of such online sites for the promotion of music and artists has enhanced opportunities for independent labels and performers to pursue a 'do-it-yourself' approach. The transfer to digital has made the production, distribution, marketing and promotion of music more accessible, but crucially, the realization of these new D-I-Y opportunities that have arisen for independent actors is largely confined to niche or 'peripheral' markets. As a number of the interviewees outlined (primarily artist managers and those working in the independent music sector), moving beyond this to gain access to the mainstream, mass marketplace still usually requires the assistance of a major label. Their accounts indicate that the level of resources and contacts required for effective large-scale distribution, marketing and promotion are still usually only attainable through a major label. As such, selling music to the masses still means doing a deal with corporate middlemen.

Hence, all of these promotional activities serve not only to bring the artist and their music to the attention of the music consumer, but also to attract investments of money and resources from a major label, and convince those corporate middlemen 'to back a horse that's going to win'.

On the back of such evidence, Negroponte's (1995, 1996) celebration of the digital world signalling a more level-playing field where the major media corporations no longer hold advantage over the smaller actor seems somewhat premature, at least in the case of the music industry.

That said, we must be mindful of the fact that the transfer to digital has allowed some outside players such as Apple to become significant actors within the music industry. Through consumer electronics, the iTunes music store, and laterally the iTunes Festival, Apple has established itself succeeded in embedding itself in the music industry.

The research interviews that inform this book also highlight another significant continuity within the process of marketing music. Despite the expansion of a more complicated and varied field of tastemakers and gatekeepers in which many more loci for the promotion of music now exist, radio is still the most potent force when it comes to influencing consumer habits.

We might also consider that in many respects, the role of new platforms regarding tastemaking and gatekeeping may be seen as extensions of, or the digital equivalents of already existing functions based on older technical platforms. Streaming can be seen as the extension of radio, and social networking sites are frequently referred to as expanded 'word-of-mouth' mechanisms by some interviewees. Equally blogs may be viewed as an additional contemporary manifestation of the music press / music critic. As evidenced by a number of interviewees, the demise of music television as a significantly effective promoter of recordings coincided with the migration of its core audience to the online world and sites such as YouTube, which in itself can be seen as a logical extension of television.

Existing research in the sphere of techno-social relations, most notably Carolyn Marvin (1988), has argued that new technological practices are frequently fashioned out of existing practices to facilitate a new technological system. In short, new technological worlds are essentially 'elaborating an old one' (ibid.: 232). In certain fundamental respects, the contemporary internet music economy is fashioned in the likeness of the older, established music economy. Furthermore this digital economy sits comfortably within the context of the broader music economy that encompasses long-established industrial practices and revenue streams across a plethora of new and previously existing platforms. In many cases, the internet is merely extending or modifying established revenue paths.

We can also observe another relatively recent trend in the record industry which further emphasizes that despite technological developments, the major labels still exercise control over record production for the mass market. This relates to the role of the record producer in the production process.

The 'cult' of the record producer

The accounts of some interviewees emphasize how the role and status of the record producer has continued to evolve in recent times. In many instances, record producers now exist as individual brands in their own right. Beyond serving to shape or define the sound of the record, many producers, courtesy of the elevated status they have come to enjoy, are widely perceived as fundamental to enhancing the public profile of the artists they produce. Lending the brand of their persona to the record can be as important as working in the studio to record or remix it with the recording artist.

The evidence afforded by a number of interviewees is that bridging the gap between a peripheral market and mass market now increasingly means employing the right producer to remix recordings for mass-market tastemakers (most notably radio), and a mass audience. The case of Damien Rice in particular, which focused on the role of record producer David Arnold in the trajectory of his best-selling debut album *O*, vividly illustrates how having the brand of a celebrity producer applied to the recording of a new artist enables the record label (Warner's in this case), greater leverage in pitching recordings to daytime radio programmers and mainstream print media. A key point here is that Arnold, and other big-name producers are largely only accessible through one of the major labels. Thus, while the recording may have been independently created and produced in the first instance and, enjoyed a commercial life up to a point, it is of necessity returned to the production phase of its development, under the direct control of a major label, in order to be re-branded for mass consumption, that is, in order to become a 'hit'. So, while new and recent digital technologies make the recording process easier and cheaper and enhance a do-it-yourself approach to promotion and distribution to a point, this only moderately reshapes the industrial structure at the level of peripheral markets. Beyond this, a process that we may term 'the cult of the producer' helps to maintain and bolster an oligopolistic industrial structure.

Implications arising from profiles of the 'consumer' in the record industry chain

Any assumption that 'early adopters' or, to draw upon BBC Radio 1 terminology, 'restless' consumers are indicative of the actions of the majority is erroneous. Yet, this assumption is perhaps implied in many media accounts that label file-sharing as rampant and, in the more extreme accounts, points to the terminal decline of the music industry. As noted, the IFPI claim 95 per cent of all music traffic on the internet to be 'illicit' file-sharing. We also noted that perspectives advanced by many interviewees in Chapter 2 which imply the perception of wide-scale internet 'piracy'. Comments such as 'people aren't paying for music anymore' (Dave O'Grady); 'wholesale theft' (John Kennedy); 'if people think that music is free, songwriters are going to stop making music because there will be no point' (Johnny Lappin) were frequently articulated. However, if the assumption based upon these claims, and commonly reported accounts in the media is that free access to music on the internet is terminally wounding the record industry, some of the other findings thrown up in the interviews and related research complicate and problematize such an assumption.

When it comes to generating big hits, the 'contented' or 'rare-to-occasional' consumers, by far the largest consumer band according to all of the accounts reported, are crucial. The sheer size of this consumer band makes their rare-to-occasional contributions to the record industry hugely significant. It is important to stress that the research drawn upon in this book did not employ any consumer studies and thus has not gleaned any information directly from end users/consumers of recorded music. However, the perspectives of many of the key informants (on the profile of their overall record-buying public) imply that file-sharing activities remain the preserve of a relative minority or niche groupings. These findings also need to be digested in the light of the various reports that combine to outline contradictory 'effects' of file-sharing as advanced in Chapter 2. In sum, the relationship between file-sharing and falling record sales must be understood as something more complex than a straightforward cause-effect association.

Here, we might also consider the potential for 'cannibalization' to be occurring, whereby the emergence of online streaming services, and also the proliferation of other sources of music (via digital, and more traditional sources) has an impact on sales. The variety of spaces where the user can now 'legitimately' access and consume music without actually purchasing it has been expanding. The 'legal' availability of music via streaming platforms such as YouTube, Spotify, Grooveshark and Pandora may also be eating into the traditional sales market.

The reinforcement of music as a copyright industry

Understanding evolving trends of ownership and control in the music business means that we must continue to place emphasis on concentration, vertical integration, horizontal integration and conglomeration, all of which continue to characterize the structure and organization of the industry. Despite the potential of the internet to demolish such structures, the industry remains oligopolistic in nature. But what this study also reinforces is that we must pay increasing attention to the issue of 'rights' ownership, particularly copyright, but also other strands of intellectual property rights in the form of patents and trademarks. Authors such as Frith (1987, 2004) and Hesmondhalgh (2007a, b) have for many years flagged the significance of studying the music industry in copyright terms. As we have already seen, issues of intellectual property lie at the heart of the vertically integrating live music value chain, the re-conceptualization of the recording artist and the converging of the music industry from a body of discrete but related sub-sectors to a more comprehensively integrated industry network. These processes all emphasize a move towards an intensification of the exploitation of rights. Within these processes, this research highlights how, to an increasing extent, the recording artist exists as a nexus from which a spectrum of rights extends, and can be exploited through multiple channels simultaneously.

Successive generations of increasingly cheaper and better technologies of production, distribution, duplication and consumption have emerged to threaten these structures. Marshall McLuhan's ideas have experienced a renaissance over the past 15 years, underpinning much commentary in both media and academic output since the internet became a technology of mass communication. The approach of McLuhan and the subsequent work of others advancing techno-centric perspectives holds significant attraction for those who see the internet (or wish to have the internet seen) as the driver of radical change in society, not least for those who argue that it is causing the radical transformation of, or even terminal decline of the music industry. Some (e.g. Negroponte, 1995; 1996) contend that digital technologies have effectively rendered copyright law obsolete, or, as a number of my research informants argue make it significantly ineffective from the point of view of protecting sound recordings. As Boyle (2008) noted, the common-sense assumption of the 'information age' is that copyright cannot any longer be protected in the wake of digital developments. The characteristics of digitizable cultural or informational texts – in Boyle's terms, that which is 'non-rival' and 'non-excludable' (Boyle, 2008: 3) – make them in essence, extremely difficult to monetize, or so goes the received wisdom. The call of the record industry has consistently been for stronger laws to protect their copyrighted catalogues in the wake of recent and new digital platforms. The grounds upon which they base this call are that their industry will not survive unless copyright laws are strengthened to counter the threats viewed as arising from these technologies, particularly the widespread 'piracy' that occurs over the internet. As the accounts of IFPI's John Kennedy and IRMA's Dick Doyle testify, the record industry presents their arguments to legislators and judiciaries in nation-states across the world on a regular and ongoing basis. The litany of court cases reported on the IFPI website and elsewhere clearly suggests that they are frequently successful in their petitioning. The severity of the threat posed by technology to the ability of the major record companies to control the exchange and flow of recorded music is lessened by the strengthening expansion of copyright law.

The fear of technology enabling individuals and groups outside the established industrial power centres to independently engage in the distribution of recorded music results in legal responses to technological innovations. Given that the majority of high-grossing copyrights are owned by the recording and publishing arms of the major music companies, it is these companies themselves that are the primary beneficiaries of longer and stronger copyright laws. Such developments and trends again resonate strongly with Winston's (1998) 'law of the suppression of radical potential' in that the pressure and actions of established music industry actors are shaping the role and outcome of the internet and other digital technologies in the music industry. We are also reminded here of Lessig's (2001) second 'futuristic vision' of the internet, where he sees it evolving as a technology of control, shaped and regulated by evermore restrictive intellectual property constraints. As we have seen, a now familiar pattern has evolved where by digital distribution technologies arrive, initially with the promise and potential of radical disruption to existing industrial interests and social practices, but only end up embroiled in conflict and struggle with regulation. There is an inherent conflict with the new potentials arising from new or emergent technologies and the established music industries. This has been the case from Lessig's (2001) account of the piano roll, to Frith's (1978) and Scannell and Cardiff's (1991) account of radio in the post–World War I years, to the cassette duplication technologies of the 1970s as detailed by Lister et al. (2008), to the internet. To apply Winston's model to the key trends reported in the earlier chapters of this book, the capacity of the internet for the circulation and distribution of music has been suppressed by the 'brake' of the established entertainment corporations and their myriad vested interests. The need of capital to create new markets is the force applying the brake that suppresses the radical potential of internet technologies with regard to the mediation of music. As we have seen, the digital world has been shaped to provide a plethora of new platforms and opportunities through which major copyright owners can exploit their intellectual property. The reality that has unfolded is one where these corporations have been using their legal muscle and economic power to disable and subsequently usurp many of the online entrepreneurs that have emerged to challenge them.

The underlying principle emerging from the various copyright infringement cases taken by the major companies and/or their representative trade bodies – against the suppliers of file-sharing software programmes, individual network users, and ISPs – is that the law is as significant in shaping the outcome of a new media as is the technology itself. The extension and application of copyright law in these cases have constrained the potential of the technologies to disrupt the roles and interests of the major music companies, their established practices and the nature and form of their relationship with their consumers. In addition, the subsequent licensing agreements and other forms of alliances between the major music copyright owners and various digital outlets/platforms illustrate how the technical possibilities arising form the technologies for digital distribution and copying can be made subordinate to corporate interests.

Finally . . .

This book has sought to provide a more in-depth understanding of the changes that have been taking place within and around the music industry since the advent of the internet as a technology for the mediation of music. Overall the patterns and trends presented in this study illustrate the resilient nature of the established music industry in the light of the widespread diffusion of digital technologies that, theoretically, hold the potential to radically diminish their role and power. Hopefully, this book has demonstrated that the terminal decline of corporate power celebrated by Napier-Bell in the midst of the 'digital revolution' proclaimed by the likes of Kelly and Negroponte remains, in the music industry at least, a distant and unlikely outcome.

Appendix:

Interviewee biographies

Bailie, Stuart: Music journalist and broadcaster

Stuart Bailie was a critic and feature writer with NME for a period of ten years, ultimately serving as deputy editor in the late 1990s. He has subsequently worked as a freelance music journalist, writing for such publications as *Q, Hot Press, Mojo* and *Uncut* as well as music columnist with *The Times* and *The Sunday Times* in London. Since 1999 he has been a producer and presenter with BBC Radio Ulster. He has also written and researched music documentaries for BBC Radio 2 and BBC Television. Since 2007 he has combined his work at the BBC with the role of CEO of the Oh Yeah Music Centre in Belfast. He founded this dedicated music recording, rehearsal and performance centre in Belfast with support from recording artists Snow Patrol, Ash and David Holmes.

Barrett, Ben: Artist manager

Ben Barrett is the manager of international recording artists Lisa Hannigan and Damien Rice. Working at Mondo Management in London she has also assisted in the management of David Gray and Orbital. Previously she worked in the sphere of live music promotion with the Mean Fiddler organization. Initially booking Irish tours for international artists, she subsequently worked for the company's London office where she promoted UK tours as well as music festivals in Boston, Chicago, San Francisco and London.

Carroll, Jim: Music journalist; ex-independent label owner; ex-major label press officer

Jim Carroll is currently music columnist with *The Irish Times* and a DJ with Dublin-based rock radio station Phantom FM. He previously operated Lakota Records, a joint-venture with Sony Records. He has also worked as a press and promotions officer with London Records where he represented acts such as Goldie, Echo and the Bunnymen and Armand Van Helden. Earlier he spent almost a decade working in the area of artist and repertoire (A&R) with such companies as GoDiscs! (Universal), WEA (Warner's) and Rondor (Universal).

Curtis, P. J.: Record producer; musician; broadcaster; educator

At the time of our interview, Curtis had 54 album production credits to his name over a period of almost 35 years. Working in the United States, Ireland and the United Kingdom, his album credits include Albert Lee, Rory Gallagher, Altan, Pumpkinhead, Liam Clancy & Tommy Makem, Dolores Keane, Maura O'Connell, Scullion, Stockton's Wing, Mary Black, Frances Black, Arcady, Sean Keane and Davy Spillane. Records he produced for Altan have won both Grammy and National American Independent Record Distributors (NAIRD) awards. Formerly, he was instrumental in setting up music performance, music business studies and music management training programmes with the CDVEC.

D'Ardis, John: Studio owner; record producer; songwriter

For the past four decades John D'Ardis has owned and operated Trend Studios, a sound recording, manufacturing and video production facility in Dublin. To this end he has worked with all the major record labels and a host of independent music and film companies. He is also a songwriter and music publisher. Along with Bill Whelan he was instrumental in the creation of the IMRO which replaced the PRS as the primary performing rights society operating in Ireland in the 1990s.

Doyle, Dick: Director General, IRMA

Dick Doyle is director general of IRMA, the umbrella trade body for the record industry in the Republic of Ireland. He is also chief executive of PPI, the organization that oversees the collection and distribution of royalties to record companies for the use of the copyright on recordings they release. He formerly worked in the the Industrial Development Agency (Ireland) before serving as personal secretary to Fianna Fail government minister Seamus Brennan during his tenure at the Irish Department of Trade and Marketing in the late 1980s/early 1990s.

Ergatoudis, George: Head of Music, BBC Radio 1

Since 2005 George Ergatoudis has worked as Head of Music at BBC Radio 1. Prior to this he served as a producer at the station while also managing BBC Radio 1Xtra's music policy. In the 1990s Ergatoudis was a senior producer with Kiss FM in London where he won a Sony Gold Award for producing *The Steve Jackson Breakfast Show*. During his time as producer at BBC Radio 1 he also won a Sony Award for his radio documentary *Last Night a DJ Saved My Life: A History of the Remix.* Before pursuing a career in radio, Ergatoudis worked with Island Records as club promotions manager at the urban/dance label 4th & Broadway.

Findlay, Bruce: Artist manager, label owner, retailer

Bruce Findlay is currently the manager of Scottish band Aberfeldy. In the past he has worked with major international acts such as China Crisis and most notably the multimillion selling rock band Simple Minds whom he managed for a period of 12 years. Formerly he ran a chain of independent record shops across Scotland (Bruce's). He also founded and operated an independent record company (Zoom).

Graham, Ross: CEO, NIMIC

At the time of interview Ross Graham was chief executive of the NIMIC, a state-sponsored initiative to provide strategy and services towards accelerating music industry development in Northern Ireland. The organization provided a range of information and consultancy services to emerging artists and industry professionals. NIMIC were to the fore in the early promotion and management of recording artist Duke Special. Formerly, Ross Graham worked as promotions manager with Island Records, now part of the Universal Music Group.

Hanrahan, Dermot: Radio and media entrepreneur; ex-music retailing executive

Dermot Hanrahan is a radio entrepreneur. For a period of 14 years he acted CEO of Dublin radio station FM104. Hanrahan is currently one of the investors behind 4FM and also has the managerial reins at

Cork station Red FM. He is also the main shareholder in Dublin-based rock station, Radio Nova. In 2007, in a joint investment with *The Irish Times* he launched www.entertainment.ie. Formerly, Hanrahan was general manager of Virgin's retail division in the Republic of Ireland.

Harford, Gerry: Artist manager

Gerry Harford has been manager of Irish band Therapy since 1990. 2012 saw the band's thirteenth international album release on Blast Records. Harford has also managed Tindersticks, singer-songwriter Nina Hynes and Norwegian heavy metal band Magdalena. Throughout the 1980s Harford worked as an independent live music promoter in Dublin.

Hayden, Jackie: Journalist; ex-major label promotions manager

Jackie Hayden is general manager of *Hot Press* magazine where he also authors a column on new and emerging Irish acts, 'First Cuts'. He formerly worked as promotions manager in the Republic of Ireland for CBS Records and Polydor Records. In the 1990s he served on the FORTE Music Industry Task Force and acted as chairman of the committee to examine the international marketing of Irish music.

Hennessy, Shay: Independent label owner

Shay Hennessy is the managing director of independent music group, Crashed Music. He was formerly general manager of Pickwick Records and K-Tel Records. He also served as press and promotions officer for A&M Records, Ireland. He is a former chair of IMRO as well and has served on the boards of IFPI and PPI.

Jenner, Peter: Artist manager

For the past four decades Peter Jenner has worked in artist management. His clients have included Pink Floyd, Syd Barrett, T-Rex, The Clash, Roy Harper, Ian Dury, The Disposable Heroes of Hiphoprisy as well as Eddi Reader and Billy Bragg who he currently represents. He is currently secretary-general of the International Music Managers' Forum.

Johnston, Úna: Music industry trade fair organizer

Based in Thurles, County Tipperary, Úna Johnston is the European manager for SXSW, a global music industry trade fair which takes place annually in Austin, Texas. She previously organized unsigned Irish artists to perform at the annual New Music Seminar in New York. She formerly operated a music event management company, Carpe Diem, whose projects included In the City and the Guinness Blues Festival.

Kavanagh, Willie: Major music label executive

At the time of interview (2007), Willie Kavanagh had worked in the major record industry for almost 30 years. He is currently the chief executive of EMI Music Ireland, a position he has occupied for more than two decades, and is also the current chairman of IRMA, the Irish arm of record industry trade body IFPI.

Kennedy, John: Former chairman & CEO IFPI

At the time of interview (2007 and 2008) John Kennedy was chairman and chief executive of the IFPI, the trade body representing the record industry, globally. He started his career as a lawyer working at several record companies. In 1983 he set up a private agency specializing in the music industry and in 1985 was awarded an OBE for his work as a trustee of the Band Aid Trust and Live Aid. In the 1990s he became chairman of Polygram Music and Film. Prior to taking up his role with the IFPI, Kennedy acted as president and chief operating officer at Universal Music International. He departed his roles with IFPI in 2010.

Lappin, Johnny: Music publisher

Johnny Lappin has been an independent music publisher since the 1970s. His clientele include Clannad, The Celtic Tenors and Sharon Shannon. He is also managing director of Liffey Music Publishing, the company set up to handle publishing for the Celtic Woman show internationally. He is chairman of the Music Publishers Association of Ireland and has also served on the boards of the IMRO and Mechanical Copyright Protection Society (MCPS).

Lindsey, Steve: Music publisher

Steve Lindsey has worked with major record and publishing companies for 25 years. He served as professional manager with Warner/Chappell Music Publishing before moving to Go Discs! Music as general manager. Following its takeover by Polygram he worked for Island Music as creative director and general manager. He has also worked as an independent music supervisor on such film productions as *Mission Impossible* and *Welcome to Sarajevo*.

Lockhart, Jim: Musician; radio producer

Jim Lockhart is keyboardist and flute player with trad-rock band Horslips, who having enjoyed significant success across Europe in the 1970s and early 1980s, have recently reformed. For more than 25 years he has worked as a music radio producer at Ireland's public service broadcaster, RTE. Over the years he has been responsible for a variety of weekday shows on both RTE1 and 2FM. He is currently head of production at 2FM.

O'Ceallaigh, Fachtna: Artist manager

Fachtna O'Ceallaigh has worked in music management since the 1970s. Until recently he was manager of international recording artist Sinead O'Connor. At the time of interview O'Ceallaigh was working with New York–based singer-songwriter Lissy Trullie. In the past he has managed Bob Geldof & The Boomtown Rats, Bananarama, and Clannad. His career in music started in the 1970s as music writer with *The Irish Press*. He also briefly managed Mother Records, an Island Records label in the late 1980s.

O'Grady, Dave: Independent record label owner; artist manager

At the time of interview (2009), Dave O'Grady was managing director of Independent Records, a Dublin-based record label which started releasing records in 1994. The label specialized in licensing independent US albums for the Irish market. He is also the manager of two Irish recording artists, David Kitt and Mundy, both of whom have achieved international releases.

O'Riordan, Michael: Independent music publisher

Michael O'Riordan is general manager of Rosette Music whose roster includes Daniel O'Donnell. He was formerly manager of Release Records, a label that dominated the domestic market in the 1960s and 1970s courtesy of numerous showband releases. He chairs the public relations committee of IMRO and has also serves on the board of the Music Publishers of Ireland.

Pandula, Petr: Independent music label owner; live music promoter; music retailer

Petr Pandula is the owner of Magnetic Music, an independent company with interests in recording, publishing, live concert promotion and record retailing. Originally working as a live concert promoter in Germany, Pandula launched Magnetic Records in 1998. The company has offices in Germany and Ireland.

Sheehan, John: Former major music label executive

John Sheehan spent 24 years as chairman of Sony Music Ireland (formerly CBS Records) until the merger of the company with BMG in 2004. Following that, he remained with the company as head of artist and repertoire (A&R) for their Irish office. He has also served as chairman of IRMA and was a member of the FORTE Music Industry Task Force and the Music Board of Ireland.

Vignoles, Julian: Television commissioning editor; radio producer

Julian Vignoles is assistant commissioning editor for entertainment at RTE television. He has also worked as a producer in Radio 2FM and as a music journalist at *Hot Press*.

Wenham, Alison: Independent record industry trade body representative

Having worked for 15 years in both the major and independent recording sector, Alison Wenham has been chair and CEO of the AIM since its formation in 1998. The member companies of this independent record industry umbrella trade body represent approximately 20 per cent of the UK recorded music market. In 2006 Wenham was elected as founding president of WIN, an umbrella organization comprising of more than 20 national/regional independent trade associations representing thousands of independent music companies globally. Wenham is also a Trustee of Creative and Cultural Skills, a Fellow of the Royal Society for the Arts, Special Music Adviser to the British Council, attends PPL and VPL Board meetings and sits on a variety of government and industry committees.

Whelan, Bill: Composer; record producer; music publisher

As a composer Bill Whelan is best known as the creator of Riverdance. As a record producer he has worked with numerous artists including U2, Kate Bush and Charlotte Church. Over the past decade he has set up a music publishing company with U2 manager Paul McGuinness, McGuinness-Whelan. He also launched Irish Film Soundtracks, a music production company aimed exclusively at film and television production companies.

Williamson, John: Artist manager

John Williamson is the owner of the artist management company Banchory Management. At the time of interview (2008 and 2009) he was the manager of international recording act Belle & Sebastian. As well as working as live music promoter, he also previously managed Scottish band Bis.

Wilson, Ian: Head of Music RTE Radio 2FM

Ian Wilson is head of music production at RTE Radio 2FM, a position that he has held since 1989. Between 1997 and 2003 he was chairman of the European Broadcasting Union's (EBU) 'Eurosonic' group, representing 68 stations across Europe. As a producer at 2FM he was the long-time producer of the Dave Fanning Show where he introduced 'The Fanning Sessions' – the recording and broadcasting of new Irish rock music talent. He also introduced 'Eurodance', one of the first live online dance events, which brought together a network of seven 'dance centres' across Europe. These shows have involved up to 48,000 'real video' participants.

Bibliography

Africa News (2011), 'Music piracy – is the tide turning?', *Africa News*, Wednesday, 12 October.

Alderman, J. (2002), *Sonic Boom: Napster, P2P and the Future of Music*. London: Fourth Estate.

Allen, K. (2006), 'Easy listening and easy buying make easy pickings for Tesco and Asda', *The Guardian* [online], Thursday, 21 December. Available at: <www.guardian.co.uk/business/2006/dec/21/lifeandhealth.supermarkets>.

— (2007), 'Survey finds pirate downloads at all-time high and set to rise', *The Guardian* [online], Monday, 30 July. Available at: <www.guardian.co.uk/business/2007/jul/30/newmedia.musicnews>.

— (2010), 'Piracy continues to cripple music industry as sales fall 10%', *The Guardian* [online], Thursday, 21 January. Available at: <www.guardian.co.uk/business/2010/jan/21/music-industry-piracy-hits-sales>.

Andersen, B. and M. Frenz (2008), 'The impact of music downloads and p2p file-sharing on the purchase of music: a study for Canada'. Dynamics and Institution of Markets in Europe (DIME), Working Paper [online]. Available at: <www.dime-eu.org/files/active/0/WP82-IPR.pdf>.

Anderson, J. (2009), 'The merger of Live Nation and Ticketmaster', *The Music Business Journal*, 5(1) (February), 4.

Associated Press and Wire (2002), 'Music stars wage campaign to stop online piracy', *The Associated Press State & Local Wire* [online], Thursday, 26 September. Available at: <www.lexisnexis.com/uk/nexis/results/docview/docview.do?start=996&sort=RELEVANCE&format=GNBFI&risb=21_T6539992730>.

Australasian Performing Right Association (2011), 'Economic contribution of the venue-based live music industry in Australia', a report by Ernst & Young [online]. Available at: <http://apra-amcos.com.au/downloads/file/GENERAL%20 %20NEWS/NationalLiveMusicResearch_Sept2011.pdf>.

Bakker, P. (2005), 'File-sharing – fight, ignore or compete: Paid download services vrs. p2p networks', *Telematics and Informatics*, 22(1–2), 41–55.

Barfe, L. (2004), *Where Have All the Good Times Gone? The Rise and Fall of the Record Industry*. Boston: Atlantic Books.

BBC (2007), 'Fopp closes down its 105 stores', BBC News [online], Friday, 29 June. Available at: <http://news.bbc.co.uk/2/hi/business/6252300.stm>.

Bell, D. (1973), *The Coming of Post-Industrial Society*. New York: Basic Books.

Berkman Centre for Internet and Society and Gartner (2005), *Consumer Taste is Driving the Online Music Business and Democratising Culture*. Berkman Centre for Internet and Society (Digital Media Project) [online]. Available at: <http://cyber.law.harvard.edu/home/uploads/511/11ConsumerTasteSharing.pdf>.

Bijker, W., T. P. Hughes and T. J. Pinch (1987), *The Social Construction of Technological Systems: New Directions in the Sociology and History of Technology*. Cambridge, MA: MIT Press.

Billboard (2011a), 'Business matters: Former emi exec says file-sharers are good consumers', *Billboard* [online], Tuesday, 26 July. Available at: <www.billboard.biz/bbbiz/industry/digital-and-mobile/business-matters-former-emi-exec-says-file-1005293592.story>.

— (2011b), 'Music's top 40 money makers 2011', *Billboard* [online], Friday, 11 February. Available at: < www.billboard.com/features/music-s-top-40-money-makers-2011–1005031152.story#/features/music-s-top-40-money-makers-2011–1005031152.story>.

Blackburn, D. (2004), *Does File Sharing Affect Record Sales?* Cambridge MA: Harvard University, Department of Economics Working Paper.

— (2007), *The Heterogeneous Effects of Copying: The Case of Recorded Music*. Cambridge, MA: Harvard University, Department of Economics Working Paper.

Boyd, B. (2011), 'Music hacks playing catch-up with the technological revolution', *The Irish Times* (Ticket supplement), Friday, 4 February.

Boyle, J. (2008), *The Public Domain: Enclosing the Commons of the Mind*. London and New Haven: Yale University Press.

BPI (2009), 'UK reports resilient music sales in 2008', BPI press release, 7 January.

— (2011), 'Music sales dip further in 2010 but digital albums hit the mainstream', press release for the BPI press release [online], Wednesday, 5 January. Available at: <www.bpi.co.uk/press-area/news-amp3b-press-release/article/music-sales-dip-further-in-2010-but-digital-albums-hit-the-mainstream.aspx>.

Brussels Court of First Instance (2007), *SABAM versus S. A. Scarlet* (anciennement Tiscali), No.04/8975/A [online], Friday, 29 June. Available at: <www.juriscom.net/documents/tpibruxelles20070629.pdf>.

Burnett, R. (1996), *The Global Jukebox: The International Music Industry*. London: Routledge.

— (2011), 'Internet and music', in M. Consalvo and C. Ess (eds), *The Handbook of Internet Studies*. Malden, MA: Wiley-Blackwell.

Burnett, R. and P. Wikström (2006), 'Same songs, different wrapping: The rise of the compilation album', *Popular Music and Society*, 32(4), 507–22.

Burrell, I. (2007), 'The big question: Is the crisis facing the music industry as bad as the big record labels claim?' *The Independent* [online]. Available at: <www.independent.co.uk/arts-entertainment/ music/features/the-big-question-is-the-crisis-facing-the-music-industry-as-bad-as-the-big-record-labels-claim-436271.html>.

Buskirk, E. van (2009), 'Google, Universal to launch music hob Vevo', *Wired*, Thursday, 9 April [online]. Available at: <www.wired.com/ epicenter/2009/04/vevo-is-real/>.

Cabral, L. (2009), 'Selling records and selling concerts', *The Economics of Entertainment and Sports: Concepts and Cases*. Draft of October 2009 [online]. Available at: <http://luiscabral.org/economics/teqching/ music.pdf>.

Casadesus-Masanell, R., A. Hervaes-Drane and S. Silverthorne (2007), 'Delivering digital goods: iTunes vs. Peer-to-Peer', in *HBS Working Knowledge* [online]. Available at: <http://hbswk.hbs.edu/item/5594. html>.

Casadesus-Masanell, R. and A. Hervaes-Drane (2010), 'Peer-to-peer file-sharing and the market for digital goods', *Journal of Economics and Management Strategy*, 19(2), 333–73.

Chapple, S. and R. Garofalo (1977), *Rock and Roll Is Here to Pay: The History and Politics of the Music Industry*. Chicago: Nelson-Hall.

CISAC (2012), *Authors' Royalties in 2010: An Unexpected Rebound*. Global economic survey of the royalties collected by the cisac member authors' societies in 2010. Paris: CISAC.

Collins, J. (2010), 'Ruling means internet users will not be cut off for engaging in music piracy', *The Irish Times*, Thursday, 12 October, p. 7.

Committee of the Judiciary, US House of Representatives (1982), 'Home recording of copyrighted works', second session hearing before the Committee of the Judiciary, House of Representatives, Monday, 12 April. Washington: US Government Printing Office [online]. Available at: <http://cryptome.org/hrcw-hear.htm>.

DFC Intelligence (2012), 'Video game software global revenues to grow to $70 billion by 2012', DFC Intelligence [online], 5 June. Available at: <http://dfcint.com/wp/?p=338>.

Digital Music News (2009), 'Last year 105,000 albums were released in the US. Only 6,000 of them sold more than 1,000 copies', *Digital Music News* [online], Thursday, 9 July. Available at: <http:// digital-stats.blogspot.ie/2009/07/last-year-a05000-albums-were-released.html>.

Dredge, S. (2012), 'Spotify says Facebook partnership and new apps should allay growth fears', *The Guardian* [online], Sunday, 29 January. Available at: <www.guardian.co.uk/media/2012/jan/29/spotify-facebook-partnership-apps>.

The Economist (2007), 'Russia's booming economy: It's not just about oil and gas', *The Economist* [online], Monday, 18 June. Available at: <www.economist/com/node/9354403>.

Eijk, N. van, J. Poort and P. Rutten (2010), 'Legal, economic and cultural aspects of file-sharing', *Communications and Strategies*, 77, 1st quarter, 35–54.

EMI (2011), 'EMI establishes a new one stop North American sync and licensing unit', press release [online], Wednesday, 6 April. Available at: <www.emimusic.com/news/2011/emi-establishes-new-one-stop-north-american-sync-licensing-unit/>.

European Court of Justice (2011), 'Judgement of the Court (Third Chamber) in Case C-70/10' [online], Thursday, 24 November. Available at: <http://curia.europa.eu/juris/document/document.jsf;jsessionid=9ea7d0f130d53b3144d03b9e4d1b92579ba8c8f4d30a.e34KaxiLc3eQc40LaxqMbN4Oa3qLe0?text=&docid=115202&pageIndex=0&doclang=EN&mode=lst&dir=&occ=first&part=1&cid=2038696>.

Financial Times (2003), 'Vivendi earnings hit by music industry crisis', *The Financial Times* [online], 17 June. Available at: <www.lexisnexis.com/uk/nexis/results/docview/docview.do?docLinkInd=true&risb=21_T6540287359&format=GNBFI&sort=BOOLEAN&startDocNo=26&resultsUrlKey=29_T6540287367&cisb=22_T6540287366&treeMax=true&treeWidth=0&csi=227171&docNo=26>.

FMQB (2008), 'Bush administration supports performance rights act', *FMQB* [online], 11 June. Available at: <http://fmqb.com/article.asp?id=743083&spid=1314>.

FORTE Task Force (1996), *Access All Areas: Irish Music – An International Industry*. Dublin: Government Publications Office.

Foster, P. (2010), 'Downloads keep going up as Britain becomes the land of 7m pirates: Music giants lose fortune in 1.2bn song thefts', *The Times*, Friday, 17 December, pp. 14–15.

Frith, S. (1987), 'Copyright and the music business', *Popular Music*, 7(1), 57–75.

— (2004), 'Music and the media', in S. Frith and L. Marshall (eds), *Music and Copyright* (2nd edn). Edinburgh: Edinburgh University Press, pp. 171–88.

Gartner (2011), *Gartner Says Spending on Gaming to Exceed $74 Billion in 2011*, press release [online], Tuesday, 5 July. Available at: <www.gartner.com/it/page.jsp?id=1737414>.

Global Gaming Factory (2009), 'Acquisitions of the pirate bay and new file-sharing technology p2p 2.0', Global Gaming Factory press release, Monday, 30 June [online]. Available at: <http://feed.ne.cision. com/wpyfs/00/00/00/00/00/0F/26/BC/wkr0011.pdf>.

Globe and Mail (2008), 'Disharmony and the music business', *Globe and Mail*, Saturday, 31 January, p. 18.

Gronow, P. (1983), 'The record industry: The growth of a mass medium', *Popular Music*, 3, Producers and Markets, pp. 53–75.

Harris, A. (2011), 'Music labels feel the music pirating pain', *Sydney Morning Herald* [online], Monday, 21 November. Available at: <www.smh.com.au/business/labels-feeling-the-music-pirating-pain-20111120–1npba.html>.

Hendy, D. (2000) 'Pop music radio in the public service: BBC Radio 1 and new music in the 1990s', *Media, Culture and Society*, vol. 22, pp. 743–61.

Hesmondhalgh, D. (2007a), *The Cultural Industries* (2nd edn). London: Thousand Oaks; New Delhi: Sage Publications.

— (2007b), *Digitalisation, Copyright and the Music Industries*, Centre for Research on Socio-Cultural Change (CRESC), Working Paper No. 30 [online]. Available at: <www.cresc.ac.uk/sites/default/files/wp30. pdf>.

— (2010), 'Music, digitalization and copyright', in Murdock G and P. Golding (eds), *Digital Dynamics: Engagments and Connections*. New York: Hampton Press.

Hickey, S. (2008), 'Industry crisis as album sales drop', *The Irish Independent*, Monday, 14 January.

Higginbottom, S. (2011), 'Oh its fast! China's broadband growth, that is', *GigaOM* [online], Monday, 24 January. Available at: <http://gigaom. com/broadband/oh-its-fast-chinas-broadband-growth-that-is/>.

Howard, T. (2008), 'Ad Track: Jingles out, cool songs in at Cannes', *USA Today* [online], Wednesday, 18 June. Available at: <www.usatoday.com/money/advertising/adtrack/2008–06– 15-cannes-music-ads-adtrack_N.htm>.

Huygen, A., P. Rutten, S. Huveneers, S. Limonard, J. Poort, J. Leenheer, K. Janssen, N. Van Eijk and N. Helberger (2009), *Ups and Downs. Economic and Cultural Effects of File Sharing on Music, Film and Games*. Delft, Amsterdam: TNO, SEO & IVIR.

IFPI (2000), *Record Industry in Numbers* [2000 edn]. London: International Federation of Phonographic Industries.

— (2004), *Record Industry in Numbers* [2004 edn]. London: International Federation of Phonographic Industries.

— (2005), *Digital Music Report* [online]. Available at: <www.ifpi.org/ content/library/digital-music-repotr-2005-pdf>.

— (2007a), 'Beijing court confirms Yahoo China's music service violates copyright', IFPI [online], 20 December. Available at: <www.ifpi.org/ content/section_news/20071220.html>.

— (2007b), 'Dutch file-sharing site closes after notice from anti-piracy watchdog', IFPI [online], 20 December. Available at: <www.ifpi.org/content/section_news/20071115b.html>.

— (2007c), *Record Industry in Numbers* [2007 edn]. London: International Federation of Phonographic Industries.

— (2008a), 'Anti-piracy raids in Mexico continue', IFPI [online], 16 June. Available at: <www.ifpi.org/content/section_news/20080619.html>

— (2008b), 'Czech police shut down illegal server', IFPI [online], 23 April. Available at: <www.ifpi.org/content/section_news/20080423.html>.

— (2008c), *Digital Music Report 2008: Revolution, Innovation, Responsibility* [online]. Available at: <www.ifpi.org/content/library/DMR2008.pdf>.

— (2008d), *Record Industry in Numbers* [2008 edn]. London: International Federation of Phonographic Industries.

— (2008e), 'Zhongsou found guilty of copyright infringement', IFPI [online], 21 May. Available at: <www.ifpi.org/content/section_news/20090622.html>.

— (2009a), *Digital Music Report 2009: New Business Models for a Changing Environment,* IFPI [online]. Available at: <www.ifpi.org/content/library/dmr2009.pdf>.

— (2009b), 'Major forum shut down in Argentina', IFPI [online], 7 July. Available at: <www.ifpi.org/content/section_news/20090707.html>.

— (2009c), *Record Industry in Numbers* [2009 edn]. London: International Federation of Phonographic Industries.

— (2010a), *Digital Music Report 2010: Music How, When, Where You Want It* [online]. Available at: <www.ifpi.org/content/library/dmr2010.pdf>.

— (2010b), 'Finland – Prison sentence for P2P hub operator', IFPI [online], 7 October. Available at: <www.ifpi.org/content/section_news/20101007.html>.

— (2010c), 'Four websites shut after largest ever online anti-piracy action in Bulgaria'. IFPI [online], 2 August. Available at: <www.ifpi.org/content/section_news/20100802.html>.

— (2011a), *Digital Music Report 2011: Music at the Touch of a Button* [online]. Available at: <www.ifpi.org/content/library/dmr2011.pdf>.

— (2011b), 'Italian ISPs ordered to block illegal torrent site', IFPI [online], 21 April. Available at: <www.ifpi.org/content/section_news/20110421.html>.

— (2011c), *Record Industry in Numbers* [2011 edn]. London: International Federation of Phonographic Industries.

— (2012), *Digital Music Report: Expanding Choice, Going Global.* [online]. Available at: <www.ifpi.org/content/library/DMR2012.pdf>.

IMF (2011), World Economic Outlook Database. Available at: <http://
imf.org/external/pubs/ft/weo/2011/02/weodata/weorept.aspx ?s
y=1980&ey=2016&sort=country&ds=.&br=1&pr1.x=40&pr1.
y=0&c=924&s=NGDP_RPCH%2CPPPPC&grp=0&a=#download>.

IMRO (1997), *Irish Music Rights Organisation 1997 Annual Report*.
Dublin: IMRO.

— (1999), *Irish Music Rights Organisation 1999 Annual Report*. Dublin:
IMRO.

— (2000), *Irish Music Rights Organisation 2000 Annual Report*. Dublin:
IMRO.

— (2002), *Irish Music Rights Organisation 2002 Annual Report*. Dublin:
IMRO.

— (2003), *Irish Music Rights Organisation 2003 Annual Report*. Dublin:
IMRO.

— (2005), *Irish Music Rights Organisation 2005 Annual Report*. Dublin:
IMRO.

— (2006), *Irish Music Rights Organisation 2006 Annual Report*. Dublin:
IMRO.

— (2007), *Irish Music Rights Organisation 2007 Annual Report*. Dublin:
IMRO.

— (2009), *Irish Music Rights Organisation 2009 Annual Report*. Dublin:
IMRO.

— (2011), *Irish Music Rights Organisation 2011 Annual Report*. Dublin:
IMRO.

Informa Telecoms and Media (2009), 'Global performance rights
payments top usd1.5 billion in 2008', press release [online],
Wednesday, 14 October. Available at: <www.lloydsmiu.com/
itmgcontent/icoms/s/press-releases/20017707909.html;jsessionid=
0B9756838AB0B567478CBB00DCC896CF.065acf6a61c52eed94766
d1ba7da5d95d4ecd58a>.

— (2011), *How Mobile Apps Bring New Business Opportunities to the
Music Industry*. London: Informa Telecoms & Media.

Irish Times (2009), 'Record firms take downloading action', *The Irish
Times*, Tuesday, 7 July, p. 4.

Jackman, S. (2011), 'No cure for piracy since the day the music
started dying', *The Australian* [online], Monday, 12 September.
Available at: <www.google.ie/#hl=en&gs_nf=1&cp=17&gs_
id=dd&xhr=t&q=september+12+2011&pf=p&biw=1280&bih
=707&sclient=psyab&oq=september+12+2011&aq=0&aqi=
g2gm2&aql=&gs_l=&pbx=1&bav=on.2,or.r_gc.r_pw.r_qf.,cf.
osb&fp=ea717b45be839139>.

Joshi, P. (2012), '2012: The year of digital', *Business Standard* [online],
Tuesday, 3 January. Available at: <http://business-standard.com/india/
news/2012-the-yeardigital-music-460571/>.

Juniper Research (2008), *Mobile Music: Ringtones, Ringbacks, Full Tracks and Payment Models 2007–2012* (4th edn). Basingstoke: Juniper Research.

— (2011), *Mobile Music Opportunities: Market Size, Strategic Analysis & Forecasts 2011–2015*. Basingstoke: Juniper Research.

Kassabian, A. (2001), *Hearing Film: Tracking Identification in Contemporary Hollywood Film Music*. New York and London: Routledge.

— (2002), 'Ubiquitous listening', in D. Hesmondhalgh and K. Negus (eds), *Popular Music Studies*. Oxford and New York: Oxford University Press, pp. 131–42.

— (2004), 'Would you like world music with your latte?: Starbucks, Putumayo and distributed tourism', *Twentieth Century Music*, 1(2), 209–23.

Kavanagh, W. (2010), 'Record industry canary down the coalmine for the digital economy', *The Irish Times*, Friday, 8 August, p. 14.

Kelly, K. (1999), *New Rules for the New Economy: 10 Ways the Network Is Changing Everything*. London: Fourth Estate.

— (2002), 'Towards a post-napster music industry', *The New York Times Magazine*, 17 March, pp. 19–21.

Kennedy, J. (2006), 'Unlocking the music market in China'. Speech delivered at the China International Forum on the Audio Visual Industry, Shanghai, Thursday, 25 May. Available at: <www.ifpi.org/content/section_views/view020.html>.

Laing, D. (2004), 'Copyright, politics and the international music industry', in S. Frith and L. Marshall (eds), *Music and Copyright* (2nd edn). Edinburgh: Edinburgh University Press, pp. 70–85.

— (2012), 'What's it worth? Calculating the economic value of live music', *Live Music Exchange* [online]. Available at: <http://livemusicexchange.org/blog/whats-it-worth-calculating-the-economic-value-of-live-music-dave-laing/>.

Latonero, M. (2003), 'The social and cultural shaping of music technology'. Paper presented at the annual meeting of the International Communication Association (ICA), Marriott Hotel, San Diego, CA, 27 May. Available at: <http://citation.allacademic.com//meta/p_mla_apa_research_citation/1/1/1/8/3/pages111836/p111836-2.php>.

Lessig, L. (1999), *Code: And Other Laws of Cyberspace*. New York: Basic Books.

— (2001), *The Future of Ideas*. New York: Vintage.

— (2004), *Free Culture: The Nature and Future of Creativity*. New York: Penguin.

Liebowitz, S. (2002), 'Record sales, mp3 downloads and the annihilation hypothesis'. Working Paper, University of Texas at Dallas.

— (2004), 'Will MP3 downloads annihilate the record industry?', in
  G. Libecap (ed.), *Intellectual Property and Entrepreneurship*. Series on
  Advances in the Study of Entrepreneurship, Innovation and Economic
  Growth, vol. 15, Emerald Group Publishing Limited, pp. 229–60.

— (2006), 'File sharing: Creative destruction or just plain destruction?',
  Journal of Law and Economics, 49(1), 1–28.

— (2008), 'Testing file-sharing's impact on music album sales in cities',
  Management Science, 54(4), 852–9.

Lister, M., J. Dovey, S. Giddings, I. Grant and S. Kelly (2008), *New
  Media: A Critical Introduction* (2nd edn). London and New York:
  Routledge.

Live Nation Entertainment (2011), *Annual Report* (Form 10-K).
  Washington: United States Securities and Exchange Commission
  [Commission File Number 001–32601].

Longhurst, B. (1995), *Popular Music and Society*. Cambridge: Polity Press.

Los Angeles Times (2009), 'Madonna, AC/DC and the year's
  highest-grossing pop acts', *The Los Angeles Times* [online], Tuesday,
  13 January. Available at: <http://latimesblogs.latimes.com/music_
  blog/2009/01/madonna-acdc-an.html>.

— (2011), 'Concert business is up 11% in the first half of 2011,
  Pollstar reports', *The Los Angeles Times* [online], Thursday, 7 July.
  Available at: <http://latimesblogs.latimes.com/music_blog/2011/07/
  concert-business-is-up-11-in-first-half-of-2011-pollstar-reports.html>.

MacKenzie, D. and J. Wajcman (eds) (1985), *The Social Shaping of
  Technology*. Philadelphia, PA: Open University Press.

Mann, C. (2003), 'The year the music dies', *Wired* [online]. Available at:
  <www.wired.com/wired/archive/11.02/dirge.html>.

Marlowe, C. (2012), 'PC games market reports record $18.6 billion for
  2011', *Digital Media Wire* [online], 6 March. Available at: <www.
  dmwmedia.com/news/2012/03/06/pc-games-reports-record-18–6-
  billion-for-2011>.

Marvin, C. (1988), *When Old Technologies Were New: Thinking about
  Electric Communication in the Late Nineteenth Century*. New York:
  Oxford University Press.

Mathieson, C. (2009), 'How the net saved live music',
  The Sydney Morning Herald [online], Friday, 3 July.
  Available at: <www.smh.au/news/entertainment/music/
  how-the-net-saved-live-music/2009/07/02/1247127624164.html>.

McDaniel, A. (2012), 'Digital music sales on track for a record year',
  Upstart Business Journal [online]. Available at: <http://opstart.
  bizjournals.com/news/technology/2012/07/06/digital-music-on-
  pace-for-a-record-year.html>.

McGuinness, P. (2008), 'Why won't the ISPs stop defending the
  past, start embracing the future and partner the legitimate music

business?'. Speech delivered at *Music Matters* conference, Hong
Kong, Wednesday, 4 June. Available at: <www.ifpi.org/content/
library/paul-mcguinness-June2008.pdf>.

McLuhan, M. (1962), *The Gutenberg Galaxy: The Making of Typographic
Man*. New York: Mentor.

— (1964), *Understanding Media: The Extensions of Man*. London:
Routledge.

Mortimer, J. H., C. Nosko and C. Sorensen (2010), 'Supply responses
to digital distribution: Recorded music and live performances'. NBER
Working Paper No. 16507.

Musictank (2008), *Let's Sell Recorded Music!* Newsletter No. 55
[online], September. Available at: <www.musictank.co.uk/events/
face-to-face-with-the-millennials/playlist.xml>.

Music Week (2012), 'BPI 2011 stats: Market down, album sales fall
5.6% – but digital up 26.6%', *Music Week* [online], Monday, 2
January. Available at: <www.musicweek.com/story.asp?sectioncode
=1&storycode=1047971&c=1>

Napier-Bell, S. (2008), 'The life and crimes of the music biz', *The
Observer*, Music Monthly, 20 January, p. 41.

National Music Publishers Association (NMPA) (2003), *International
Survey of Music Publishing Revenues*. New York: NMPA.

Negroponte, N. (1995), 'Being digital: A book (p)review', *Wired*
[online], Issue 3.02, February. Available at: <www.wired.com/wired/
archive/3.02/negroponte.html?pg=2&topic=>.

Negroponte, N. (1996), *Being Digital*. New York: Vintage.

Negus, K. (2011), *Producing Pop: Culture and Conflict in the Popular Music
Industry*. London: out of print book. ISBN 0–340–57512–3. Goldsmiths
Research [online]. Available at: <http://eprints.gold.ac.uk/5453/>.

New York Times (2011), 'At new try at curbing piracy', *The New York
Times* [online], Sunday, 17 July. Available at: <www.nytimes.
com/2011/07/17/opinion/sunday/17sun3.html>.

NPD Group (2008), *NPD Digital Music Study* [online]. <http://npd.com/
press/releases/press_080226a.html> [accessed on 26 February
2012].

Oberholzer-Gee, F. and K. Strumpf (2010), *File-Sharing and Copyright*
[online]. Available at: <http://musicbusinessresearch.files.wordpress.
com/2010/06/paper-felix-oberholzer-gee.pdf>.

Orlowski, A. (2007), 'Apple, Tesco "most to blame" for biz crisis' *The
Register* [online], Friday, 19 October. Available at:.

Ovum (2011), *Digital Music Industry to Hit Revenues of $20bn by 2015*.
Ovum press release, Wednesday, 9 March. Available at:.

Panay, P. (2011), 'Re-thinking music: The future of making money as a performing musician', in *Re-Thinking Music: A Briefing Book*. The Berkman Center for Internet & Society at Harvard University.

Parfitt, B. (2009), 'NPD: 2008 video game revenues top $21bn', *MCV* [online], Friday, 16 January. Available at: <www.mcvuk.com/news/read/npd-2008-video-game-revenues-top-21bn/013605>.

Peitz, M. and P. Waelbroeck (2004), 'The effect of internet piracy on music sales: Cross-section evidence', *Review of Economic Research on Copyright Issues*, 1(2), 71–9.

— (2006), *Why the Music Industry May Gain from Free Downloading: The Role of Sampling*. International University in Germany Working Paper No. 41/2005.

Peterson, R. A. and D. G. Berger (1990), 'Cycles in symbol production: The case of popular music', in S. Frith and A. Goodwin (eds), *On Record*. London: Routledge, pp. 140–57.

Pope, C. (2009), 'Has music had its day?', *The Irish Times*, Monday, 27 April, p. 15.

Preston, P. (2001), *Reshaping Communications*. London: Thousand Oaks; New Delhi: Sage Publications.

Preston, P. and J. Rogers (2010), 'The three Cs of key music sector trends today: Commodification, concentration and convergence', in Dal Yong Jin (ed.), *Global Media Convergence and Cultural Transformation: Emerging Social Patterns and Characteristics*. Hershey, PA: IGI Global, pp. 373–96.

Price Waterhouse Coopers (2007), *Global Entertainment and Media Outlook: 2007–2011* [online]. Available at: <www.pwchk.com/webmedia/doc/633186450910103120_e&m_outlook_index2007.pdf>.

PRS for Music (2009a), *Economic Insight*, Issue 15, Monday, 20 July.

— (2009b), 'UK music tour revenues up 30% to more than £400m in 2008', PRSformusic [online], Friday, 3 July. Available at: <www.prsformusic.com/aboutus/press/pages/default.aspx>.

— (2010), *Economic Insight*, Issue 20, 4 August.

— (2011), *Economic Insight*, Issue 23, 4 August.

Resnikoff, P. (2009), 'The RIAA: Just how many lawsuits and letters', *Digital Music News* [online], Sunday, 28 June. Available at: <www.digitalmusic news.com/stories/062809riaa>.

Rob, R. and J. Waldfogel (2006), 'Piracy on the high C's: Music downloading, sales displacement and social welfare in a sample of college students', *Journal of Law and Economics*, 49(1), 29–62.

RTE (2007), 'HMV's annual profit plunges', RTE Business News [online], Thursday, 28 June. Available at: <www.rte.ie/business/2007/0628/hmv.html>.

Rushe, D. (2010), 'Rock concert sales plunge as recession forces promoters into discounts', *The Guardian* [online], Thursday, 30

December. Available at: <www.guardia.co.uk/business/2010/
dec/2010/dec/30/rock-concert-sales-plunge>.

Sarno, D. 'The internet sure loves its outlaws', *The Los Angeles Times*
[online], Sunday, 29 April. Available at: <http://articles.latimes.
com/2007/apr/29/entertainment/ca-webscout29>.

Scannell, P. and D. Cardiff (1991), *A Social History of British
Broadcasting, Vol. 1: Serving the Nation 1922–39*. Oxford: Blackwell
Publishers.

Sisario, B. (2009), 'Music sales fell in 2008, but climbed on the
web', *The New York Times* [online], Thursday, 1 January. Available
at: <www.nytimes.com/2009/01/01/arts/music/01indu.html?_
r=1&pagewanted=print>.

— (2012), 'Concert revenue was up in 2011, led by u2', *The
New York Times* [online], Thursday, 5 January. Available
at: <http://mediadecoder.blogs.nytimes.com/2012/01/05/
concert-revenue-was-up-in-2011-led-by-u2/>.

Smirke, R. (2010), 'In the city day 1: Biz looks to china's music market',
Billboard [online]. Available at: <www.billboard.biz/bbbiz/content_
display/industry/news/e3id03412c644d4e5cdeb331c2f4e18e7d4>.

— (2011), 'UK's 2011 Singles Sales Reach Record-Breaking Numbers',
Billboard [online], Tuesday, 20 December. Available at: <www.
billboard.biz/bbbiz/industry/record-labels/uk-s-2011-singles-sales-reach
-record-breaking-1005706212.story>.

Smith, T. (2006), 'Digital music to cover lost cd sales', *The Register*
[online], Monday, 23 January. Available at:.

Sony BMG Music Entertainment (2006), 'Sony BMG Entertainment
sign content licence agreement with YouTube'. Sony BMG Music
Entertainment, Monday, 9 October. Available at: <www.sonymusic.
com/posts/61-sony-bmg-music-entertainment-signs-content-license-
agreement-with-youtube>.

Sony Music Entertainment (2004), 'Sony music entertainment and
bmg unite to create sony-bmg music entertainment'. Sony Music
Entertainment press release, Tuesday, 5 August.

Sterk, D. (2011), 'p2p file-sharing and the making available war',
Northwestern Journal of Technology and Intellectual Property, 9(7)
(Spring), 495–512.

StubHub (2009), 'Stubhub concert ticket sales report', *International
Business Times* [online]. Available at: <www.ibtimes.com/prnews/
20081212/2008-stubhub-concert-ticket-annual-report.htm>.

Sunday Business Post (2008), 'Artistic license: Heed the music lessons',
The Sunday Business Post, 6 April.

Sunday Times (2008), 'Music industry in a flat spin', *The Sunday Times*,
Arts, Culture and Entertainment, 27 January, p. 5.

Sweney, M. (2011), 'UK music industry revenue falls £189m' *The Guardian* [online], Thursday, 4 August. Available at: <www.guardian.co.uk/media/2011/aug/uk-music-industry-revenue-falls>.

Toffler, A. (1970), *Future Shock*. London: Pan.

— (1980), *The Third Wave*. New York: Bantam Books.

Topping, A. (2010), 'Twitter power: How social networking is revolutionising the music business', *The Guardian* [online], Saturday, 5 September. Available at: <www.guardian.co.uk/media/2010/sep/05/twitter-power-social-networking-music>.

Verna, P. (2009), *Global Music: Tuning into New Opportunities*. New York: eMarketer.

Wikström, P. (2009), *The Music Industry*. Cambridge and Malden, MA: Polity Press.

Williams, R. (2003/1974), *Television: Technology and Cultural Form* [edited by Ederyn Williams]. London: Routledge.

Winseck, D. R. (2011), 'Political economies of the media and the transformation of the global media industries: An introductory essay', in D. R. Winseck and Dal Yong Jin (eds), *The Political Economies of Media: The Transformation of the Global Media Industries*. London: Bloomsbury, pp. 3–48.

Winston, B. (1995), 'How media are born', in J. Downing, A. Mohammadi and A. Sreberny Mohammadi (eds), *Questioning the Media* (2nd edn), pp. 54–74. London: Sage.

— (1998), *Media, Technology and Society: A History from the Telegraph to the Internet*. London and New York: Routledge.

World Bank (2011), 'Russia overview', on the World Bank website. Available at: <www.worldbank.org/en/country/russia/overview>.

Wray, R. (2008), 'Interview: EMI's guy hands', *The Guardian* [online], Tuesday, 15 January. Available at: <www.guardian.co.uk/business/2008/jan/15/6>.

Zentner, A. (2006), 'Measuring the effect of file-sharing on music purchases', *Journal of Law and Economics*, 49(1), 63–90.

Index